THE BOOK OF
GUNS
&
GUNSMITHS

THE BOOK OF
GUNS
&
GUNSMITHS

Anthony North and Ian V Hogg

COLLINS PUBLISHERS
GLASGOW/LONDON

A QUARTO BOOK

© Copyright 1977 Quarto Limited

First published 1978 by
William Collins Sons & Co. Ltd.

ISBN 0411604–6

This book was designed and produced by
Quarto Publishing Limited
13 New Burlington Street, London W1
Art Editor: Dave Sumner
Editor: Nicholas Fry
Picture Research: Anne-Marie Ehrlich

Phototypset in England by
Filmtype Services Limited, Scarborough

Printed in Spain by
Printer Industria Gráfica S.A.
Tuset, 19 Barcelona
San Vicente del Horts 1977
Depósito Legal **B. 39633-1977**
Mohn-Gordon Limited, London

Frontispiece: The lock of an air-gun made by
J. G. Kolbe, probably for King George II (see page
129). Victoria and Albert Museum.
Title page: Detail from a 17th century engraving by
Jacob de Gheyn (see page 55).
Endpapers: A pair of percussion pistols in a mahogany
case with plated turn-off barrels and walnut stocks
inlaid with silver. Signed 'Egg London', about 1830;
Victoria and Albert Museum, London.

Contents

Editorial Note

This book follows the technical progress of small arms, from the invention of gunpowder to the development of modern gas-operated mechanisms for automatic fire. This progress has been governed by a variety of factors.

Up to the middle of the 19th century, there was little technical difference between weapons used in sporting and military contexts. Improvements in methods of ignition and loading, the introduction of rifling and refinements in ammunition were due as much as anything to the natural urge of gunmakers to refine their product. Firearms were made by craftsmen, and solidity, refinement and careful finish were qualities which every gunmaker traditionally strove for. It is this early period which is covered in Part One.

With the advent of modern mass-warfare the picture has changed completely. The demand for large quantities of arms which can be cheaply and quickly produced has led to a usurpation of the traditional gunsmith's art by the methods of industrial mass-production. The technical development of modern small arms, also, has been largely governed by military requirements, and it is this development which is covered in Part Two.

If the traditional arts of the gunsmith survive, it is in the manufacture of sporting guns and to a certain extent of hand-guns. Today's sporting guns fall into a special category. They represent either a continuation of long-established methods of manufacture and design, or an adaptation of principles developed in modern military weapons. In either case they have contributed little to the mainstream of modern small-arms design, and for this reason they are not represented in this volume.

Facing page: An illustration from the manuscript *Belli Fortis* by Conrad Kyeser of Eichstätt, written in about 1400, showing a figure firing a hand cannon. From a reproduction of the manuscript in the University of Göttingen.

Part One

The Origins and Development of Firearms

Chapter One

Hand Cannon and Matchlocks

10

The series of illustrations shows gunpowder-making at the end of the 14th century, from a contemporary German manuscript.

IN SPITE of the far reaching effects on civilization of the invention of gunpowder and the development of the gun, their early origins are shrouded in obscurity. The earliest evidence for the existence of what was considered by contemporary writers as an invention of the devil, is often contradictory, and usually in the form of later versions of earlier sources.

Leonardo da Vinci, who was to make important contributions to the technological development of firearms in the early 16th century, made a drawing of a steam-gun which threw 'iron balls with a great noise and fury'. He described it as an invention of Archimedes, implying that the Greeks were aware of the propellent properties of steam if not of gunpowder. A fallacious theory put forward by two 18th century scholars stated that gunpowder was invented in India by the Hindus.

As early as the 16th century, the contribution of the Chinese to the development of gunpowder was acknowledged. William Camden, in his work *Britannia*, published in 1586, states 'some have sayled a long course as farre as China, the farthest part of the world, to fetch the invention of guns from thence'. The evidence that gunpowder was a Chinese invention is based on a number of military treatises which describe, and in particular instances

Previous page: An illustration from Diebold Schilling's Chronicle of Bern, completed in 1483. From a reproduction of the manuscript in the Burgerbibliothek, Bern.

illustrate, devices using gunpowder. One of these treatises, the *Wu Ching Tsung Yao*, dating from 1040, describes what are basically fireworks. As the text is known only in a 15th century copy, to which later additions have probably been made, it is not reliable evidence.

Modern scholars and students of the subject have carefully sifted the evidence contained in Chinese texts and have concluded that gunpowder of a sort was known by the Chinese at the beginning of the 11th century and was being used in hollowed pieces of bamboo to drive missiles by the mid-13th century The discovery was probably brought to Europe at that time, possibly through Moorish Spain by the Arabs, whose works on medicine and mechanical devices were widely read.

What is always considered to be the earliest genuinely datable evidence for the existence of gunpowder in Western European texts is contained in some manuscripts written in the 13th century by Roger Bacon, a Franciscan friar studying at Oxford. He was the author of several treatises on alchemy and philosophy. In three of his works, the subject of gunpowder is mentioned. Unfortunately, two of the references to gunpowder are in the form of anagrams, and their interpretation is still the subject of controversy. In a 17th century copy of Bacon's *De Secretis Operibus Artis et Naturae, et de Nullitate Magicae*, there is an anagram which has been translated to form a workable formula for gunpowder. Another form of the anagram – as yet unsolved – is contained in the British Museum's 15th century copy of the same work. As the original is known to have been written about 1260, these could be the earliest European references to gunpowder. Sadly, the vital anagram is not in the only known 13th century copy of the treatise, and it is believed that the cypher was not the one normally used by Bacon.

However, the *Opus Maius*, dating from 1267, and the *Opus Tertius*, of about 1268, con-tain direct references to gunpowder and its properties. In the latter, Bacon describes what is, in fact, a firework. He refers to it as a 'child's toy, of sound and fire made in various parts of the world'. Bacon describes how powder of saltpetre, sulphur and hazelwood charcoal should be enclosed 'in an instrument of parchment the size of a finger'. Such a device, according to Bacon, 'can make such a noise that it seriously distresses the ears of men if one is taken unawares'. The concluding sentence of this passage contains thoughtful reflections on the potential of gunpowder: 'If the instrument were made of solid material, the violence of the explosion would be much greater'. This accurate and graphic account of the power and effect of gunpowder does suggest that Bacon had actually seen the 'child's toy' that he describes, and implies that he may have appreciated its potential.

In addition to the works of Roger Bacon, other European texts mention gunpowder at about the same period. A book called *Liber Ignium Ad Comburendos Hostes* (The Book of Fires for Burning Up Enemies) by Marcus Graecus, supposedly originally written in the 8th century, describes the use of gunpowder for rockets and what were probably 'bangers'. No texts earlier than about 1300 are known and it is generally thought that entries concerning gunpowder were inserted later.

Another well-known source of recipes for gunpowder is the book *De Mirabilibus mundi*, said to have been written by St. Albertus Magnus, who died at Cologne in 1280. Several of the recipes are similar to those found in the *Liber Ignium* of Marcus Graecus, and it is by no means certain that St Albertus Magnus was the author, as surviving editions of the book are of a much later date. Neither the *Liber Ignium* nor *De Mirabilibus Mundi* can be accepted as reliably dated sources. It seems likely that one heavily plagiarised the other, but which is the original is not at all clear.

It is significant that hardly any of the early descriptions of gunpowder, apart from the Chinese, mention its potential use in driving a missile. Some authorities believe that one of the earliest illustrations showing gunpowder used in a gun is to be found in an Arabic manuscript preserved in a museum at Leningrad. The original is said to date from about 1300, but the Leningrad copy, which is somewhat unreliably dated, supposedly dates from about 180 years later. It shows soldiers, possibly Mongols, using incendiary weapons. One of the illustrations shows what appears to be a wooden tube containing arrows and a charge. The text tells how the tube should be partially filled with gunpowder and used to fire both arrows and other missiles. Another illustration shows a bearded warrior holding a device very similar to the later hand-gun – a tube attached to a long pole with long cords suspended from it. If the later copy of this manuscript is faithful to the original, this would be one of the earliest representations of a gun. This would suggest that if the Chinese knew of the propellant properties of gunpowder by the mid-13th century, then the discovery was in Arabic hands by 1300.

The chief contacts between Islam and the West during this period took place in Moorish Spain, and there are a number of interesting early references in Spanish texts to the use of gunpowder. The original documents have been lost, and scholars have had to rely on later versions of the text. A transcription of the *Chronicle* of Alfonso XI, printed at Valladolid in 1551, makes reference to the use by the Moors of 'many balls of iron that they hurled by means of cannon' at the siege of Algeciras in April 1343. Although this reference is a 16th century copy of a 14th century original, it is interesting to note that at least one manuscript from Spain, *El Poema de Alfonso*

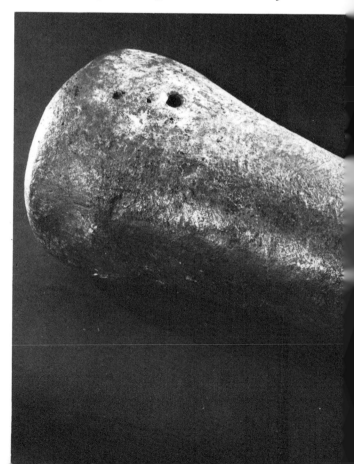

Onçeno in the library of the Escorial, has two references to the use of artillery at Algeciras in 1343. One describes the King of the Moors instructing his son Abdalla to carry food and what is referred to as 'la polvora para el trueno' – powder for the cannon. From this and other references, it seems reasonable to suppose that the Moors had a well-developed artillery by the mid-14th century.

The year 1326 provides two important documents for the early history of guns. In that year, members of the Council of Florence instructed that 'arrows or iron bullets and metal cannon' should be constructed for the defence of the Florentine Republic. Also in 1326, Walter de Milemete finished an illuminated manuscript for Edward III of England. This book, entitled *De Nobilitatibus, Sapientiis et prudentiis Regum*, dated 1326, was a homily on the duties and responsibilities of the crown. One illustration shows a gun shaped like a vase, placed on a flat board supported by trestles. An arrow or bolt appears in the mouth of the device. A knight clad in mail is somewhat diffidently applying a lighted match to the top of the container.

A manuscript in the British Museum, probably also by Walter de Milemete, shows a similar shaped gun with a group of trembling figures waiting for it to be fired. These guns are probably what contemporary documents describe as 'iron pots for shooting arrows'. The curious bulbous shape was due to the need to have a substantial amount of solid metal where the explosion actually occurred – that is, at the breech of the gun. The trembling knights watching their braver comrade applying his match to the cannon suggest that the process was fraught with peril. In 1861, a small cast bronze bottle-shaped cannon similar in shape to that shown in the Milemete manuscripts, was excavated in Loshult, Sweden. The small size of the gun suggests that it was almost certainly designed to be used in the hand. There are no apparent external means of fixing the gun to a pole or stock. It seems likely therefore that the gun was either attached to a stock by hoops which have since been lost, or more probably, simply rested in a wooden frame. What appears to be a wooden frame is also shown in the Milemete manuscript from the British Museum.

Between 1326 and the end of the 14th century, there is an almost complete lack of gun illustrations. This has led some authorities to suggest that the illustrations in the Milemete manuscript were inserted at a later date. However, most modern scholars now accept that the illustrations are contemporary.

Some light has been thrown on this otherwise dark period by the discovery of a number of unpublished illustrations of siege guns. These come from 14th century French and English manuscripts. One of these illustrations in a French manuscript, probably written before 1397, shows a soldier firing a gun

One of the earliest surviving guns is this bronze cannon from Loshult, Sweden. Dated about 1300, it is now in the National Historical Museum, Stockholm.

An early iron gun is this hand cannon
from Vedelspang. German or Danish,
about 1400; Tøjhusmuseet, Copenhagen.

similar in design to an iron gun of 'hooped' construction taken from the moat of Bodiam Castle, Sussex, and now in the Rotunda at Woolwich.

For the earlier part of the century, we must rely on documentary evidence. Fortunately, a substantial number of extracts relating to gunpowder and guns, taken from the Privy Wardrobe Accounts, were published in 1911. The Privy Wardrobe was the English Crown department dealing with all the supply of arms to the Royal forces. The accounts contain payments made in 1345 for the repair of '*gunnis cum saggitis et pellotis*', guns with arrows and bullets. In 1388, there is a reference to '*111 canones parvos vocatos handgunnes*', which seems to be the earliest recorded reference to hand-guns. References to the purchase of gunpowder, show that initially it was quite expensive. In 1346, William of Staines supplied 1600lb of powder at 18 pence per lb but by 1449 a certain

William Cantlow charged only eightpence. The principal reason for the initial high price was possibly the shortage of saltpetre.

Harrassed clerks preparing inventories and accounts in the later Middle Ages rarely had the time to indulge in lengthy descriptions of the objects they were listing, so we know very little of the actual appearance of the guns they describe. Most of the surviving guns which date from before 1400 are without decoration. However, there is at least one gun from the period which is quite lavishly decorated. It is a late 14th century gun of bronze, now in the National Historical Museum, Stockholm. It was found in the sea off Mörkö, in Sweden. It bears the inscriptions 'Maria plea' and 'Hielp Got help uns' in Gothic lettering against a cross-hatched ground, and at the breech end is a bust depicting a bearded man. Immediately below this figure is a substantial lug. There are numerous references in 15th century inventories to 'hakenbüchse' – guns with hooks – and it seems very likely that this is one of them.

Another similar early gun, but one without any decoration, is in the Germanisches Museum, Nuremberg. This is of interest because it was found in a ruined castle in Hesse-Schloss Tannenberg, which is known to have been destroyed in 1399.

The bronze hand cannon found in the sea off Mörkö in Sweden. German, late 14th century; National Historical Museum, Stockholm.

Facing page, top: Swiss hand cannon with wooden stocks, dating from about 1400. The one at the top is a 'Hakenbüchse' – a gun with a hook. Historisches Museum, Bern. **Bottom:** a famous piece of early artillery, Mons Meg at Edinburgh. Made at Mons in Belgium, 1449.

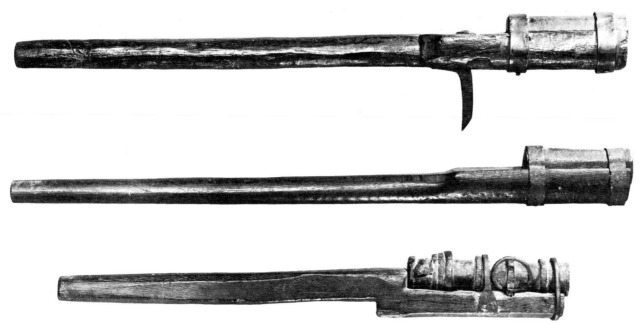

Most surviving early guns are of bronze, but there are a few in iron. One of the best known was found at Vedelspang in Schleswig. Like the Tannenberg gun, it was found in the ruins of a castle, which was destroyed in 1426. The Vedelspang gun is of iron and the back extends to form a long iron stock, terminating in a conical knob. A hook is attached by an iron band around the barrel. The knob was possibly used to prevent the gun sinking into the ground when it was discharged.

Few early guns have their original stocks, but isolated examples do survive. In the Historisches Museum, in Bern, are some hand-guns which appear to have the originals. The guns can be dated to about 1400 and are attached to thick wooden poles by means of loops which either completely surround the stock and barrel, or are nailed to it. In one example from Bern, the end of the gun is butted up against the stock, which is cut with a recess for this purpose. It is interesting to speculate what sort of recoil, if any, such guns might have had.

By 1400, the number of guns fitted with hooks or with stout bands joining the stock to the barrel, suggests that gunpowder had become powerful enough to necessitate such precautions. One of the iron guns from Bern is made of a series of tubes held together by thick iron rings which were fitted over the tubes when white hot. The famous 15th century bombard Mons Meg, from Edinburgh Castle, is made in this way. The full story of Mons Meg is a clear demonstration of how valuable archives are to the military historian. A diligent search of the Duke of Burgundy's General Account Books revealed that Mons Meg was made in Mons for Duke Philip the Good of Burgundy, in June 1449, by Jehan Cambier,

Illustrations from a manuscript of 1410 showing a figure grinding gunpowder and others holding and firing hand cannon. Codex 34; Imperial Library, Vienna. **Below:** A wagenburg, as shown in an illuminated manuscript of 1437. Codex Vindobana 3062; Austrian National Library, Vienna.

his chief supplier of artillery. In 1457, the Duke ordered that it be sent to Scotland through the port of Sluys to 'assist the affairs' of James II of Scotland. It has remained there ever since. This mighty bombard has been adorned with a host of epithets throughout its long history, ranging from the description in a 1578 inventory of artillery as 'ane grit peice, of forgit yron callit Mons' to an account of the ordnance of Edinburgh Castle where it is described as 'the great Iron Murderer called Muckle Meg'. In 1497, the bombard was taken in solemn procession to Holyrood House, and soon became a symbol of Scotland's independence.

A number of 15th century manuscript illustrations show how hand cannon were used. A splendid depiction of a wagenburg – literally 'stronghold of wagons' – from a manuscript dated 1437 shows an incident from the Hussite Wars in which John Ziska, the Bohemian leader of a peasant army, inflicted defeats on the German and Hungarian armies. A soldier armed with a hand-gun can be seen firing over the side of one of the armoured wagons and other cannon can be seen on the top. The gunner is holding the stock with his left hand and appears to be aiming by sighting along the barrel. Another interesting manuscript illustration depicting not only hand cannon being used, but also a large bombard, is to be found in a British Museum manuscript of the works of Quinte-Curce dated 1468. A group of armoured soldiers is attacking the walls of a castle; the long stocks are tucked under their right arms and are held adjacent to the barrels with the left hand. The soldiers are using their right hands to apply lighted matches to the touch-holes. The large bombard is made in two segments and is supported on a stout block with trestles.

A technical improvement, enabling the gunner to use both hands to support and aim his gun, was made in about 1400. This was the invention of the 'serpentine' lock. An illuminated German manuscript of 1411 illustrates the device. It consisted of a long lever in the form of an extended Z which was pivoted through the stock. If the lighted match were fixed to a hole in the top part, pressing the long lever underneath up towards the stock would automatically push the match towards the touch-hole. This improvement not only allowed the gunner to hold his gun in a more steady manner, with two hands, but also freed him from the worry of holding a lighted match for long periods. The idea of the 'serpentine' was perhaps suggested by the very similar trigger device

Facing page: Soldiers armed with hand cannon are shown besieging a castle in this illumination from a manuscript of the works of Quinte Curce, completed in 1468; British Museum.

18

A major technical advance in the 15th century was the invention of the serpentine lock. Guns equipped with these locks appear in a number of contemporary manuscripts. **Left:** illustrations from a Froissart manuscript of 1468, formerly in Breslau State Library. **Below:** illustration from a manuscript dated 1411. Codex Vindobana 3069; Austrian National Library, Vienna.

A bronze Lanzknecht gun. German, 1500; from the Duke of Brunswick's Collection.

found on crossbows. Another improvement, already employed in the 14th century, was the use of a primitive pan to contain the powder for firing. On the gun from Loshult, this is simply a recessed area around the touch-hole. However, the gun from Mörkö has a square pan dished in the centre, raised above the level of the rest of the barrel.

Although the 'serpentine' lock was a major technical advance, improvements were made to it throughout the 15th century. By the last quarter of the century, the idea of the extended Z-shaped lever had been discarded in favour of the snap-matchlock. The lever and pan were moved and now worked on a flat plate attached to the side of the stock. A downward curving lever, the cock was fitted with a tube to hold the tinder. The match was held into the pan by a spring placed on the inside of the lock-plate. At the back of the cock was an extension; when the cock was pulled from the pan, this projection was caught by a sprung stud, or sear, which passed through the side of the lock-plate. The support of the sear was withdrawn by pushing a button fitted to the lock-plate, and the cock, with its lighted tinder or match, then fell into the pan from the pressure of the spring.

A more popular form of matchlock was the sear-lock. With this type of lock, the cock was kept away from the pan. A lever underneath the stock – similar to the serpentine – was connected through levers to the cock, which moved into the pan when the first lever was pulled towards the stock. This form of lock remained popular until the late 17th century, particularly for military weapons. By the mid-15th century, not only the lock had been moved to the side of the stock, but also the touch-hole and pan, now often fitted with a flat covering plate which could be drawn aside by hand to allow the powder to be placed inside. This protected the powder from rain or wind.

Several of the early illustrations of guns being fired, such as the illustration of the 'wagenburg', show the soldiers sighting along the barrels of their guns. Now that the lock had been moved to the side of the gun, it was found that the round pole which served as a stock was inconvenient. During the 15th century, a new type of stock was developed which was designed to be held at the cheek or shoulder. The term by which it is normally described is 'Lanzknecht stock', because so many of the illustrations of lanzknechts from the late 15th and early 16th centuries show them carrying guns with stocks of this form. The typical Lanzknecht stock is made from a long flat piece of wood 'stepped' towards the muzzle and, unlike the earlier stocks, supports the whole length of the barrel.

A typical Lanzknecht stock is shown in this 16th century woodcut by Hans Sebald Beham of a lanzknecht loading his weapon.

Left and facing page: illuminations from Diebold Schilling's *Berner Chronik* (Chronicle of Bern), completed in 1483, showing soldiers armed with pikes, crossbows and guns. From a reproduction of the manuscript in the Burgerbibliothek, Bern.

Improvements in the method of attaching the barrel to the stock were made in the latter part of the 15th century. By then, instead of being attached by bands over the top, most barrels had projecting flanges underneath pierced with holes so that they could be secured by pins passing through the flanges and through the stock. The illustrations from Diebold Schilling's Chronicle of Bern, which was completed in 1483, show soldiers armed with guns of this type.

Although we have no detailed contemporary accounts of the performance of early guns and the efficiency of gunpowder, some interesting experiments were recently carried out with a reproduction of a 14th or 15th century hand-gun. For this experiment, the recipe for gunpowder given in Albertus Magnus's *De Mirabilibus Mundi* was followed, namely six parts of saltpetre, two parts of charcoal and one part of sulphur. Muzzle-velocity and penetrative power were measured as well as accuracy and some of the results were interesting. It was found that gunpowder could be made a more explosive mixture and thus a more powerful and efficient propellant if the separate ingredients were first moistened for mixing, then dried. The mixture failed to explode at all unless it was really well rammed,

and the long stocks of early guns may have assisted this process by providing rigidity. Also the muzzle-velocity was considerably increased if the barrel was made longer. Although the reconstruction of the gun was held by clamps to a stout frame, its accuracy was limited to about 10 yards. Experiments suggested that one of the biggest influences on the actual design of early guns, must have been the discovery of a form of corned powder, i.e. powder moistened for mixing, sieved and dried.

Another significant element in the development of gunpowder was the discovery that saltpetre, previously collected from deposits which occurred naturally in stables and cellars, could be produced artificially in 'nitre beds'. A German manuscript of 1405 describes the preparation of these beds, composed of earth, dung, urine and lime, to produce saltpetre by nitrification.

No early history of the origins of firearms would be complete without an account of the mysterious monk, Black Berthold. According to some traditions dating back in Germany to the early 15th century, Berthold was a monk, possibily of Greek or Danish extraction who became interested in some branches of alchemy. His researches led him to experiment with mercury, sulphur and saltpetre in an attempt to make gold. One version of the legend tells how he applied heat to the mixture and was somewhat puzzled when the explosion blew his laboratory to pieces. Another story tells how Berthold wished to test the Aristotelian concept that substances with hot and cold natures would not mix. He mixed sulphur, saltpetre and charcoal in a mortar and placed it over a fire. The explosion not only confirmed Berthold's belief in the wisdom of Aristotle, but also led him to speculate on the potentially destructive powers of the substance with which he had been experimenting.

Over page: The German monk, Black Berthold, often credited as the inventor of gunpowder, experimenting in his workshop. From *The Gun and its Development* by W. W. Greener, 1910.

Chapter Two

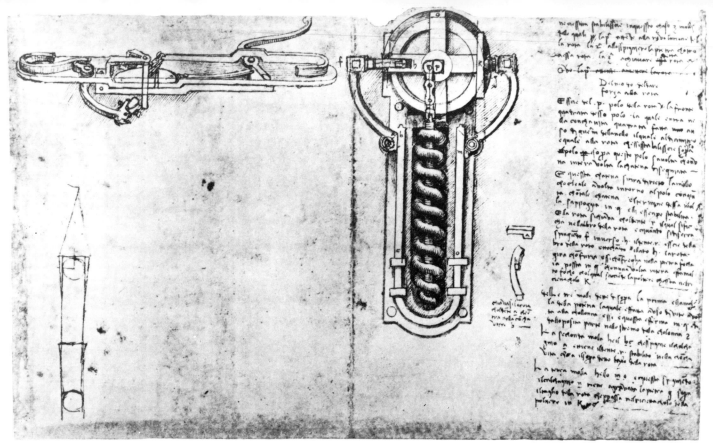

IF THE first 200 years in the history of firearms were important for the development of basic elements, such as the gun and gunpowder, then the 16th century was important for the actual mechanical developments that occurred.

There were two important inventions made during this century, which greatly influenced not only the development of firearms but also the whole field of warfare. The first of these was the invention in about 1500 of the wheel-lock. Basically, the wheel-lock worked like an old-fashioned cigarette lighter. Some iron pyrites were held in jaws against a toothed wheel, which was wound up against a spring. When the wheel was released, it spun rapidly, producing sparks which fell into the powder, causing the explosion.

There are two theories about the invention of this mechanism. One is that it was invented by Leonardo da Vinci, the other that it was the invention of an unknown German gunsmith of approximately the same period. The attribution to Leonardo is based upon two sketches contained in the well-known album of his drawings, in the Ambrosiana, Milan, the Codex Atlanticus. Regrettably, the precise chronology of these drawings cannot be established for, sometime after Leonardo's death in 1519, many of the drawings and sketches were taken out of the original notebooks and mounted as an album. This completely destroyed any chronology the drawings might have had and we are left with what amounts to a miscellaneous collection done at various periods during Leonardo's lifetime.

There are about 4000 drawings and the wide range of subject matter makes it difficult to establish the date of a particular drawing with any precision. It has been suggested that the two showing wheel-locks which are on folio 56 V b of the manuscript date from the period when Leonardo was in the service of Lodovico, Duke of Milan, between 1482 and 1499. The only reason for this suggestion appears to be that it is known that the artist designed military engines for the Duke during this particular period. Another authority has made a careful study of the changes in Leonardo's handwriting in an attempt to provide a chronology for the miscellaneous collection of drawings contained in the Codex Atlanticus.

On this rather insubstantial evidence, it has been suggested that the two drawings date from about 1508. The drawings are placed side by side on the page and depict two wheel-lock mechanisms, one depicted at a slight angle as seen from above, the other drawn in plan. The second drawing is shown in more detail and shows a flat rectangular plate pierced with four small holes. At one end, held in by straps

The invention of the wheel-lock was an important step in the development of firearms. The sketches of wheel-lock mechanisms shown above are from the album of drawings by Leonardo da Vinci known as the Codex Atlanticus, dated about 1500. Ambrosiana, Milan.

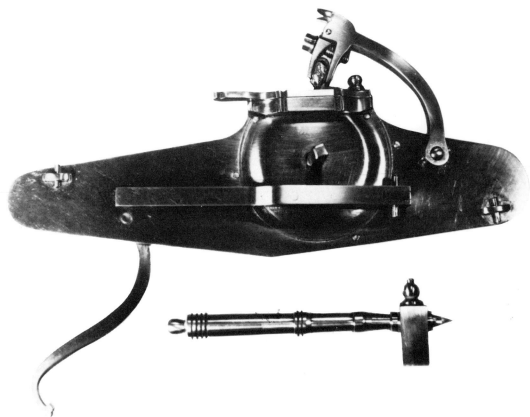

in the form of a cross, is a wheel with a raised rim. A square-topped bolt runs through the centre of the wheel and the frame of crossed straps. Above the straps is a circular washer, and the bolt is attached to a chain which joins a rod of circular section. What appears to be a spring in the form of a helix surrounds the rod and fits into a recess in the plate. Another spring looking like an elongated U is held to the plate by pins and clips. This runs round the lower end of the rod and helical spring. At each side of the plate, touching the U-shaped spring, is a short bar curving inwards and pinned at one end to the edge of the plate. At the opposite end, the bars terminate in a square section. On the left side this forms jaws to hold what appears to be a piece of pyrites; on the right it holds a bar fitting into a notch in the edge of the wheel, thus forming the trigger.

It is interesting to note that Leonardo apparently did some rough drawings of ideas for this particular mechanism. These show the rod and surrounding spring, and there are a number of drafts of ideas for the linking chain. Although this particular mechanism could be attached to a gun, the shape of the plate on which it is mounted rather suggests that it was designed to be used as a tinder lighter. This is borne out by Leonardo's written notes which describe it as being designed to produce fire. The other

mechanism, which is unfortunately not drawn in detail, is possibly designed for use on a gun, for the shape of the lock-plate is very similar to those used with contemporary match-locks. The lock is very similar to the fully-developed wheel-lock of a few years later. A wheel is wound up against a mainspring, to which it is linked by a chain; a scar is withdrawn from a recess in the wheel by pressing on a lever similar to those found on crossbows. The pyrites are held in the jaws of a downward curving cock made from a rectangular bar.

Evidence that Leonardo's drawing of this second mechanism may be a design for a wheel-lock was supplied some years ago when an amateur gunsmith made an exact replica of this lock. He found that the lock would not work for various technical reasons, the most important being that the shape of the spring as drawn was far too angular, and the position of the trigger screw interfered with the main spring. After various slight improvements had been made to the design, and the wheel had been hardened, the mechanism worked perfectly.

The evidence for the first drawing being a design for a wheel-lock tinder lighter is over-whelming, but the evidence for the second drawing being a design for a wheel-lock mechanism for a gun is much less substantial. It is unlikely that it was intended for practical use.

Above: a modern reconstruction of one of the wheel locks drawn by Leonardo da Vinci.

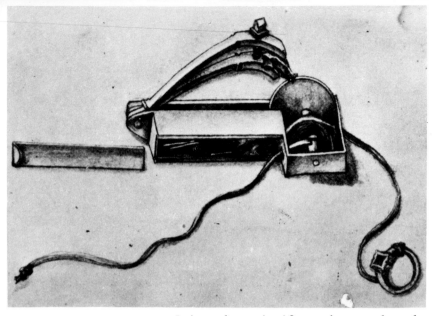

Very similar to Leonardo's wheel-lock designs are these drawings of wheel-lock tinder lighters from the lost manuscript of Martin Löffelholz, dated 1505. In the bottom drawing the end of the chain attached to the U-shaped main spring can be clearly seen.

It is perhaps significant that much early evidence of the wheel-lock comes from Germany. References to the rules of the Geislingen shooting range banning what were described as 'self-igniting guns', and payments made in 1509 to Hans Luder 'wheel-lock and gunmaker' have been shown to be false. However, there is definite documentary proof of wheel-lock guns in use at an early date in Germany. The Augsburg chronicler, Wilhelm Rem, gives an account of a rendezvous in 1515 which also has something to say about the wages of sin.

The chronicler's account reads: 'How Laux Pfister shot a whore at Constance, in the year of Our Lord 1515. On the day of Three Holy Kings, there was at Constance a certain young citizen of Augsburg who invited a handsome whore. And when she was with him in a little room, he took up a loaded gun in his hand, the lock of which functioned in such a way that when the firing-mechanism was pressed it ignited itself and so discharged the piece. Accordingly, he played around with the gun and pressed the firing-mechanism and shot the whore through the chin so that the bullet passed out through the back of her neck. So he

had to compensate her and give her 40 florins and another 20 florins per annum for life. He also paid the doctor 37 florins and the other costs amounted to some 30 or 40 florins.'

The gun could only have been a wheel-lock. In 1507, according to an account book of the steward of Cardinal Ippolito d'Este (1479–1520), a servant going to Germany from Hungary on a pilgrimage was given four florins to buy '*Unum piscidem de illis que incenduntur cum lapide*' – a gun of that kind that is caused to fire with a stone. Ten years later, in Styria, Emperor Maximilian I banned the use of what he described as 'guns that ignited themselves', and a year later extended the ban to the Empire. A letter to the Emperor in 1518 suggests new laws to deal with persons who carry guns secretly under their clothing, and suggests that he should make it illegal 'to carry or bear guns that ignite themselves'. All this suggests that wheel-locks were being made in such quantities in German territories during the first quarter of the 16th century that they were becoming a social nuisance.

A German manuscript, formerly in the Staatsbibliothek of Berlin, but now mislaid, throws some light on the problem of the Leonardo drawings. This manuscript was a quarto volume containing line and wash drawings of technical devices and recipes. On the frontispiece were the arms of Martin Löffelholz, of Nuremberg, who died in 1533, and of his wife Anna Haugin, together with the date 1505. On one of the folios were drawings of two wheel-lock tinder lighters, which have close similarities to the Leonardo wheel-lock drawings. Especially significant is the form of the pan and the shape of the head of the cock of the second of the two tinder-lighters shown in the Löffelholz manuscript. These are virtually identical to the Leonardo tinder lighter. No one knows which came first, and the mystery is

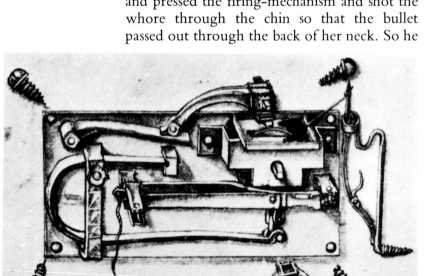

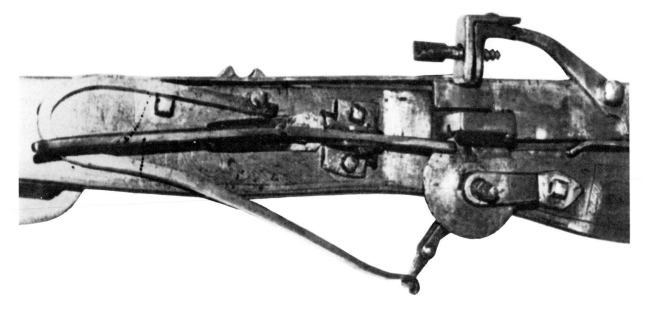

unlikely to be solved until the original Löffel-holz manuscript is found.

What are generally considered to be the earliest surviving wheel-locks, are preserved in the Palazzo Ducale in Venice. These are on three combined guns and crossbows and are similar in construction, consisting of a steel bow fitting into a slot cut in a square-sectioned iron tiller. A gun barrel with octagonal muzzle projects from the front. On the right side of the tiller is a square pan fitted with a cover which swivels at the corner. The wheel-lock mechanism is attached to the side of the tiller by screws, and is very like one of the tinder-lighters shown in the Löffelholz manuscript. There are certain improvements on the locks of the Venice cross-bows which suggest that they are later. The lock, for example, has substantial jaws closed by a vertical screw, and the lower end where it pivots is thicker and more substantial.

The crossbows are difficult to date pre-cisely because they are, unfortunately, not described in any of the Venetian inventories. The most complete of the crossbows has some decorative traces, consisting of some rather feeble etched trophies and scrollwork, of the

with the Löffelholz tinder-lighters, this seems to suggest a date of about 1510. There is no clear evidence as to where the crossbows were made, although the style of the etched decoration does suggest northern Italy.

It is necessary to return to Germany to find the earliest wheel-lock gun with a firm date. Again it is found on a combined weapon, a crossbow and gun preserved in the Bayerisches Nationalmuseum. As with several early firearms it is a coat-of-arms which provides the evidence. The tiller is painted with the arms used by Archduke Ferdinand I, before he became King of Bohemia in 1526, and bears his initials and those of his wife, Anna of Bohemia, whom he married in 1521. The lock is a considerable

sort often found on Italian 16th century armour. Comparisons have been drawn between the etching on this crossbow and on Milanese armour of about 1510, now in the Musée de l'Armée, Paris. Taken together with the tech-nical relationship which these wheel-locks share

Some of the earliest surviving wheel-locks are found on combination weapons. **Top:** the lock from an Italian combined gun and crossbow preserved in the Palazzo Ducale in Venice, dated about 1510.
Above: The combined crossbow and wheel-lock gun of Archduke Ferdinand of Austria, made before 1526. Bayerisches Nationalmuseum, Munich.

Left: Internal view of the lock of the combined crossbow and wheel-lock gun of Archduke Ferdinand of Austria.
Centre: The steel wheel-lock pistol with external mechanism in the Germanisches Museum, Nuremberg. Italian, about 1530.

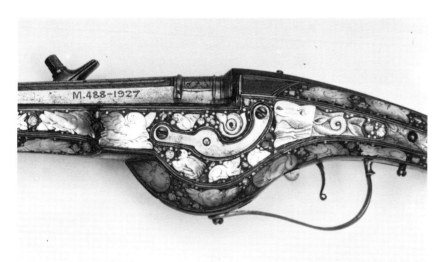

improvement on those previously considered. Nearly all the mechanism is placed behind the lockplate. The cover of the pan slides automatically and the sear-lever is operated by a button worked by means of two bars. The cock-spring is shaped rather like a sickle. Guns with springs of this very distinctive form were probably produced in Nuremberg.

In general, the German form of wheel-lock spread throughout Western Europe as the 16th century progressed, but there were countries which developed their own distinct type. One of the most important of these was France, which as early as 1540 had its own type of construction. In French wheel-locks, the mainspring is not attached to the inside of the lock-plate, but is placed in a recess cut in the stock and is pinned into position. Also, the wheel-spindle is not held in place by a bridle, but passes through the stock on the opposite side where it is held by a plate. Italian wheel-locks often had a mainspring on the outside of the lock-plate. A wheel-lock pistol made entirely of steel, with a substantial external

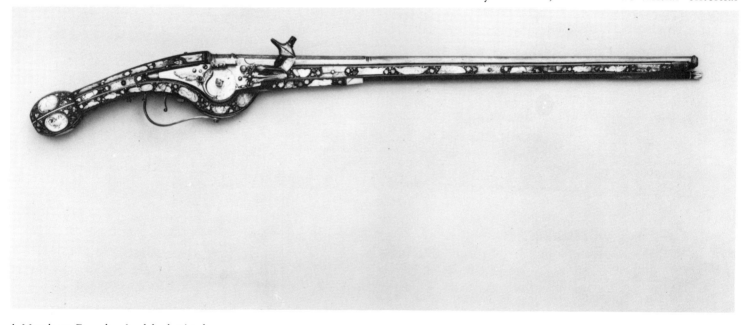

A Northern French wheel-lock pistol, the walnut stock inlaid with mother of pearl, staghorn and brass wire. About 1610; Victoria and Albert Museum. The reverse side, illustrated in the detail above, shows how the spindle passes right through the stock.

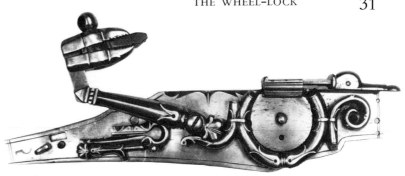

A self-spanning wheel-lock of chiselled iron, stamped with a mark attributed to Bartholme Marquart, who worked for the Spanish court. South German (Augsburg), about 1540; Victoria and Albert Museum.

Two wheel-lock spanners in the Victoria and Albert Museum: a spanner of gilded iron; German, early 17th century (**left**). And a combined priming flask and spanner of engraved iron; German about 1650.

mainspring, is preserved in the Germanisches Museum, Nuremberg. It has been dated to about 1530.

Various experimental wheel-locks were made which were modifications of the usual form. In the Victoria and Albert Museum is a self-spanning wheel-lock (a lock that winds itself up) dating from 1540–50, unfortunately detached from its original gun. It has been attributed to Bartholme Marquart. These self-spanning wheel-locks worked by means of cog-wheels. When the lock was drawn back from the pan it automatically revolved the wheel. Very few have survived and they were probably never popular. It is difficult to get sufficient 'pull' on the lock because of the sharp edges of the cock, and the mechanisms are usually very stiff. A special spanner was devised to wind up the mechanism of a wheel-lock. One end was pierced with a square hole to take the end of the wheel-spindle, and the opposite end was often chiselled to form a screw-driver, used to dismantle the lock or remove the pyrites held in the cock. The first examples were elaborately chiselled and pierced, and many were fitted with a swivel by which they could be suspended from the belt.

In addition to a clearer chronology of firearms in the 16th century, there is also a little more information available on the gunsmiths themselves. The dry, laconic entries listing only the name of the gunsmith and the price he was paid were beginning to be augmented, allowing us a glimpse of the craftsmen and their particular specialities. Alonso Martinez de Espinar, writing in 1644, tells of the Marquart family of gunsmiths. According to Espinar, the gunsmith Master Simon and his brother Master Pedro were 'very great masters of barrels and wheel-locks'. He says they were brought from Germany by the Emperor Charles V 'as the best that he found there'. Other

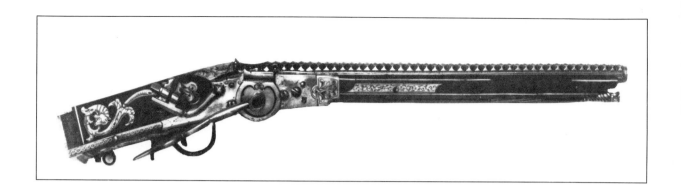

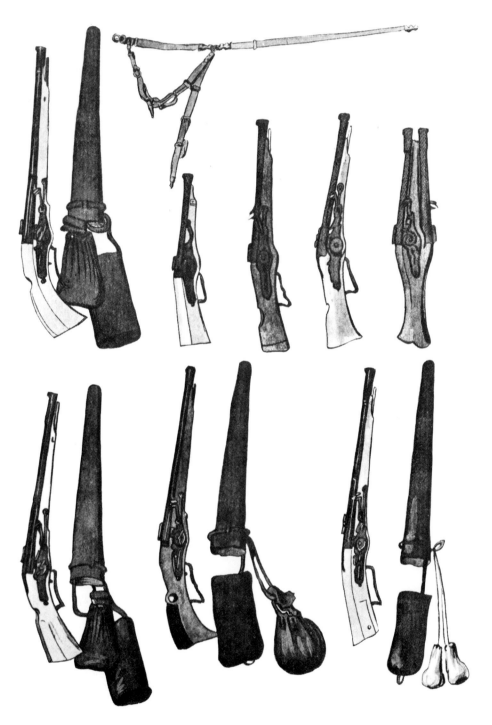

Two items from the Real Armería in
Madrid. The French wheel-lock carbine
of Charles V dating from about 1540,
and an illustration from the *Inventario
Illuminado* showing firearms and their
protective cases.

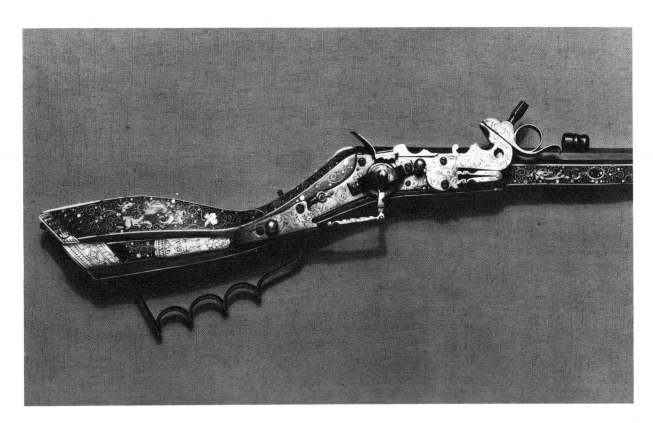

biographical details are given including the interesting facts that 'they have used as marks the same sickles as their father, each one in a shield, and the cypher of his name, and at either side a sickle'.

The Marquart family originated in Augsburg where they were established as clockmakers as early as 1479. The first member of the family to work on guns was apparently Bartholme, who started a gunmaking business in 1527. The transition from clocks to guns was comparatively easy, the complicated and intricate springwork of a wheel-lock needing exactly the skills that a well-trained clockmaker possessed. Bartholme is known to have been elected to the city council of Augsburg in 1549, and he died in 1552. A number of his guns survive, including a small wheel-lock carbine and a wheel-lock pistol with two barrels. Both are in the Real Armería in Madrid.

The Real Armería contains an important collection of early wheel-lock firearms, several of which belonged to the emperor Charles V of Spain. Some show interesting constructional features. The earliest example of French wheel-lock construction is to be found on a carbine in this collection. The ebony stock is inlaid with staghorn panels engraved in a manner characteristic of French work found at a later date. The

lock-plate has a semi-circular notch cut in the back edge as well as a detached mainspring, both characteristic French features. It dates from about 1540 and almost certainly belonged to Charles V. Fortunately, illustrated inventories were prepared of the emperor's armoury, one in 1544, the *Inventario Illuminado*, and another after his death, the *Relación de Valladolid*, prepared in 1560 by order of his son. The first consists of two folios of water-colour drawings of some of the Emperor's arms, the second lists those arms belonging to the Emperor with brief descriptions of 27 firearms. The *Inventario Illuminado* must be considered as one of the most important documentary sources for the history of arms and armour. The firearms are shown in some detail, next to their protective cases. These closely resemble the leather cases made for knives, large numbers of which survive from the 16th century. They were presumably made of boiled leather, the two halves being held together with thongs.

The wheel-lock enjoyed wide popularity for sporting and military guns until the 18th century. One particular form of wheel-lock gun, the Tschinke, continued in use until then and was widely exported. Like the Italian form of wheel-lock, the Tschinke had the mainspring fitted to the outside of the lock-plate. Its name

Above: A wheel-lock sporting rifle or Tschinke, the walnut stock inlaid with engraved staghorn and mother of pearl. Silesian (Teschen) about 1650; Victoria and Albert Museum.

derives from the town where it originated, Teschen in Silesia, now in Poland. As well as an external mainspring Tschinkes have a button for setting the sear and a characteristic 'dog-leg' shaped butt. These guns are really small-bore rifles designed to be used for shooting at sitting birds. The earliest dated examples are found from about 1610 and guns of this form continued to be popular in Germany until about 1730.

In certain countries including England and the Low Countries military wheel-locks were used until the latter part of the 17th century. One rare group of wheel-lock pistols made in Germany have both mechanism and spindle concealed behind a round-sectioned lock-plate. These concealed locks date from about 1660.

There is at least one pair of wheel-lock pistols which were made in the 19th century. The French gunmaker Le Page made a pair of rifled duelling pistols with wheel-locks signed by him 'Le Page à Paris 1829'. These were clearly made as a curiosity and were given subsequently by a member of the Le Page family to the Musée de l'Armée in Paris. The wheel-lock was expensive to make and complicated to repair, hence the relationship between clock-makers and makers of wheel-locks. It was normally reserved for the luxury guns of the aristocracy. Nevertheless its invention produced something of a revolution in tactics on the battlefield for it indirectly led to the invention of the pistol. For the first time, fire would be held until needed, and the large number of German engravings showing wheel-lock pistols being used by horsemen testifies to its impact on the contemporary military scene. A number of 16th century German engravings depict armed riders carrying a holster containing a pistol with a distinctive butt terminating in a large ball. In the middle of this century, pistol stocks usually terminated in a small facetted globe but in the latter half of the 16th century the characteristic form of the German wheel-lock developed. The barrel was set at an angle to the stock, and the butt terminated in a large ball. It should be noted that these ball-butts were not intended to be used as clubs as they were far too fragile. The majority of such pistols produced in the mid-17th century are lavishly inlaid with stag-horn. These pistols were carried in holsters almost completely covering the stock, and the large ball enabled them to be quickly drawn. It is a fitting tribute to the value placed on the wheel-lock by military authorities that the great Gustavus Adolphus of Sweden (1611–1632), killed at the battle of Lützen in 1632, carried two plain but business-like wheel-lock pistols when he fell.

Above: Armoured riders firing ball-butt pistols. Engravings from J. J. von Wallhausen's *Art Militaire du Cheval*, Frankfurt-am-Main, 1616.

Two ball-butted pistols of characteristic German pattern, the stocks of both inlaid with engraved stag-horn. The first example has a lock of French type with a separate mainspring; South German (Nuremberg), dated 1593. The second bears the initials of the stock-maker, B.H., and the barrel is engraved with maker's marks and dated 1579 (see detail). Both Victoria and Albert Museum.

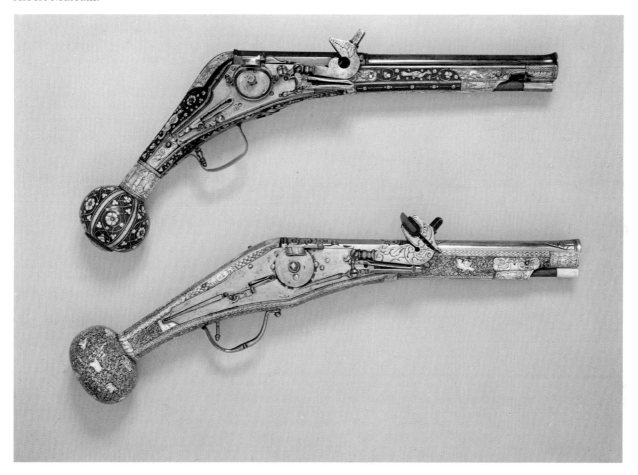

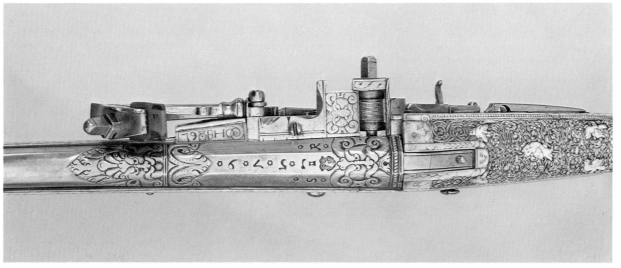

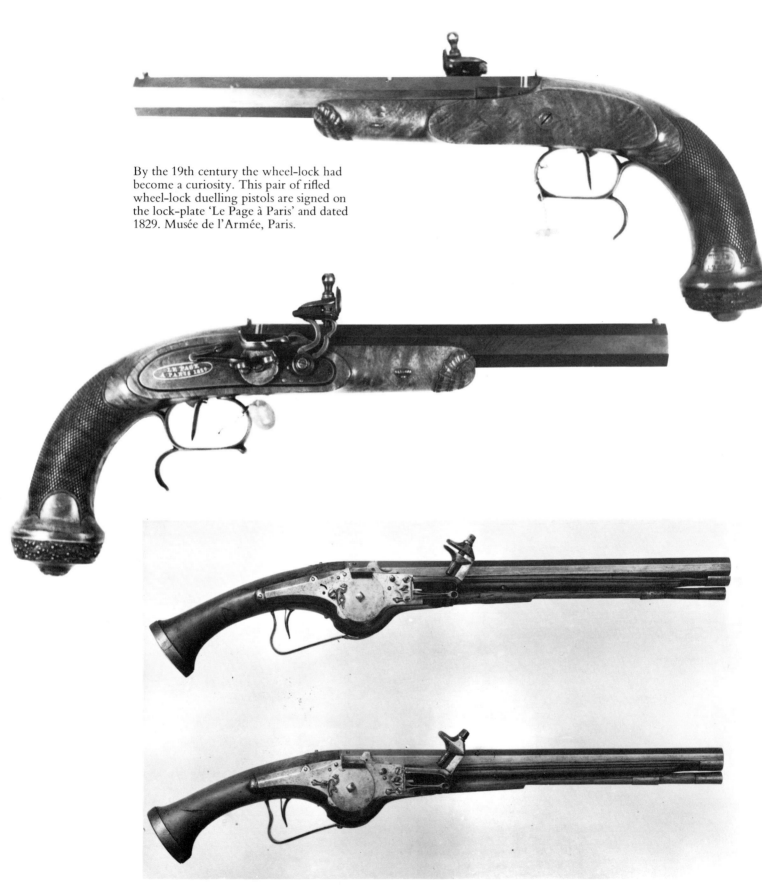

By the 19th century the wheel-lock had become a curiosity. This pair of rifled wheel-lock duelling pistols are signed on the lock-plate 'Le Page à Paris' and dated 1829. Musée de l'Armée, Paris.

The pair of wheel-lock pistols used by Gustavus Adolphus, king of Sweden, at the battle of Lützen. German or Swedish, about 1630; Livrustkammaren, Stockholm.

A curious gun, of the type known as a rasp-lock, survives in the Historisches Museum, Dresden. It is made of iron and has a gradually flaring muzzle. At the end of the barrel and immediately behind it run repeating Gothic 'Is' arranged to form decorative bands. It has always been known as the 'Monk's Gun'. In an inventory taken in 1606, it is described as being the 'invention of the known inventor of gunpowder, Black Berthold – used to find out the effect of gunpowder'. It is preserved in almost perfect condition and shows little sign of ever having been used. It is quite unlike any other known firearm in operation, for the lock is worked by a screw passing through a box attached to the side of the gun. By tightening the screw, the cock with pyrites can be lowered on top of the box which contains a long square fire-steel with a ring at one end. The gun was loaded with gunpowder and priming powder was put into the pan which has an aperture through which the steel runs.

To fire it, the ring is pulled sharply back, the grooved surface of the steel being dragged along the surface of the pyrites and sending a shower of sparks into the pan.

It has been maintained by at least one authority that the 'Monk's Gun' is the direct ancestor of the wheel-lock. Indeed, the form of the jaws does resemble those of the Leonardo wheel-lock. It is also fitted with a substantial belt-hook at the lower end. No other firearm like this has ever been discovered and it is, therefore, very difficult to date. The Gothic lettering suggests a date not later than 1550, but it could well have been made before 1500. It bears what appears to be a maker's mark which is somewhat indistinct. The comparison with the jaws on the Leonardo lock suggests that 1500 may be the correct date. Until more documentary evidence is found, or another dated or dateable example is discovered, the 'Monk's Gun' must remain an interesting curiosity, and also something of an enigma.

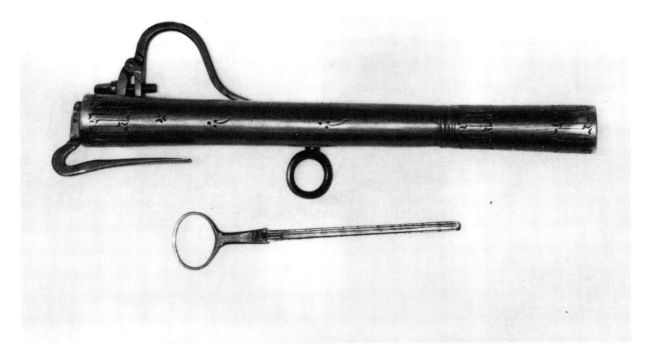

The German rasp-lock known as the Monk's Gun, of blued iron with Gothic letters. About 1500; Historisches Museum, Dresden.

Chapter Three

The Snaphance and Flintlock

The earliest dateable snaphance; on the
barrel is the mark C.K. together with
that of Nuremberg. About 1550;
Livrustkammaren, Stockholm.

ALTHOUGH THE wheel-lock was effective when it worked, its expense and complicated mechanism soon led gunsmiths to experiment with simpler and cheaper forms of ignition. The principal method of making fire during the 16th century was to strike flint and steel together in some tinder. An unknown gunsmith took

Two 17th century poachers sum up the
original associations of the word 'snaphance', having evidently just 'snapped
up' a hen. Engraving by Abraham
Bosse, Antwerp about 1630.

this idea and adapted it for guns and produced the earliest form of flintlock.

As with other forms of ignition, the first accounts of a lock using this principle appear in documents. A Swedish Royal account in 1547 mentions a 'snapplas' – a snap-lock. An ordnance, printed in Florence in the same year, placed a ban on various firearms including what are described as 'archibusi da fucile'. 'Fucile' was the word used to describe the piece of steel used to strike fire from flint. The 'snap-lock' consisted of a cock with jaws holding a piece of flint facing a flat plate. The plate is hinged above the pan. The cock is pulled back against a mainspring until caught by a small lever, the sear, which is attached to the trigger. On pulling the trigger, the lever is withdrawn from the cock and it snaps forward against the steel causing it to move from the top of the pan and admit the sparks to the powder in the pan.

The snapping action of the cock was likened by the Dutch to a 'snapping-hen' and thus the cock became known as a snaphaan or snaphance. The earliest use of the word in English is pejorative, meaning a thief or robber – the snapping action presumably referring to someone who snaps things up. Authorities are generally agreed that the earliest snaphance gun is preserved in the Stockholm Royal Armoury. The gun can be dated on its style to the mid-16th century.

A contemporary account describes how 35 harquebuses from Nuremberg were to be fitted up with 'snap-locks' in the Royal Armoury at Arboga in Sweden. The Stockholm gun has a Nuremberg mark on the barrel which, together with its provenance, strongly suggests that it may have been one of the 35. The barrel also bears a maker's mark, C.K. The jaws for the flint are very long, and are held by a vertical screw, and the heel of the cock is drawn out to form a long rear spur. The part which acts on

Some 17th century snaphance locks in the Victoria and Albert Museum. **Top to bottom:** a Russian snaphance lock, iron chiselled and parcel gilt; the late 17th century Swedish lock of Baltic type, of engraved and chiselled iron with long split jaws similar to those of the Löffelholz tinder lighter; and a German lock of about 1660, showing both the outside and the internal mechanism. This last lock typefies the later form of snaphance, with small jaws and internal mainspring.

the spring is very foreshortened. The pan-cover is operated by hand, with the flat-plate against which the cock strikes the steel attached to a long facetted bar. When the lock is fully cocked, it is held by a sear projecting from inside the lock through the lock-plate which is retracted by pulling the trigger, causing the cock to fall forward.

The closest parallels for locks of this sort are certain German snaplocks, and it has been pointed out that the jaws closely resemble those of the Löffelholz tinder-lighter. With the collectors' and enthusiasts' love of subdivisions and typology, these have been described as Baltic locks. However, as it is known that the Swedish Royal workshops contained a number of German craftsmen, there seems no reason why the snaphance-lock should not originally have been a German invention.

Locks of this form were very popular in Scandinavia and in Russia, where they were made until the 17th century. A detached lock, now in the Victoria and Albert Museum, presents a curiously anachronistic appearance as the form of the plate has the elegant lines associated with the best late-17th century flintlocks. However, the cock is of the Baltic type, with long split jaws and vertical screw, so reminiscent of the Löffelholz tinder-lighter of some 200 years earlier.

The further chronology of the snaphance can be followed by an examination of some dated German guns. All bear dates of either 1571 or 1572 on the barrels. One, from the Germanisches Museum, Nuremberg, has a long downward curving plain stock. It is particularly interesting because the lock is fitted not only with a snaphance but also with a matchlock operating on the same lock-plate. This snaphance is a much improved version of the earlier forms. The barrel bears two sets of maker's marks, W.W. and M.F., together with the date,

The snaphance gun in the Pitt-Rivers
Museum, Oxford. French or English,
late 16th century.

1572. On these later snaphances the spring is inside the lock-plate, the jaws are small and are fitted to a curved, bar-shaped cock. The sear no longer protrudes through the lock-plate, but catches in a notch in the tumbler, inside the lock-plate. Instead of a manually operated pan-cover, a bar on the outside of the lock-plate, linked to the pan cover, is struck by an extension on the cock which automatically opens the pan as the cock falls. The Nuremberg gun, together with its two companions, poses something of a puzzle to historians. Whereas the three guns are all apparently German, another related example has what might be described as French connections. This is a fine snaphance gun in the Pitt-Rivers Museum, Oxford. It has a stock inlaid with engraved staghorn and a very similar lock to the dated group. On the lock-plate is a mark inlaid with brass. The same mark occurs on some French wheel-locks so the whole group may be French. To confuse the issue even further, the stock of the Pitt-Rivers snaphance is inlaid with horn done in a characteristic Dutch or English manner. As with so many attempts to precisely locate the origins of these firearms, the more one searches, the more confusing the issue becomes.

In England a number of fine snaphance

guns and pistols were produced. A number of these are to be found scattered around the world in collections as far afield as Russia, Venice and Bohemia. Three pairs of snaphance pistols are in the Oruzheinaia Palace in the Kremlin, part of a gift made by James I to the Czars Boris Godunov (1598–1605) and Mikhail Feodorovich (1613–45). In Levens Hall, Cumberland, are preserved a pair of snaphance pistols made for Sir James Bellingham, former owner of the house. They are dated 1601 on the barrels, and are inscribed on the fence of the lock with the owner's initials. The stocks are plain with lemon-shaped butts. The locks are fitted with an L-shaped safety catch on the opposite side of the lock. This is a characteristic feature of most late 16th and early 17th century English guns and pistols.

In contrast to the austere Levens Hall pistols, some very finely decorated English firearms have survived. A large snaphance musket, together with a wheel-lock pistol and a powder horn, have long been in the possession of the Raymond family of Belchamp Hall, Essex. By tradition, these and other objects were the property of Sir William Harris of Shenfield, who married into the Raymond family in the early 17th century. The musket is

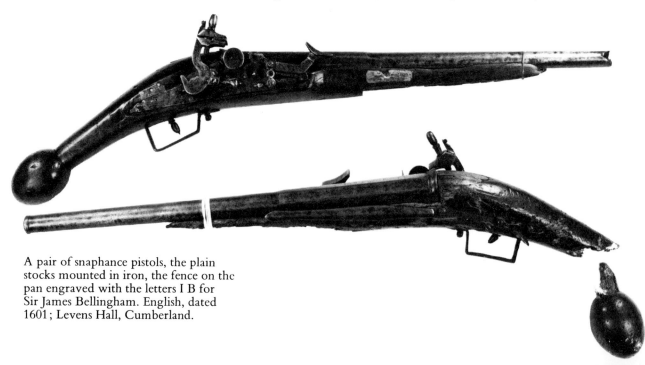

A pair of snaphance pistols, the plain
stocks mounted in iron, the fence on the
pan engraved with the letters I B for
Sir James Bellingham. English, dated
1601; Levens Hall, Cumberland.

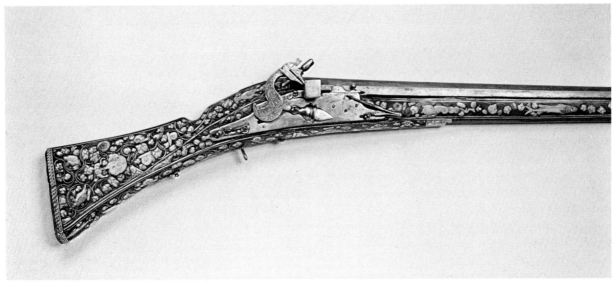

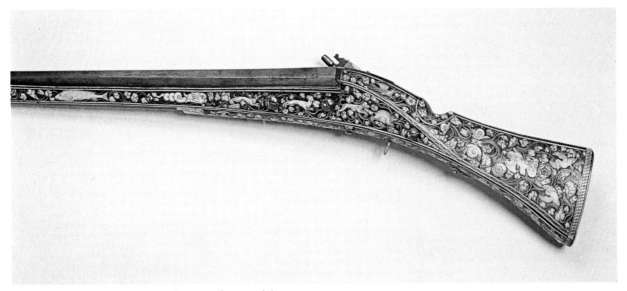

Two finely decorated English firearms from Belchamp
Hall, Essex. A wheel-lock pistol, the stock inlaid with
engraved staghorn, the barrel and lock damascened in
gold and silver; English, about 1580. And a snaphance
musket; English, dated 1588.

44

The small snaphance pistol recently acquired by the Armouries at the Tower of London. English, about 1600.

dated 1588 on the horn butt-plate, and the stock is inlaid with bone in a characteristically English design. This gun is by the same hand as a fine English petronel in Copenhagen. The wheel-lock pistol is of considerable interest, because not only is it one of the few English wheel-locks identified, but it also survives with much of its decoration preserved. It dates from about 1580 and the powder horn is decorated in a similar manner to the wheel-lock, and is also almost certainly English. Another fine English snaphance pistol was recently acquired by the Tower Armouries. It still retains traces of its gold damascening, and the butt is inlaid with horn and mother of pearl.

In Scotland, the snaphance was popular for a considerable time after it had been abandoned elsewhere. The exact relationship between English and Scottish snaphances has yet to be fully discussed, but there is evidence to suggest that the originality and individuality of Scottish firearms may well have influenced English gunmaking in the early 17th century. Again, the Tower Armouries provide an interesting example of the Scottish snaphance in the form of a pair of pistols from the Collection of Lady Seafield, formerly belonging to Ludovic Grant. Characteristics of the Scottish examples of the snaphance are the long tapering lock-plate, the comb-like projection on the back of the cock and the form of the jaws.

A rare form of lock which combines features both of the wheel-lock and the snap-hance is the segment or quadrant lock. Instead of a revolving wheel, there is a steel quadrant to be cocked. This moves forward on pulling the trigger and slides against pyrites. It is said to have been invented by Rafaelle Verdiani, an Italian gunmaker, and a gun fitted with this lock signed by him, dated 1619, is preserved in the Tower of London.

A lock that was widely used in the Mediterranean area is that known to collectors as the Miquelet. The word is derived from Catalonian dialect, but there is no evidence to show that it was ever applied during the 17th century to the kind of lock it is used to describe.

It seems to be simply a collector's term introduced during the 19th century. The Spanish lock was known to contemporary writers as a 'patilla' and had very distinct features. The large V-shaped mainspring was placed on the outside of the lock-plate, the screw for tightening the jaws on the cock is in the form of a large ring, the front of the cock is filed down to a chisel edge and is held by two sears which protrude through the lock-plate, one for half-cock, the other for full-cock. The 'L'-shaped battery combines the pan cover and steel.

The so-called Roman lock, which also had an external mainspring, was popular in Italy until about 1650. It is thought that the 'miquelet' came to Spain through the Spanish territory of Flanders in about 1610, possibly from Scandinavia or Germany. According to Spanish legend, this form of lock was invented

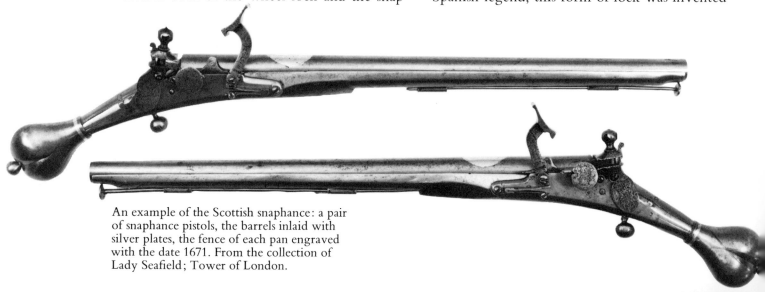

An example of the Scottish snaphance: a pair of snaphance pistols, the barrels inlaid with silver plates, the fence of each pan engraved with the date 1671. From the collection of Lady Seafield; Tower of London.

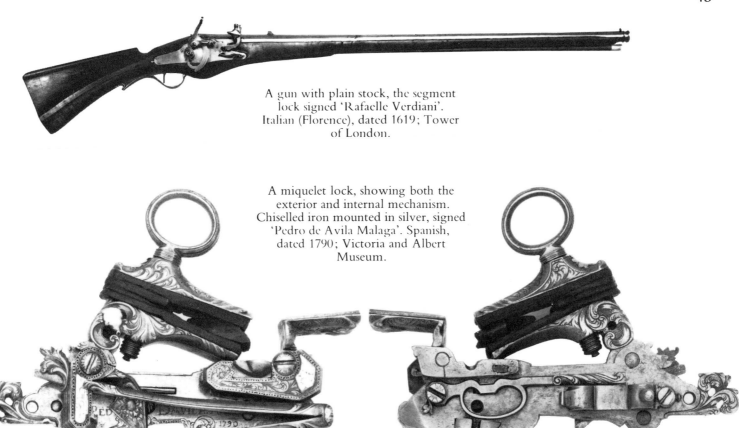

A gun with plain stock, the segment
lock signed 'Rafaelle Verdiani'.
Italian (Florence), dated 1619; Tower
of London.

A miquelet lock, showing both the
exterior and internal mechanism.
Chiselled iron mounted in silver, signed
'Pedro de Avila Malaga'. Spanish,
dated 1790; Victoria and Albert
Museum.

by Simon Marquart, but there is evidence to suggest that it was already in use by about 1610. The earliest examples are to be found on three wall guns now in the Real Armería, in Madrid. These have all been dated to about 1625. One bears the sickle mark of Simon Marquart, the younger, and is the only known lock of this form by this maker.

In the Victoria and Albert Museum, there is an interesting pair of late 17th century blunderbuss pistols fitted with miquelet locks, the barrels of which are engraved with the owner's name. The stocks are ornamented with a roughly engraved silver overlay, characteristic of Ripoll, a well-known centre of Spanish gunmaking. The miquelet-lock continued in use in Spain until the early 19th century, although later versions are heavily influenced by the French flintlock and bear little relationship to the sturdy and vigorously decorated locks of the 17th and 18th centuries.

The true French flintlock was introduced some years before the so-called English lock but because it has close connections with the snaphance, it is convenient to discuss it first. Like the snaphance, on the English lock the sear protrudes through the lock-plate. Examples have also been excavated from American sites such as Williamsburg and Jamestown. Over the years, these sites have yielded many interesting fragments of firearms, including some rare English military wheel-locks. The English lock had the pan-cover and steel made as one unit, and a small extension on the tumbler which caught in the sear to give the half-cock position. English locks often have a 'dog-catch' on the outside of the lock-plate, which catches in a notch cut in the cock. Locks fitted with the catch are called 'dog-locks'.

One of the earliest 'dog-lock' pistols has an interesting American connection. In Pilgrims' Hall, Massachusetts, is a pistol belonging to John Thomson who sailed to America to join the Pilgrim Fathers in 1622. He presumably brought the pistol with him from England. He is said to have used it on many occasions in fights with the Indians. A series of pistols fitted with 'English locks' are preserved in the splendid

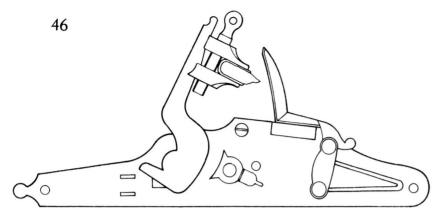

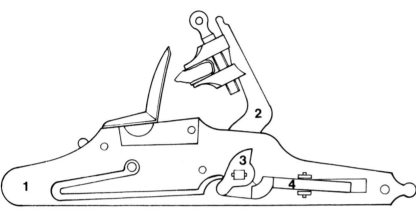

The mechanism of an English dog lock, about 1640. 1, lock-plate; 2, cock; 3, tumbler; 4, combined sear and trigger-lever. The wedge-shaped extension on the tumbler is caught in a notch in the sear, giving the half-cock position.

armoury of the Popham family at Littlecote House, Berkshire. Sir Edward Popham held the house for Parliament during the English Civil War and much of the equipment he provided for his troops still survives in the house including an unparalleled collection of English pistols, dating from about 1640.

There are also some interesting long guns fitted with early dog-locks. Preserved in the museum at Alton, Hants, are two English guns dating from the 17th century. One is a long gun, or birding-piece, fitted with an English 'dog-lock', which came from Mill Court and is associated with the Civil War in southern England. The other, more interesting gun is very short and is also fitted with a dog-lock. In size, it closely resembles a carbine, with its shapely downward curving stock, but it has also been suggested that it may have been a youth's birding-piece. The metal mounts are unmarked, but on the right side of the butt are carved the letters R.S. The barrel is of

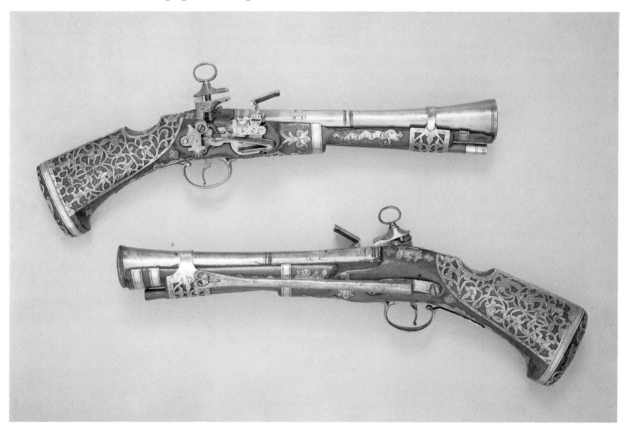

A pair of miquelet blunderbusses, the mounts of engraved silver. Spanish (Ripoll), about 1690; Victoria and Albert Museum.

octagonal section and is of small calibre. The plain dog-lock has a shapely tapering lock-plate which suggests a date around the middle of the century.

A birding-piece in the hands of a skilful shot was a very effective weapon. At the siege of Sherbourne Castle in 1645, a Royalist sniper shot a number of Sir Thomas Fairfax's officers with a birding-piece from the safety of a high tower. His skill was probably due to his peace-time occupation, for he is described in a contemporary account as a 'keeper of parks'.

It is fortunate for historians that Louis XIII of France (1601–43) took an intelligent interest in all matters relating to firearms. He had a substantial collection, which is by no means merely the taste of a rich and powerful monarch with the money to indulge his whims. Much of the collection consists of severely plain military weapons without the slightest trace of decoration – interesting only from the point of view of mechanism or mechanical design. The collection did, of course, also include some very luxurious arms. Of outstanding importance is the fact that an inventory was taken of royal possessions at the order of Louis XIV in 1673. This included the firearms in the Royal collection. Each firearm was given a number, usually roughly stamped into the stock – often underneath the barrel, or roughly engraved on the top strap of the barrel. By comparing the numbered inventory descriptions with the numbered firearms, many of the firearms formerly in Louis XIII's collection have been identified. The collection includes a short wheel-lock birding piece with plain flairing stock, probably used by the king when he was a boy. His physician, Jehan Héroard, writing about the king in his diary, tells how at the age of 10 he already owned seven guns. The collection seems to have survived intact until the French Revolution, but was broken up after 1815.

Louis XIII of France took an active interest in firearms, of which he acquired a substantial collection. This painting from the school of Rubens, 'Louis XIII of France crowned by Victory', shows a number of arms including two different types of wheel-lock at his feet.

Dr Torsten Lenk defined the flintlock in a monumental work on the subject published in 1939, and most writers have followed it. He stated that to be a true flintlock, it had to have the steel and pan-cover made as one unit, with a vertically moving sear engaging in two recesses in the tumbler, on the inside of the lock. The two recesses in the tumbler gave either half-cock or full-cock. Although several early flint-locks have now been recognised, two guns are of outstanding importance. Both satisfy Lenk's criteria. One is in the Metropolitan Museum, New York, the other is in the Hermitage, Leningrad. The first gun, once in the Renwick Collection, was formerly in the Cabinet d'Armes of Louis XIII, and is described in detail in the Royal Inventory as entry 134.

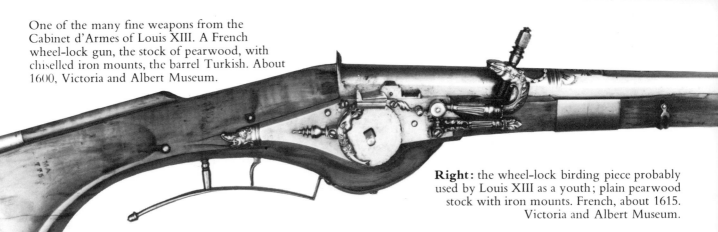

One of the many fine weapons from the Cabinet d'Armes of Louis XIII. A French wheel-lock gun, the stock of pearwood, with chiselled iron mounts, the barrel Turkish. About 1600, Victoria and Albert Museum.

Right: the wheel-lock birding piece probably used by Louis XIII as a youth; plain pearwood stock with iron mounts. French, about 1615. Victoria and Albert Museum.

Lenk did not have an opportunity of examining the gun himself, but had to rely on photographs and other people's opinions of it. On top of the barrel near the breech, is stamped a maker's mark consisting of a crossbow set between two letters. The letters were read by Lenk as I.B. As the inventory mentions that the gun was made at Lisieux, and the Bourgeoys family of gunsmiths were known to be working there at that time, Lenk looked for a member of the family with the same initials and came up with Jean le Bourgeoys, who died in 1615. He suggested that this flintlock must therefore date from 1615 or

before. When this gun was sold at auction in 1972, it was discovered that the first initial was a P not an I. The obvious candidate was, therefore, Pierre le Bourgeoys, who died in 1627. It should also be noted that in 1962 Sir James Mann, in his catalogue of the arms and armour in the Wallace Collection, had already indicated that a wheel-lock pistol attributed by Lenk to Jean le Bourgeoys was by Pierre.

The invention of the true flintlock must have taken place before 1627, somewhat later than Lenk suggested. The Renwick gun, apart from being an exceptionally important technical document, is a splendid work of art. The barrel

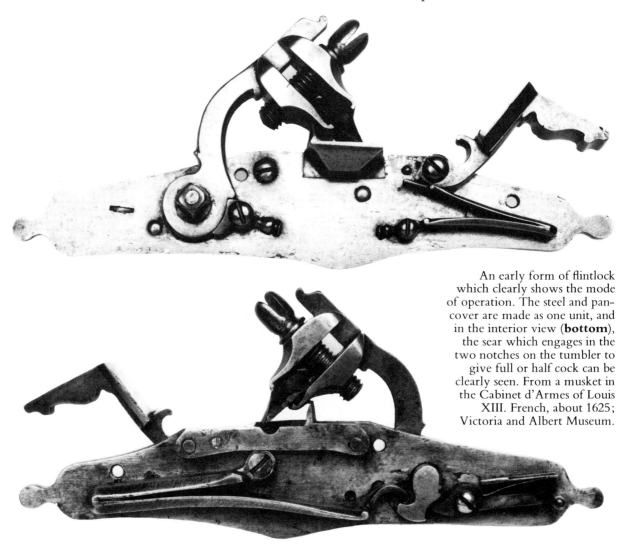

An early form of flintlock which clearly shows the mode of operation. The steel and pan-cover are made as one unit, and in the interior view (**bottom**), the sear which engages in the two notches on the tumbler to give full or half cock can be clearly seen. From a musket in the Cabinet d'Armes of Louis XIII. French, about 1625; Victoria and Albert Museum.

Details of the lock, barrel and stock of gun number 134 from the Cabinet d'Armes of Louis XIII. A flintlock fowling piece bearing the crowned cipher of the king and the mark of Pierre le Bourgeoys of Lisieux on the barrel. French, 1615–20; Metropolitan Museum, New York. Photo Sotheby's.

Marin le Bourgeoys (died 1634), painter, sculptor, maker of musical instruments, and gunsmith.

is blued and decorated with gilt scrollwork at the breech, in the centre and at the muzzle. The stock is of ebonised pearwood, with the butt terminating in a scroll inlaid with silver wire. Set in the stock are silver birds, snails and other animals in brass and a floral inlay in mother of pearl. On the side of the stock, opposite to the lock, is inlaid a crowned L for Louis XIII. The lock and other steel mounts are etched with scrollwork and gilt – altogether a gun fit for a king. This gun is very light, quite short and would have been the ideal size for the young monarch. It was bought for the Metropolitan Museum, New York, for the record price of £125,000.

In the Hermitage, Leningrad, is another fine gun with the arms of France and Navarre on a round plate on the butt. These arms were used by Henri IV of France and his successors. In the stock is roughly engraved the number 152, and a description exactly corresponding to this gun is to be found in the Inventory. On a plate beneath the stock is engraved 'M. le Bourgeoys a Lisieul'. Marin le Bourgeoys, born in the middle of the 16th century, started his career as a painter. He was certainly a painter until 1583, when he was paid for some decorations he did in Lisieux for the entry of the Duc de Joyeuse. He is recorded in 1589 as 'peintre ordinaire' to the Duc de Montpensier, Governor of Normandy.

He came from a family specialising in the manufacture of locks, watches, crossbows and guns, so had a sound technical background. Appointed to be 'valet de chambre' to Henri IV in 1598, perhaps as a means of avoiding the stringent guild regulations, he seems to have spent all his working life in Lisieux. He apparently became interested in other crafts, for he is recorded as a sculptor and a maker of musical instruments. He also made a terrestrial globe for Henri IV, which was placed in the Louvre with other examples of his work. However, Marin soon became interested in guns for in 1605 he is described as a gunsmith, and records mention that he had already made an air-gun with a copper barrel. In that year he was given money for travel to Paris, so that he could present the king with a hunting-horn, a crossbow and a gun 'all of his own making'.

The Hermitage gun is an even more luxurious production than the previous one. The blued barrel is enriched with gold damascening, the gilt-bronze mounts are etched and chiselled and the stock is inlaid with silver and brass wire. In contrast, the lock is rather plain with traces of lightly engraved scrolls. The scrolls and ornamention are so similar to the other Louis XIII guns that it seems likely that, if Pierre le Bourgeoys made the gun, then the decoration was carried out by his brother Marin le Bourgeoys.

There are other pieces of evidence which suggest that these early flintlocks are slightly later in date than was previously thought. The Hermitage gun signed by Marin le Bourgeoys has a classical bust on the stock almost identical to one appearing on a flintlock gun in the Musée de L'Armée signed by François Duclos and dated 1636. A poem by François Poumerol

One of the earliest 'true' flintlocks. A
sporting gun bearing the arms of France
and Navarre and the maker's signature,
'M. le Bourgeoys a Lisieul'. Probably
made for Henri IV of France; from the
Cabinet d'Armes of Louis XIII. French,
1605–10; Hermitage, Leningrad. The
detail shows the classical bust adorning
the stock.

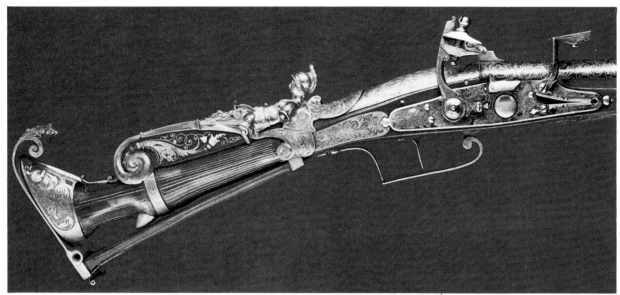

published in 1631 and addressed to Louis XIII
discusses the advantages of the snaphance over
what is described as the 'new' flintlock. This
reference is only relevant if the flintlock was
still considered to be a comparatively recent
invention in 1631. On the basis of the above, the
gun in the Metropolitan Museum should now
be dated to about 1615–20 and the gun in the
Hermitage to about 1605–10.

It is not recorded which member of the
Bourgeoys family actually invented the new
lock, however the considerable reputation for
technical skill and mechanical innovation which
Marin le Bourgeoys possessed must make him a
very strong claimant. While the French adopted
the 'true' flintlock very quickly, other countries,
particularly Italy, retained the wheel-lock' and
the snaphance until comparatively late. Although Northern Italian makers ceased making
wheel-locks in the latter part of the 17th century,
they stubbornly clung to the snaphance lock
until nearly the end of the 18th century.

A compromise solution was adopted
by some gunsmiths. Before the middle of the
century, they used the system of the French
flintlock, while maintaining the steel and

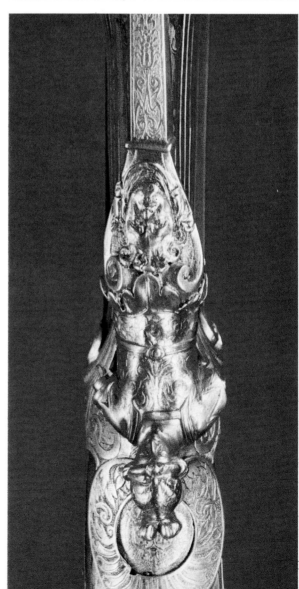

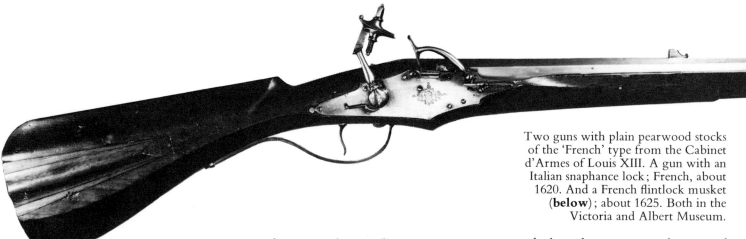

pancover as two separate elements. The true flint-lock was also adopted with pan and cover made in one, and the two systems co-existed until the 19th century.

In addition to the mechanical improvements in this period, there were a number of changes in the actual shape of firearms. Wheel-lock pistols of the late 16th century tended to be angular with the butts terminating in large balls. After 1600, these pistols were rather elongated with much smaller butt-terminals. French wheel-locks, in particular, have long elegant lines with the stock extending underneath the lock to house the mainspring. Italian wheel-lock pistols are almost straight, often with a sharply tapering butt swelling out at the end rather like the handle of a dagger. The shape of some English pistols of the 1640s retained the old wheel-lock form, with a housing for a wheel-lock plate, but, in fact, having snaphance locks. This feature is also found on certain Russian snaphances, made in the Kremlin armoury workshops by Dutch craftsmen. In general, the introduction of the flintlock lock-plate led to the pistol having slender lines, the long tapering narrow lock-plate admirably suiting the gently curving stocks.

The development of long guns was rather different. It is often forgotten that the stocks of mid-16th century guns were not designed to be held against the shoulder. They were supported by the arms and pressed against the right cheek. The butt was flattened on one side to allow firing from this position. At some point in the 16th century, the butt of certain guns developed an angular form, curving sharply downwards behind the breech. This type of stock is normally called the Castilian, or Spanish, stock and was almost certainly first developed in Spain.

The occupation of the Low Countries by the Spaniards, under the Duke of Alva in the late 16th century probably brought this form of stock to the notice of Northern European forces. Its advantages were obvious, for it allowed the gun to be held firmly and, by cutting the end of the stock straight, it could be held against the chest. In consequence, it allowed more powerful charges to be used, and guns with large calibres to be developed. Gradually, the shape of the Spanish stock became higher and thinner, and a recess for the thumb was cut near the breech. The invention and development of the flintlock had as much influence on guns as it had on pistols, and the narrow lock-plate led to a general narrowing of the stock. The recess for the thumb was now extended down the stock, forming a high tapering comb. In addition, the sharp corners were rounded and the stock took on the basic elements of the modern form. Because of its rapid adoption in France, it is usually called

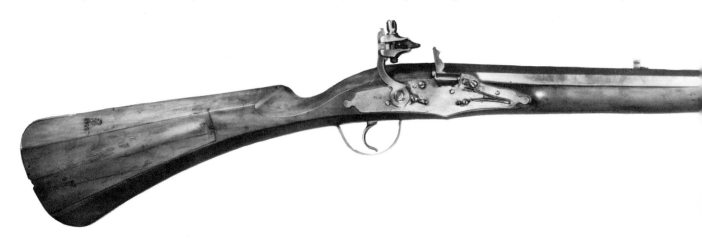

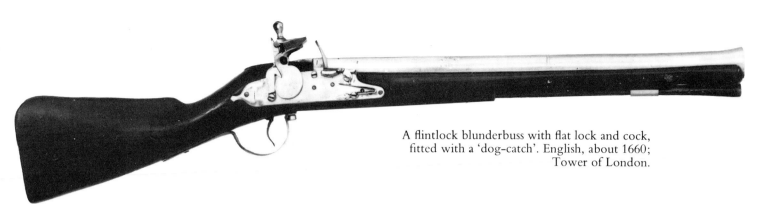

A flintlock blunderbuss with flat lock and cock, fitted with a 'dog-catch'. English, about 1660; Tower of London.

the 'French' stock. At some time around 1650 it was found more advantageous to place the gun against the shoulder and, towards the end of the century, the butt was slightly recessed to enable it to fit more snugly in this position.

From 1550 to 1650, the form of the barrel underwent various changes. There were three basic types of barrel in use up to 1600, those in the form of a simple round tube, octagonal barrels, and a combination of the two. In a few instances, the octagonal barrel was retained until the 18th century, generally for sporting guns. The tschinke and similar weapons were usually fitted with octagonal barrels. Experiments to produce lighter barrels were made in the 17th century, principally under the influence of the Italian and French gunsmiths. The barrels of the Cominazzo family were particularly prized. Felix Werder of Zurich (1591–1673) specialized in firearms with bronze and brass mounts, and special brass barrels. These were made of a brass alloy and were exceptionally thin and light. Modern science has solved the problem of how they were made by establishing that the brass alloy was toughened by cold hammering.

Military literature, particularly of the latter part of the century, abounds with technical terms for guns. The more common types of gun generally employed for military purposes included the musket, a long heavy gun, and the carbine, a short gun which seems to have been designed especially for use on horseback; a harquebus, similar to a carbine, was a birding-piece used for sport. Terms such as petronel and caliver were widely employed and seem to have been applied to a form of carbine.

The great length and weight of some 16th and 17th century guns necessitated the use of a rest to support the barrel. This was a short wooden pole, fitted with a V-shaped metal fork at one end, on which the gun was placed. The other end usually terminated in a spike which was stuck into the ground. Although the majority of rests are plain, some very elaborate English examples have survived, dating from the 17th century with the poles inlaid with bone and mother of pearl.

One of the best known forms of carbine is the blunderbuss. The name comes from the colourful German word for this type of gun, 'thunder gun'. 'Blunder-bushes' are mentioned in English inventories as early as the mid-17th century, and this type of firearm was always especially popular in England. The stocks are usually of plain wood, fitted with brass furniture. Most barrels are also of brass. Early blunderbusses have wide bell-shaped muzzles which were thought at the time to make the pellets spread over a wide area. Although gunsmiths realized that this was incorrect, and returned to the normal barrel form, blunderbuss barrels retained their distinctive profile because of large mouldings at the muzzle.

Blunderbusses were especially popular for defence against highwaymen, and some have the name of the particular coach inscribed on the barrels. Certain late blunderbusses were fitted with an additional form of protection – a short bayonet on a spring.

Gervase Markham, a military authority writing in 1625, recommended that harquebusiers 'should have active and nimble bodies, joined with good spirits and ripe understandings'. He goes on to recommend the sort of equipment they should carry: 'a harquebus of three foot three inches long and the bore of

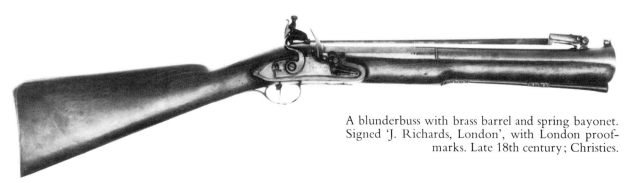

A blunderbuss with brass barrel and spring bayonet. Signed 'J. Richards, London', with London proof-marks. Late 18th century; Christies.

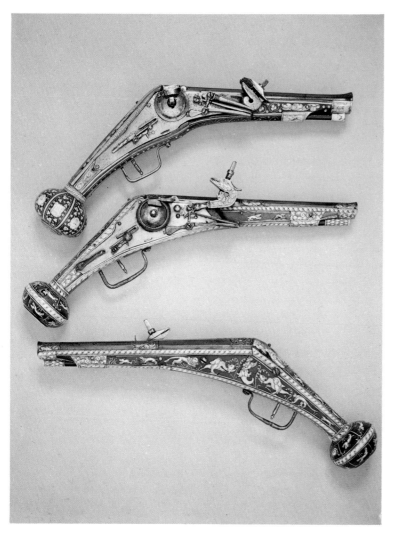

Three wheel-lock pistols with barrels of combined round and octagonal form. The stocks are inlaid with engraved staghorn. The top one bears the mark of Peter Danner of Nuremberg, the bottom pair the marks of the town of Augsburg and the barrel-smith Jäger. About 1575; Victoria and Albert Museum.

20 bullets in the pound, with flash priming-box and moulds, cartridges which will serve either for this or any other piece on horseback'.

The musket, as described by Sir Thomas Kellie in 1627, had a barrel four feet long. Charles I ordered that all muskets designed for use by the Trained Bands should be of this length. Many of the muskets in use during the English Civil War were of the matchlock variety. The match was usually made from twisted strands of cord which had been treated with chemicals so that they would burn slowly. If the weather was wet, or if the match was used up, the musketeer was helpless.

During the siege of Devizes, Wilts., in June 1643, Sir Ralph Hopton found there was not sufficient match for his musketeers; he accordingly ordered his officers to search and take 'all the bedcords they could find and to cause them to be speedily beaten and boiled' – a splendid example of military initiative which saved both Hopton and his musketeers.

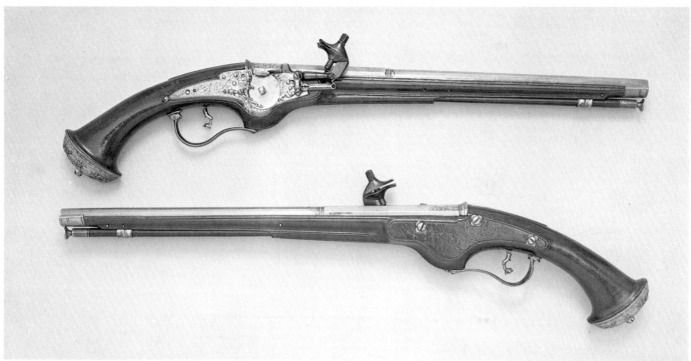

A pair of wheel-lock pistols with barrels, lock-plates and mounts of gilt and engraved brass. Probably by Felix Werder of Zurich. About 1640; Victoria and Albert Museum.

Facing page, top: an English musket rest of about 1630 and a French matchlock gun of about 1570. Victoria and Albert Museum. **Bottom**: a Dutch engraving of 1607 by Jacob de Gheyn, showing a matchlock being fired from a musket rest.

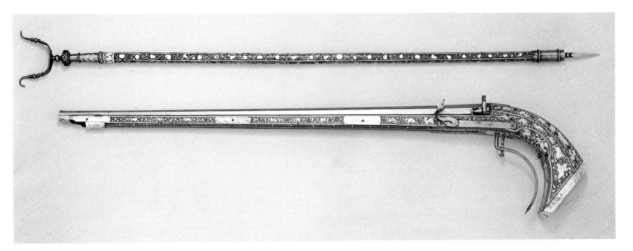

12

17 — Drive your panne

18 — Shut your panne

19 — Cast of your Loose pouder

20 — Blowe of your Loose pouder

21 — Cast about your musket.

Traile your rest.

23 — Open your charge

24 — Charge your musket

25 — Draw forth yo.r scouring stick

26 — Shorten your scouring stick

Put in your bullet & Ra. home.

Withdrawe yo.r scouring s

Shorten yo.r scouring s

Returne your Scouring s

The Battle of Edge Hill during the
English Civil War, 1642. From an
engraving by Van der Gucht
made in 1730.

57

The match was usually lit at both ends and was first blown on to produce a good steady glow. The glowing matches of a number of musketeers often gave away their position. At the siege of Lathom House, during the Civil War, the besieged Royalists stuck lighted matches in balls of clay to draw Parliamentarian fire. Another hazard when carrying lighted match was accidental explosion. At Edgehill, for example, a soldier 'clapped his hand carelessly into a barrel of powder with his match between his fingers, whereby much powder was blown up and many killed'.

Considerable pains were taken by professional soldiers to teach their less enthusiastic pupils about the proper management of their firearms. In England, from Elizabeth's reign, the Trained Bands met once a month during the summer to learn how to use their arms. However, as one of their teachers ruefully observed, the only thing they ever learned was how to drink. He complained that many of his pupils spent their time in the inns and taverns tippling when they should have been exercising in the field. Sir Thomas Venn, in his *Military and Martial Discipline*, published in 1672, observed that the God they worshipped in their training was not Mars but Bacchus. In order to prevent accidents, and also for reasons of economy,

recruits were usually taught to shoot by first using 'false fires', that is only priming-powder, leaving out the main charge and the ball.

Some Trained Bands were taught by professional soldiers known as muster-masters. The professionals obviously appreciated the value of proper training. One noted that 'trayning of the shotte is the firste and most requisite parte of the travelle of the muster-master'. They were also aware of the dangers of poor equipment. Humphrey Coningsby, describing the duties of a muster-master, says that he should have 'a specyall eye to the cockes of their peeces and the pypes of their flaskes. That the springs therof be not broken, nor lame, but sownd and quick'.

One of the advantages of all the military treatises produced in the late 16th and early 17th centuries is the wealth of information on the effectiveness of firearms. Sir Edward Cecil, writing in 1621, observed that '200 paces is as much as a mans ayme will serve to hitt any reasonable mark in the world, and that our musquets will reach. . . .' Humfrey Barwick, a well-known military writer, states in a treatise on firearms written in 1594 that a musket would kill a man in proved armour at 200 yards, unproved armour at 400 yards and without armour at 600 yards.

Facing page: another figure by Jacob de Gheyn; note the powder horn hanging from his belt, and the glowing cord match held in his hand. He is surrounded by a series of engravings from H. Hexham's *Art Militaire* of 1639, illustrating musket drill 'as practised in the warres of the united Netherlands'.

Chapter Four

18th Century Firearms
and Duelling Pistols

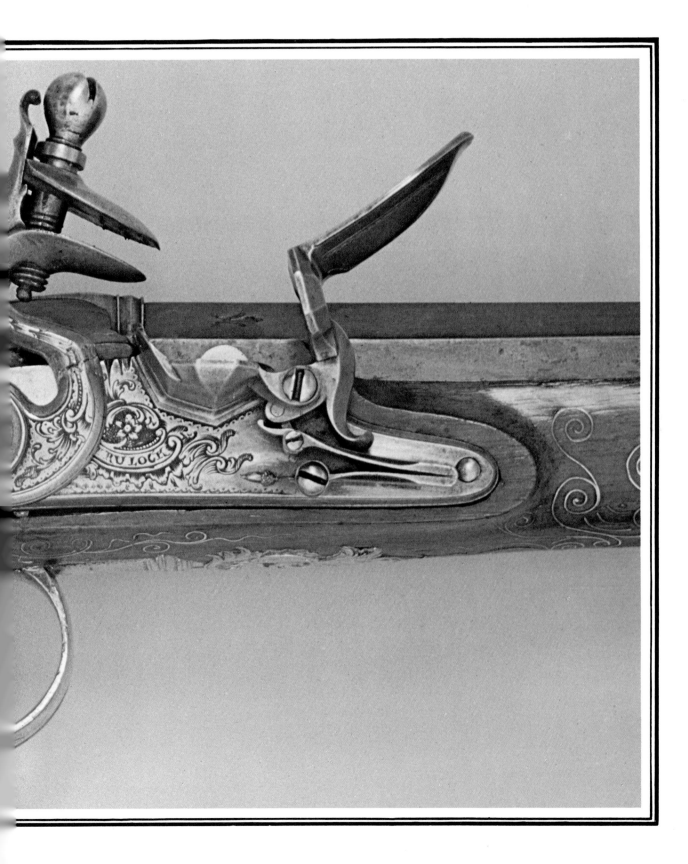

Previous page: Detail from one of a
pair of flintlock pistols, the silver mounts
with Dublin hallmarks, the Spanish
barrels stamped 'Sarasva', the locks
signed 'Trulock'. Irish, about 1770;
Victoria and Albert Museum.

THE PERIOD from 1660 until the early 19th century has justifiably been described as the age of the flintlock. The number of technical innovations to improve the lock were comparatively few, mainly because the basic mechanism could hardly be improved.

The actual design changed very little, although there were distinct national forms. One of the changes was in the shape of the lock-plate. Up to 1660, lock-plates were long and flat, but in about 1680, the lower edge of the lock-plate began to develop a slight downward curve. At the same time, the surface of the lock-plate was made convex. This fashion owed much to French influence, and is found on firearms until the last quarter of the 18th century. However, at the end of the previous century a number of locks were made in the old shape, with flat cocks fitted to flat lock-plates with sharply bevelled edges. After 1750, this shape of lock again came into fashion, although the cock underwent some alteration. Up to about 1650, cocks are generally flat and fairly thin in section. The elegant 'goose-neck' cock was introduced in about 1660. This was of half-round section and was thicker than the earlier forms. After 1630 the buffer, a small metal stop which prevented the cock from falling too far, was generally discarded although it is found on certain English and Scottish firearms at a later date. Instead, the lower end of the steel was extended and recurved to serve the same function.

The powder manufactured throughout the 17th century was comparatively slow burning, which meant that a longer barrel was necessary to allow the ball to gain full power from the charge. During the early years of the next century, great efforts were made to improve gunpowder. The new powder burned more quickly, enabling gunmakers to reduce the length of the barrels very considerably. A pistol barrel of about nine inches became standard after 1715. There were also changes in the form of the stock of both pistols and guns. Up to the middle of the century, pistol stocks were generally plain with an oval butt. After 1640, pistol butts were usually covered with a metal plate, and within 20 years this butt-plate had two extensions running up the stock. Their length was progressively increased until, by the early 18th century, they reached almost to the end of the lock-plate. After this the length was gradually reduced, as was the size of the butt cap. In the last quarter of the 18th century, an increasingly large number of pistols, especially duelling pistols, were made without butt caps.

The long gun was shortened towards the end of the previous century. The butt was made with cleaner lines, the lower edge proceeding in a straight line back from the trigger guard, with a recess in the butt for the shoulder. As with pistols, gun butts in the early part of the 18th century were fitted with a substantial metal plate at the end with two vestigial extensions on each side. This plate was reduced in size as the century progressed, and the comb at the top of the stock, particularly on French and German muskets, was very pronounced.

The technical changes made to the mechanism of the flintlock from 1660 to 1800 were principally attempts to make the flint-lock function more rapidly and efficiently, rather than attempts to find an alternative system of ignition. By 1650, the tumbler was supported through a metal bracket attached to the inside of the lock-plate. The tumbler was also made with a square bar which protruded through the lock-plate and fitted into a square hole in the cock and was secured by a screw. One mechanical innovation re-introduced in the middle of the 18th century was the detent. This feature is found on certain French and Italian firearms of the 17th century, but was at that time comparatively rare. The purpose of the detent was to stop the sear from catching in the half-cock recess of the tumbler when the cock fell into the pan. It was simply a small lever, pivoting on the tumbler which occupied the half-cock recess.

One of the problems with the flintlock mechanism was the considerable time lapse between the trigger being pressed and the main charge igniting. A feature introduced in about 1775, in order to speed this process, was

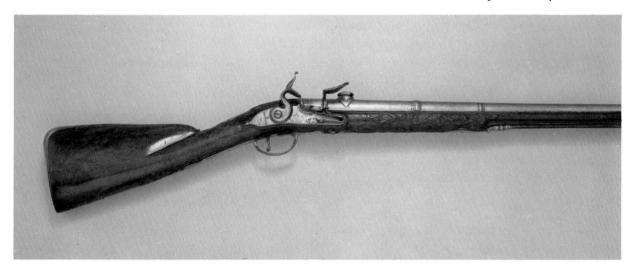

Two 18th century flintlocks which typify the development of the long gun in this period: An English breech-loader (**top**) with mounts of silver and iron, the lock signed 'R. Rowland'; about 1720; Bradford City Museum. And a French gun of about 1770, with mounts of silver and gilded iron, the barrel inlaid with brass; Victoria and Albert Museum.

the roller-bearing. The steel was extended on the opposite side to the buffer to take a small roller-bearing. This reduced the friction on the steel and allowed it to move more quickly, admitting more sparks to the pan. A swivel had been introduced between the tumbler and the mainspring on better quality firearms in about 1770, and this helped to reduce the 'drag' on the lock caused by friction. In the mid-18th century gunsmiths noticed that the touch-hole became badly distorted and enlarged through frequent use, and that the pan became badly corroded. One solution was to line the pan and touch-hole of the best firearms with gold. Joseph Manton claimed to have introduced the use of platinum for the same purpose. As

it was a harder metal, the plug around the touch-hole could be made thinner, thus increasing the speed of ignition.

In 1812, Manton also patented what he described as a 'gravitating stop which, being applied to the lock of a gun or pistol will render the same less liable to be accidently discharged while loading if it should have been inadvertently set at full cock'. The stop was a weighted lever linked to a pawl which pivoted on the outside of the lock plate. If the gun was held in a position for loading — with the muzzle pointing upwards — the weighted lever automatically engaged in a recess cut in the edge of the cock, preventing it from falling into the pan.

Other safety devices, however, had

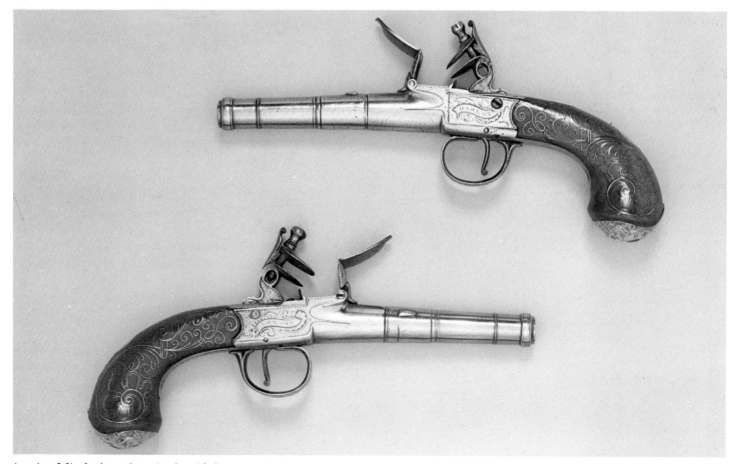

A pair of flintlock pocket pistols with box-locks (see page 64) and brass 'turn-off' barrels, the latter signed 'Hadley London'. The silver butt-caps bear Birmingham hallmarks for 1777–8. Victoria and Albert Museum.

The English gunmaker Joseph Manton (1766–1835) and the patent for one of his many inventions, a system for 'The breeching of guns on an improved principle'.

been put on flintlocks before the gravitating stop. The use of the back-catch for the 'dog-lock' has already been discussed; in the late 17th century another safety device was introduced, and is found on most high quality guns and pistols. It consisted of a bolt which slid into a notch on the edge of the cock. On pistols, this was often linked with a mechanism which was in turn linked to the trigger-guard, which could be moved to lock the cock, pan-cover and steel.

Included in the patent for a gravitating stop were other inventions of Manton's: 'An inverted breeching which contains cavities to permit the escape of any water . . . when used in rainy weather . . . a lip added to the hammer of guns and pistols', which prevented water from entering the pan, and an unlikely sounding device which caused the click caused by the drawing back of the cock to be 'a pleasant and musical sound'.

A number of better quality firearms, made after 1780, are fitted with waterproof pans. The pan was made with a projecting rim over which the cover fitted, with a small hole drilled through the fence behind, to drain off excess moisture.

A type of lock which is found on a large number of small pistols in the 18th century is the box-lock. Instead of being placed on the side of the lock-plate, the cock and other mechanism are contained between the two plates. Usually, the lower end of the cock is cut with recesses and acts as the tumbler. The cock is supported by a screw passing through both containing plates.

Two attempts were made towards the end of the 18th century to make a flintlock in which no screws except the ones on the cock were used. The London gunmaker Jonathan Hennem produced one such lock in which spring pivots were substituted for the usual screws. A more successful screwless lock was developed by another London gunmaker, Henry Nock. It is based loosely on the box-lock principle with most of the mechanism held between two plates. One of the plates is held by a locking lever. By simply lifting the lever and slightly turning one of the retaining plates, the whole lock can be readily dismantled. In terms of simplicity and technical brilliance, this lock is a masterpiece. However, as with so many good inventions, it did not receive the attention it deserved and was taken into service by the Board of Ordnance on only a very limited scale.

Henry Nock, born in 1741, was a lock-maker by trade. He developed a new lock for muskets in 1770 and, together with William Jover and John Green, patented a covered flintlock in 1775. He made some Ferguson rifles for the East India Company and also won a contract from the Royal Navy to supply seven-barrelled volley guns, a number of which survive. Nock's volley-gun was also made in a sporting version which seems to have been more successful, judging from the number that survive. He started to make sporting guns in 1784, when he occupied premises in Ludgate Hill, London. One of his more important inventions was the development of a special breech, which he patented in 1787. It consisted of two chambers, the powder firing in a small chamber first before igniting the main charge. In 1789, Nock was made gunmaker-in-ordinary to the King and, in 1802, was elected as master of the London Gunmakers' Company. He died two years later.

One of the best-known types of firearm developed in the 18th century was the duelling pistol. Although some affairs of honour continued to be settled with swords until the 19th century, a vogue for duelling with pistols began in England in about 1770. At that time the doyens of fashion, such as Beau Nash at Bath, were advocating that swords should not be worn socially, so gentlemen were obliged to seek other weapons with which to salve their wounded pride. Pistols made especially for duelling have a number of recognizable characteristics. Firstly, they are made in matched pairs. The barrels are usually about 10 inches long and are of small bore, generally about ·57.

As with other contemporary pistols, the early examples are usually fully stocked, that is to say the barrel is supported by the stock up to the muzzle. The steel mounts are usually of a dark colour but some silver-mounted duelling pistols are known. The butts have a a graceful curve and are usually quite thin, to

A dismantled example of Henry Nock's screwless lock, from a heavy cavalry pistol of about 1800. Tower of London.

Top: This pair of English flintlock duelling pistols is uncharacteristically luxurious, with fine silver mounts bearing the London hallmark for 1770 and the maker's mark I.K. The locks are signed 'Twigg'. About 1770; Sotheby's. **Bottom of page:** A cased pair of flintlock duelling pistols with browned barrels signed 'Wogdon London'. Note the pronounced curve of the stock, characteristic of Wogdon pistols. About 1775; Sotheby's.

provide a firm grip, and are cross-hatched with lines to prevent the butt slipping in the palm. Great efforts were made to give the pistol a nice balance, so that, when held correctly with arm outstretched, it would automatically aim at the target. The butts are usually rounded at the end with a slight 'turn' at their extremity. Few have butt-plates and, if found on duelling-pistols, they are fitted absolutely flush to the surface of the stock. For the purposes of aiming, they are always provided with a back-sight. In contrast to so many other firearms of the period, these pistols are marked by their almost total lack of decoration. Any that appears is usually limited to small areas of engraved ornament on the lock and trigger guard with occasional gold inlay on the barrel. The gunmaker's skill was chiefly applied to the mechanism, and the duelling pistol exhibits all those qualities, such as restraint in decoration and mechanical excellence, which made the work of English craftsmen of the 18th century so much admired.

It has been suggested that the earliest duelling pistols were made by Joseph Griffin, of Bond Street. This theory is based on resemblances between some pistols made by Griffin and Tow in about 1778, and a flintlock pistol by the same makers with hallmarks for 1777–8. The principle points of resemblance lie in the shape of the stock, which has the thin section and rounded butt found with the duelling pistol. Anyway, it is clear that, by 1775, a number of London gunmakers were making pistols especially for the duel. In their earliest form, the barrels of these pistols are octagonal at the breech, changing to the familiar round section about halfway to the muzzle. Shortly before 1780, however, a number of duelling pistols were made which were fitted with barrels

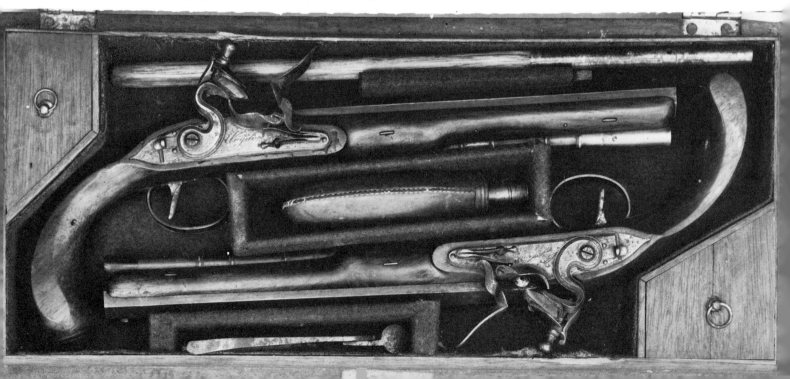

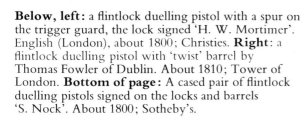

Below, left: a flintlock duelling pistol with a spur on the trigger guard, the lock signed 'H. W. Mortimer'. English (London), about 1800; Christies. **Right:** a flintlock duelling pistol with 'twist' barrel by Thomas Fowler of Dublin. About 1810; Tower of London. **Bottom of page:** A cased pair of flintlock duelling pistols signed on the locks and barrels 'S. Nock'. About 1800; Sotheby's.

of octagonal section throughout the whole of their length.

A considerable amount of ingenuity went into the actual mechanism of the duelling pistol. Two technical improvements were introduced in about 1780 which provided a quicker, smoother action for the flint-lock: the roller bearing and the swivel on the tumbler. Both these features allowed the lock to function more efficiently. By reducing the friction of the moving parts, they permitted the flint to strike the steel with less delay – an important point when both parties fired at each other simultaneously. Certain duelling pistols were fitted with what are known as set-triggers. The mechanism

is set by pushing forward the trigger, depressing a lever which engages in a spring-operated catch. The catch and lever were indirectly connected to the sear. When the trigger was pulled, however lightly, a spring struck the sear and released the cock. A small screw fitted adjacent to the trigger connected to this device could be adjusted to give a light or heavy 'pull' on the trigger as required.

One of the most famous makers of pistols of this kind was Robert Wogdon, who had premises in Haymarket, London. This maker specialized in duelling pistols and advertised his pistols as being dead accurate at a range of 20 yards. The stocks of Wogdon pistols have a pronounced curve and the steel furniture is usually very plain. Wogdon enjoyed a high reputation, but other makers, such as Durs Egg, Henry Nock, Samuel Nock and H. W. Mortimer also produced fine work. The city of Dublin also became a centre for the production of duelling pistols. Makers such as John Rigby and Thomas Fowler made fine pistols which were, and still are, keenly sought after. There are numerous contemporary accounts of duelling.

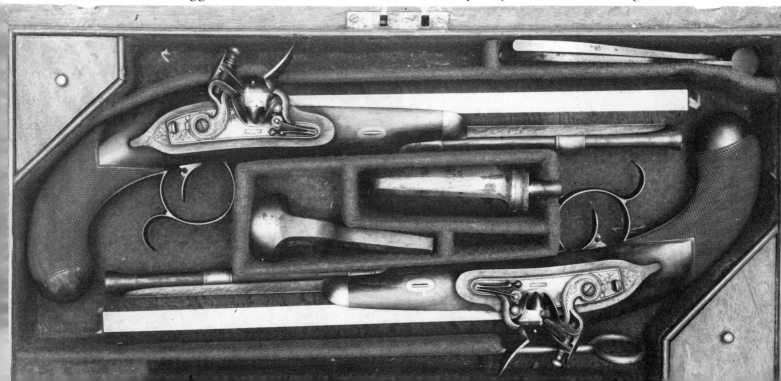

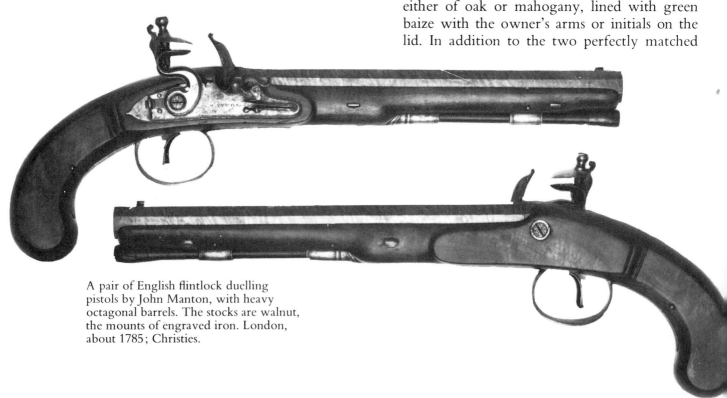

This elegant pair of flintlock pistols has barrels of brass and silver mounts. The locks are signed D. Moore. The silver trigger-guards bear London hallmarks for 1802–3, but the pistols themselves date from about 1760. Victoria and Albert Museum.

One of these tells of some duelling pistols which had been in an armoury in Ireland from 'the reign of Elizabeth', one of them called Sweetlips, the other Darling. Presumably these antique pistols, which are described as having brass barrels, were remounted some time during the 19th century. Joseph Manton is said to have introduced a new style of pistol at the end of the 18th century. The comparatively short barrels were of octagonal section, deliberately made heavy so that they would not shoot 'high'. In spite of their weight, the bore was always rather small, about ·40. Manton is also said to have invented what was known as 'secret rifling'. The barrels of all duelling-pistols by tradition were smoothbore. Manton managed in certain duelling-pistols to cut so fine a series of rifled grooves in the barrel that they would be invisible at the muzzle of the weapon.

By about 1805, some gunmakers were fitting their pistols with a special trigger-guard which had a small loop projecting from the base which

was for the middle finger. This was supposed to give a firmer grip and thereby ensure a steadier aim.

A fashion grew up after this for pistols with saw-handle butts – perhaps started by H. W. Mortimer. The butts are fitted with a spur at the top and are reputed to have a much better balance. As their name suggests, they turn down at a sharp angle rather like the handle of an 18th century saw. The percussion-lock and its rivals were all fitted to duelling pistols. Some fine examples survive, fitted with Forsyth's sliding primer and Manton's pellet-lock, the stocks retaining their traditional form. A number of late duelling-pistols were made fitted with locks for the percussion-cap. By 1840, duelling in England had more or less died out and gunmakers ceased to make these highly-specialized firearms.

At the height of their popularity duelling pistols were sold fitted in a case containing a large number of accessories. The case was made either of oak or mahogany, lined with green baize with the owner's arms or initials on the lid. In addition to the two perfectly matched

A pair of English flintlock duelling pistols by John Manton, with heavy octagonal barrels. The stocks are walnut, the mounts of engraved iron. London, about 1785; Christies.

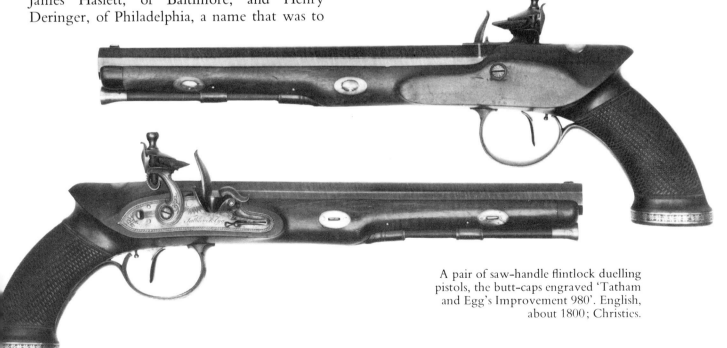

pistols – matched not only in physical appearance, but also in weight – the case would contain a powder-flask and measure, a bullet-mould, a cleaning 'jag', a rod with an attached 'worm' for taking out the charge, a screwdriver, a pricker for cleaning out the touch-hole, a mallet for tapping the ramrod, and a hand-vice for removing the mainspring. There was also a metal bottle for oil, a pouch with spare flints, a wad-cutter and spare material for making wads.

Although England is always thought of as the home of the duelling pistol, some fine examples were produced on the continent and in America. Simeon North, of Middletown, Connecticut, produced many solidly made military pistols of various models, including those of 1799, 1813 and 1828, and also made presentation pistols and some fine duelling pistols. His pistols are usually half-stocked and are closely related to current London fashions in the shape of the stock and barrel. Other American makers of duelling pistols include James Haslett, of Baltimore, and Henry Deringer, of Philadelphia, a name that was to

become legendary in the middle of the 19th century for his small percussion-cap pistol.

In France, the practice of duelling with swords did not really decline until the Revolution in 1789 and even after that the 'arme blanche' was always the favoured weapon for the duel. With the rise of Napoleon, duelling with pistols became more widespread. French duelling pistols are usually fully stocked to the muzzle and the butts are generally very angular. The French, unlike the English, had no objection to rifling, so most duelling pistols are fitted with rifled barrels. Of octagonal section, the French barrels are larger in the bore than their English counterparts. Instead of being chequered, the stocks are usually fluted. After 1820, it was not usual to fit ramrods so the accessories of French duelling pistols include brass or steel loading rods and a mallet to drive the charge home. Many of the best Parisian gunmakers made these pistols, but those specially celebrated include the Le Page and Renette families.

A pair of saw-handle flintlock duelling pistols, the butt-caps engraved 'Tatham and Egg's Improvement 980'. English, about 1800; Christies.

An elaborate example of a cased pair of pistols with matching accessories. They are breech-loading centre-fire target pistols with ebony stocks fitted with mounts of chiselled iron in the Gothic style. Austrian (Vienna), about 1860; Victoria and Albert Museum.

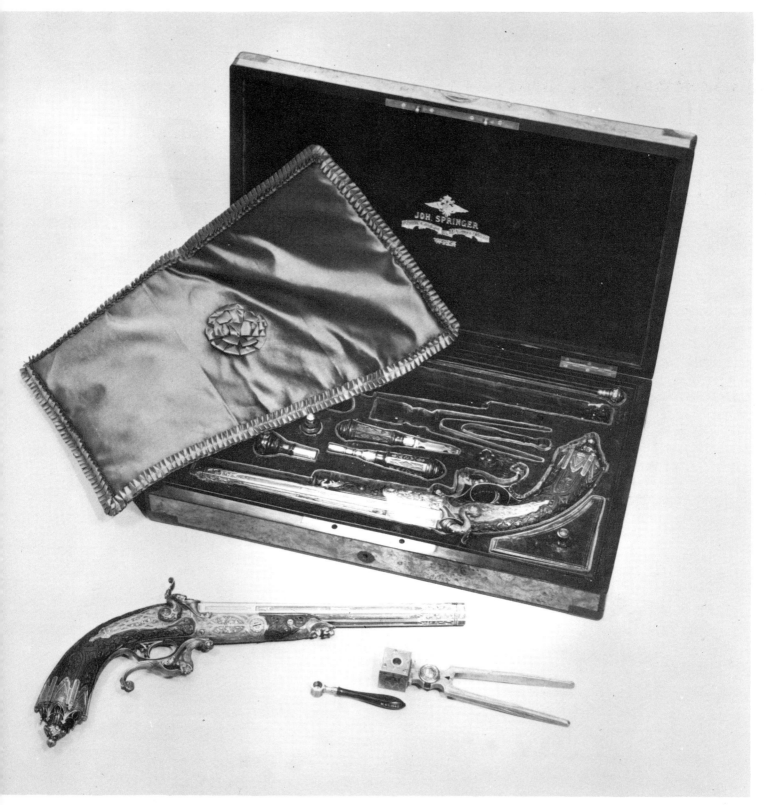

One of a pair of percussion cap pistols, the browned barrels signed 'I. Christoph Kuchenreuter', the locks signed 'Manton'. English, about 1800; Sotheby's.

Germany has always favoured the sword for settling matters of honour, consequently the number of pistols made there for duelling is comparatively small. However, one of the most famous of all the great gunmaking families, the Kuchenreuters of Regensburg, made cased pairs of pistols which could be used for duelling, in the second half of the 18th century. The stocks are usually plain, but later examples are chequered after the English fashion. Their pistols often have plain mounts of silver or brass. The rifled barrels have the name of the maker inlaid in silver on the top, and the end of the stock is usually in the characteristic German 'birds-head' form.

Any consideration of this subject would not be complete without an account of an actual duel. In the spring of 1816, an English major named Green went to the theatre in New York. In the adjacent box was a Mr Price in the company of some ladies. Price accused Green of staring 'too steadfastly' at some of the ladies under his protection. Green replied that in looking at the woman, 'he only exercised a privilege common to every man in England, of regarding beauty in whatever place or rank it was found' and apologised if he had unwittingly given offence. After Green had departed, Price is said to have regaled the company with an account of how he had made a British officer

'knuckle to him'. On hearing of this at a later date, Green immediately challenged Price. As duelling was illegal in New York, they crossed the Hudson River to Hoboken, a 'retired and silent situation for the murderous operations of the laws of honour'. Green won the toss for the ground and chose the south side. They fired at each other at a distance of 12 paces, but neither was hit. After fruitless efforts by the seconds to bring about a reconciliation, they fired again. Again neither was hit. Green then announced that he felt that both sides had vindicated their honour. Price strongly disagreed and insisted that fire be continued until one or other fell. By mutual consent, each party advanced three paces until, with only six paces separating them, Price 'received his antagonist's ball through the brain and fell dead upon the spot'. Green fled to Europe, 'to avoid all trouble from this calamatous affair'.

Another account of the same duel says that Major Green had insulted one of the ladies in the next box. He had apologised, but was openly despised by his fellow officers for having apologised to a 'damned Yankee'. According to this account, Green was forced to return and provoke Price to fight by striking him. A marble statue to Price was erected on the site of the duel with an inscription regretting 'his fall in such a sanguinary conflict'.

'A duel between George Garrick and Mr. Baddeley, 1770.'

The practice of duelling with pistols
spanned more than a century. **Below**:
'Duel between Wilkes and Martin',
from an 18th century engraving.
Facing page: the duel between the
Duke of Wellington and the Earl of
Winchelsea, 1829. **Above**: a duel in
France, 1880.

Chapter Five

Alexander Forsyth and the Percussion System

The Reverend Alexander James Forsyth (1768–1843)

FROM THE 17th century, chemists and military writers experimented to try to improve the explosive force of gunpowder and the range and power of firearms. It was found that the explosive power could sometimes be improved by adding a fulminate to the powder. This was obtained by dissolving certain metals, such as antimony, mercury, or even gold, in acid. However, the powder obtained by precipitation was found to be extremely unstable and volatile – as early experimenters found, sometimes to their cost.

At the end of the 18th century, in spite of such setbacks, Edward Howard, an English chemist, devised a reasonably safe method of making a fulminate from mercury. This was one of the first essentials for the successful development of the percussion-lock. It is one of the many ironies in the history of firearms that one of the most efficient and widely adopted systems of ignition should have been developed by a minister of the church. The Reverend Alexander James Forsyth was born in 1768, and after university education at Aberdeen, he was installed as the minister of the parish of nearby Belhelvie. Not only was the minister interested in chemistry, but he was also very fond of shooting. In his workshop, not far from the Manse, he did some experiments to improve the explosive power of gunpowder. As his predecessors in this dangerous field of endeavour had found, the fulminate was no substitute for gunpowder and the minister was inevitably blown out of his own workshop by one of these experiments.

He then tried using the fulminate as a priming powder to set off the main charge. However, he found that it burned so fast that it failed to ignite the charge. He then made the simple, but important, discovery which was to enable him to bring about a minor revolution in firearm design. He found that, if instead of using a spark from a flint to set off the fulminate, it was hit with a hammer, the fulminate would explode much better. This discovery is the essence of the percussion-lock. Forsyth used a heavy tube, which had a small touch-hole and was fitted with a pan. He placed a normal charge of gunpowder, held by a wad, in the barrel, and put some fulminate in the pan. When hit with a hammer, the fulminate exploded and almost instantaneously set off the main charge.

The speed of the ignition was an obvious advantage. As a shooting man, Forsyth must have often cursed his flintlock fowling piece with its smoke, bright flash and long delayed ignition. He immediately set about devising a lock which would work on his newly-discovered principle. An essential feature was the making of a container to hold the fulminate which, at that period, came only in the form of a powder. His lock was mechanically similar to the flintlock, but with important differences. Instead of jaws holding the flint, the cock now came in the form of a square-headed hammer. The steel and the priming pan were removed and a small round plug was screwed into the side of the barrel. A touch-hole was pierced through this into the barrel, with a cavity in it. The magazine, shaped like a 'scent bottle', containing the fulminate, was attached

Previous page: The premises of the London gunmaker Joseph Egg, from a 19th century engraving.

Facing page: A double-barrelled Forsyth patent gun, with damascus barrels and engraved iron locks, here shown dismantled in its case. About 1816; Sotheby's.

The percussion lock invented by Alexander Forsyth. The 'scent-bottle' magazine (1), having deposited its charge of fulminate into the round plug or 'roller' in the side of the barrel (2), has been revolved to the firing position, and the hammer (3) is in contact with the spring-loaded firing pin (4).

to the plug in such a way that it could be turned around it. When it was placed in line with a cavity, a small portion of the fulminate was allowed to drop into the cavity. The 'scent bottle' could also be turned in order to bring a firing pin loaded with a spring directly underneath the hammer. The gun was loaded and the lock cocked in the normal way. When the trigger was pressed, the hammer fell down on the pin, which hit the fulminate, and the explosion set off the main charge. One of the main considerations was that it was quick, easy and also cheap to convert the old flintlock mechanism to the new system. It retained all the mechanical advantages, and simply replaced the flint and steel with a quicker and more efficient ignition system.

With his new invention, Forsyth set off for London in April 1806. He was fortunate in having some influential relations, for his cousin Henry Brougham, of Penrith, was later to become Lord Chancellor. Through the good offices of Brougham, the lock was shown to various sportsmen. Sir Joseph Banks was particularly impressed and drew it to the attention of Lord Moira, Master General of the Ordnance. Moira recognised the military possibilities and

persuaded the reluctant Forsyth, who was anxious to return to his home and flock in Scotland, to undertake some experiments with the new lock in the security and secrecy of the Tower of London.

Initially, all went well; a device for testing powder and an early experimental lock were produced at this time and are still preserved in the Tower. However, the workmen involved, were accustomed to making flintlocks. Because of the dangerous and volatile nature of the fulminates used, in Forsyth's own words, 'much time was spent in making and breaking a great variety of locks and compounding a multitude of detonating powders'. With Moira's encouragement, he eventually produced a lock for a carbine and a lock for a three-pounder cannon. Both are preserved. Under Forsyth's direction, the carbine – a Baker cavalry model – was converted from flintlock to the new percussion form of lock.

In March, Forsyth was paid £300 and was asked to go with one of his workmen and take the new percussion lock to Woolwich for trial. Here the lock was fitted to a musket barrel and the trial took place under the watchful eye of a Lieutenant-Colonel Bloomfield. Its object was to find out if the new lock was more economical in its use of powder than the rival flintlock. The performance of the new lock failed to impress the observers, and Forsyth was told to remove himself, and what was referred to as 'his rubbish', from the Tower by a new and unsympathetic Master General of the Ordnance. He was paid the balance of his expenses and was only too delighted to return to the peace and quiet of the Manse after his brush with military bureaucracy.

However, his visit to London had one lasting result. In April 1807, he took out a patent, drawn up by his friend James Watt, for what was described as 'an advantageous method of discharging or giving fire to Artillery and all other fire-arms, mines, chambers, cavities and places in which gunpowder or other combustible matter is or may be put for the purpose of explosion'. This patent was so carefully worded that it prevented nearly all attempts by others to produce any new locks based upon the percussion system. Forsyth spent a considerable part of the remainder of his life fighting, and winning, lawsuits over the infringements of his patent.

In June 1808, with the backing of James Brougham, Forsyth took a lease on premises at 10 Piccadilly, London, and founded Alexander Forsyth and Co. From these premises guns and pistols of the highest standard were produced

including some beautiful duelling pistols. A number of improvements to Forsyth's invention were made by the firm. Forsyth had the advantage of employing James Purdey, one of England's most distinguished craftsmen.

One improvement to the Forsyth lock was the introduction, in about 1813, of the sliding-primer. With this system, the primer was linked to the hammer by means of a short bar. As the hammer is drawn back for cocking, the primer is drawn over the top of the pan and a small quantity of fulminate falls into the pan. This sliding-primer was fitted to both long guns and hand firearms and far more examples survive of this form of Forsyth percussion lock than of the earlier rolling primer.

Forsyth died in 1843, having received little financial reward for his invention. Having tried for many years to extract his due reward for a system – by then widely adopted by the military – Forsyth was finally granted the sum of £1,000 by the Board of Ordnance some three months after his death. Alexander Forsyth and Co. exhibited at the Great Exhibition of 1851, and continued in business until September 1852, when it closed.

In spite of its clear wording and wide application, the patent had no validity abroad. It was, therefore, the Continent that saw nearly all the experiments to try to develop Forsyth's invention. In April 1810, a Parisian gunmaker, François Prélat, produced an exact copy of the Forsyth lock and proceeded to patent it under his own name. Another well-known French gunmaker, Le Page of Paris, who held the position of Arquebusier du Roi, produced a number of firearms which were directly derived from the locks patented by Forsyth.

Forsyth's patent did not expire until 1821 and even in England, there were various attempts to make locks based on his system. These rival efforts were mostly devoted to

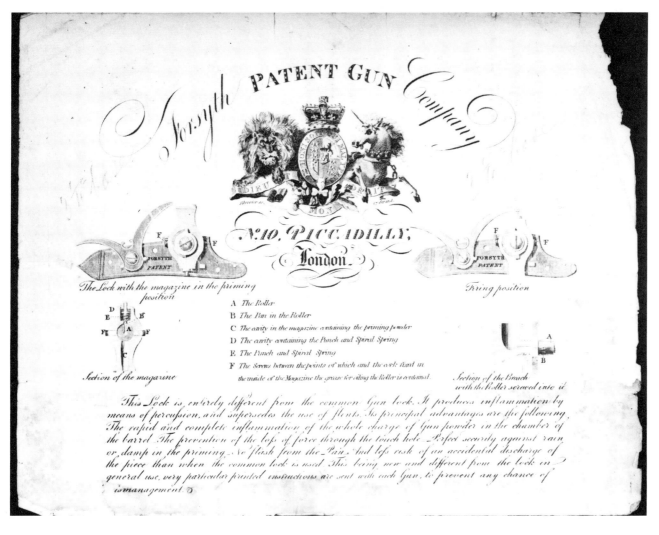

The trade card of the London gunmaker
Joseph Egg, who patented a magazine
lock in 1822.

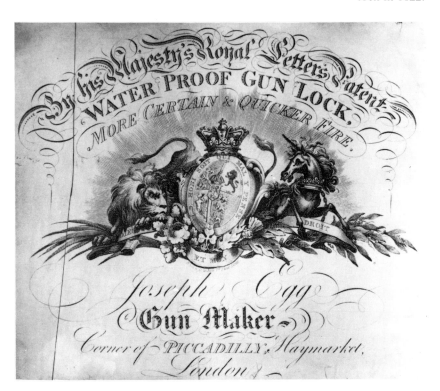

In 1818, Manton patented a tubelock which was much more successful. A very slender cylinder of copper was filled with fulminate and pushed into the touch-hole. The hammer had a head cut in the form of a blade, rather like a screwdriver. When the hammer fell, it struck the middle of the copper tube and set off the fulminate inside. The one major advantage of this system was that the fulminate was in a container protected from damp and rain. These locks would not misfire, even in the worst weather conditions. As with the other percussion locks, this was widely imitated on the Continent and other versions of it were also made in England.

Joseph Egg, another London gunmaker, produced a magazine lock in 1822, which incorporated the principles of the pellet lock. On top of the barrel were set tubes containing the pellets which moved into the pan through gravity. In 1825, Isaac Rivière took out a patent for a percussion-lock which resembled the earlier box-lock. All the mechanism was concealed

changes in the way the fulminate was used. One of the most interesting was that patented by Joseph Manton in February 1816. Even this great gunmaker, who went to considerable lengths to circumvent the patent with his pellet-lock, was dismayed to hear from Chief Justice Abbott in 1818 that his lock 'was an imitation of Mr Forsyth's' and was prevented from taking out a patent for it.

Manton advertised his new invention as 'the greatest improvement in guns ever', and went on to say that a gun fitted with the new invention would fire 'much stronger and 10 times quicker'. In this system, the detonating powder was formed into small pellets made from fulminate of mercury coated with iron oxide. The hammer contained a detachable tube into which the small pellet was dropped. A hollow pin was then fitted into the tube holding in place the pellet. When the hammer fell, the pin struck the pellet and detonated it and set off the main charge. This lock was also pirated in France and patented under another gunsmith's name in 1821. The Manton pellet lock had disadvantages. For example, every time the lock needed to be re-primed the tube had to be taken out and the pin removed.

The trade card of Isaac Riviere, inventor
of another form of percussion lock
resembling the box-lock.

81

The new forms of percussion lock were
often fitted to existing guns. This
English sporting gun of about 1805 is
fitted with a tube-lock by Joseph
Manton. Tower of London.

and only the top part of the hammer showed
above the lock.

One of the problems with all the percussion locks was finding a safe and convenient
method of storing the fulminate. One solution
was to enclose the fulminate in another material,
and in the 1820s a number of gunmakers enclosed
it in a small disc, usually of waxed paper or
cardboard, but sometimes of soft metal. The
disc was then placed in a cavity next to the
barrel of the gun.

The gunmaking trade went to considerable lengths to find a really satisfactory method
of using a fulminate in a percussion lock. With
all the various experiments, it would have been
surprising if a satisfactory solution to the problem had not been found. The answer was the
percussion cap. A projecting vertically pierced
nipple was screwed into the side of the barrel,
over the top was placed a small container with
a hollow base so it would sit firmly on the
nipple, and in the container was placed a small
quantity of fulminate of mercury. A hollow

recess was made in the head of the hammer to
allow it to fit over the projecting nipple when
it fell onto the latter.

The actual invention of the percussion
cap is, and was at the time of its invention,
the subject of some controversy. It is not possible simply to search the patents for the earliest
mention of it, because Forsyth's patent pre-
cluded the possibility of the idea being patented
in England without infringement.

A number of claimants have appeared
for this invention. Captain Lacy, writing in
1842, put the whole issue of the invention of
the copper cap very succinctly when he observed
in his book *The Modern Shooter*, 'Although the
copper cap be a diminutive, yet there have been
as many claimants to the honour of the invention as, of old, there were contending cities for
the honour of having given birth to Homer'.
These include Joseph Egg, who called himself
'Inventor of the Copper Cap' on some of his
trade labels, and Colonel Peter Hawker, the
noted 19th century sportsman. According to
Lacy, Egg assured him that he had made the
first percussion cap from 'an old penny-piece'.
Lacy was also assured by James Purdey that he
had produced a brass-cap, made from the tip of

Among the many variants of the
percussion lock inspired by Alexander
Forsyth's invention was this lock by
William Moore. English, about 1830;
Tower of London.

an old umbrella, at least two years before Egg. In the sixth edition of his famous *Instructions To Young Sportsmen*, Colonel Hawker tells how he took a drawing of a perforated nipple and the detonating powder in the crown of of a small cap to Joseph Manton, who in a few weeks produced a gun working on this system. It is certain that Manton converted one of Hawker's guns to the new system in 1819, but it is possible that the invention was not the work of a gunsmith, but of an artist named Joshua Shaw. Shaw's account of his own work was given much later to the English ironmaster Henry Wilkinson. In this account, Shaw states that he was already working with metal cap primers in the shape of top hats in 1814. He went to America in 1819, and took out a patent for a copper cap system of ignition on June 19th, 1822. The French gunmaker Prelat, who is often mistakenly credited with an early patent for a percussion cap, apparently only produced copies of mechanisms that were already existing. He built up a thriving business by the simple device of importing firearms from England and then taking out a patent in France for any new technical developments he discovered in the mechanism of these weapons.

Forsyth's patent lapsed in 1821, but it was not until 1823 that the first English patent for the percussion-cap was taken out. The new lock did not find immediate favour with either sportsmen or the military. The first caps were

An engraving from the ninth edition of Colonel Peter Hawker's *Instructions to Young Sportsmen* (1844), showing the Colonel on horseback with his friend Joseph Manton standing beside him, holding a gun.

unpredictable in their power – some scarcely detonated the main charge, others blew the entire lock off. There was a substantial body of opinion that still preferred the reliable flintlock. Gunsmiths catered for both the conservative and the pioneer, providing firearms fitted with both systems. In 1822, Sampson Davis patented what he called a Devolving Pan lock which combined both percussion and flintlock on one lock plate. The lower of the two jaws holding the flint was designed to be used as a hammer. The pan and nipple are combined and can be aligned to bring the required feature in line with either the hammer for percussion, or the cock for the flintlock. One of the dangers of the percussion cap was the possibility of its actually exploding in the face of the shooter, and this led to certain guns being developed in which the hammer operated underneath the stock or at the side. The first patent for a percussion cap ignition actually taken out in England was for an under-hammer lock. It was taken out by John Day, of Barnstaple, in 1823. The adoption of the percussion lock for military forces did not take place in Britain until 1838. In France, some percussion firearms were issued as early as 1829, but it was not fully adopted until 1840. In America, by 1842, the percussion lock had been made official for all troops. The principle behind this system – detonation by percussion – is the same principle that is used in modern cartridge firearms today.

The premises of a 19th century gunmaker
– Deane's at the Monument, London.

Chapter Six

Firearms and their Decoration

Previous page: Detail of a German wheel-lock rifle, showing the walnut stock inlaid with engraved staghorn. Mid-17th century; Victoria and Albert Museum.

AS HAD happened with the manufacture of armour and edged weapons, the firearms industry developed in those areas which had a ready supply of raw materials, such as iron-ore. Prominent from an early period were the gun-making centres of Germany and Spain. The city of Nuremberg was famous for the making of locks, whereas Eibar and Suhl were noted for barrels.

Each manufacturing centre had its own mark, which was stamped on all its products. Each maker was required by guild regulations to register his mark with the particular guild for which he worked. The town-mark was usually based either on the name of the city or town, such as Suhl, or on its coat-of-arms, as with Nuremberg. The maker's marks usually incorporated his initials, often with a suitable device. The mark of the French gunmaker Pierre le Bourgeoys, for example, consists of a crossbow between the letters P. B. because the Bourgeoys family were initially cross-bow makers. Makers could be identified by comparing the marks on their products with the registration books or plates left in the guildhall. These would give the full name of the maker next to his mark, and the date when he entered and completed his apprenticeship.

The different craftsmen working on firearms worked at first for separate guilds. In the 17th century it was usual for the complete process of firearms manufacture to come under the guilds of gunmakers which had been established in various countries. This was not not always the case, for an account of a mid-18th century lawsuit, involving a gunmaker, describes the London firearms trade as being divided into 21 different branches 'each looked upon as so many distinct trades'. The different trades listed included such diverse tasks as 'trigger and nail filer', and 'screwer together'. Often the gunmaker who sold the finished

An example of a watered steel barrel, from an 18th century Turkish gun. Victoria and Albert Museum.

product to the customer had only assembled the work of a number of different hands. Because of the diversity of manufacturing centres in Europe, a firearm could contain the work of a number of specialists of different nationalities. Spanish barrels, for example, were particularly sought after by the gunsmiths of England and France, and it is not uncommon to find an 18th century French firearm fitted with a Spanish barrel.

From their inception, firearms have needed the skills of a number of craftsmen with different specialities: a carpenter to make the stock, a locksmith to make the mechanism, and a barrel-smith to make the barrel. The stock-maker went to great lengths to find suitable wood, such as walnut, often fitting several pieces together as it was very difficult to find a suitably-grained wood without flaws, of sufficient length. The lock-plate and the lock were forged and then chiselled and filed to the required shape.

The manufacture of barrels was a particularly skilled trade. These were made either by drilling out the centre of a solid rod, or by hammering a long thin strip of iron around a rod and welding the seams together. The resulting tube was then bored and finished off with a file. The so-called 'Damascus' or 'stub-twist' barrels fashionable in the 18th and 19th centuries were made by wrapping the thin strip around a rod – rather like making a cardboard tube – and lap-welding the edges. The resulting spiral structure was brought out by washing the surface with a weak acid.

The barrels produced by oriental gunmakers were always highly prized and many European makers mounted up these finely watered barrels for their clients, fitting them with European locks and stocks. These barrels were made by forging together rods of low carbon-content iron and high carbon-content steel and making the barrel by one of the methods already described. After finishing, the surface was etched with acids which brought out the contrast between the dark steel and light iron. This produced the 'watered' effect which was so much admired. At an early date, gunmakers discovered that they could artificially colour the surface of the barrel by using oxidising agents. The barrels and locks of many firearms were treated in this way. The range of colours which could be produced by this method was considerable, although various shades of blue or brown were the most popular. After manufacture, each barrel was proved by firing from it a measured charge, considerably more than was normally used, so as to establish that the barrel would not burst.

Very few of the surviving hand firearms, from before 1530 are decorated. There are, of course, exceptions such as the late 14th century hand-gun from Mörkö, and the Monk's Gun at Dresden. One of the possible reasons for this is that, in their earliest forms, firearms were made for practical use and not for discriminating aristocratic patrons. The earliest finely decorated examples were almost certainly made for use in sport. Some finely decorated Spanish matchlocks dating from about 1560, are preserved in Vienna. The barrels, damascened in gold with floral scrolls, have stocks covered with black velvet, held by a series of gilded rosettes.

A number of guns survive from the 1530s, having stocks with inlaid designs executed in horn or ivory, often stained in different

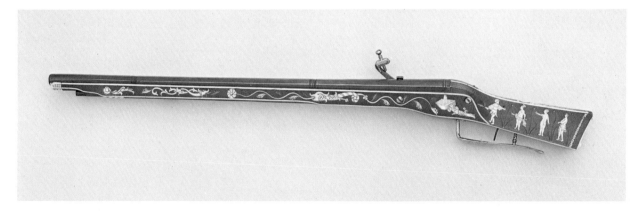

Two views of a wheel-lock gun, the stock inlaid with engraved staghorn. German (Nuremberg) about 1550; Birmingham City Museum and Art Gallery.

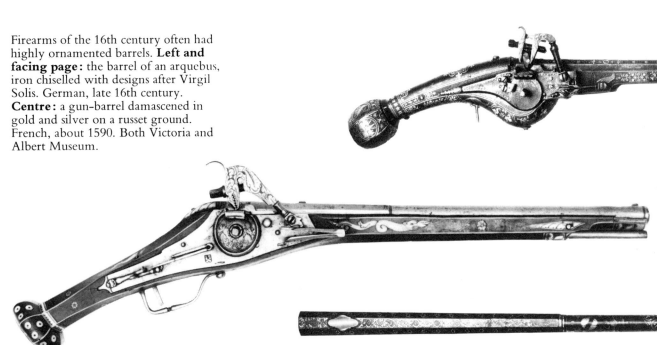

Firearms of the 16th century often had highly ornamented barrels. **Left and facing page:** the barrel of an arquebus, iron chiselled with designs after Virgil Solis. German, late 16th century. **Centre:** a gun-barrel damascened in gold and silver on a russet ground. French, about 1590. Both Victoria and Albert Museum.

colours for decorative effect. The earliest inlaid stocks are of comparatively simple design, but in Augsburg and Nuremberg, in the 16th century, the gunsmiths had access to the pattern books of major engravers such as Virgil Solis and Peter Flötner. Consequently, many of the motifs of the finest stocks can be traced back to the work of these masters.

The usual method of ornamenting the metal parts of firearms was to engrave or decorate the surface of the barrel and lock with gold or silver damascening. Damascening consisted of hatching the surface with a series of fine lines and hammering the precious metals into the surface in the required design. In the finest work, the actual design was engraved into the surface of a barrel or lock, and gold and silver wire tapped gently into the grooves. A few early 16th century firearms survive, in which the barrels are chiselled in relief and gilt. Chiselled barrels posed severe practical problems as any chiselled decoration had to be in

German designs for ornaments on butt plates, after woodcuts or engravings by Virgil Solis, Jost Amman and Paul Flindt. Late 16th century; Victoria and Albert Museum.

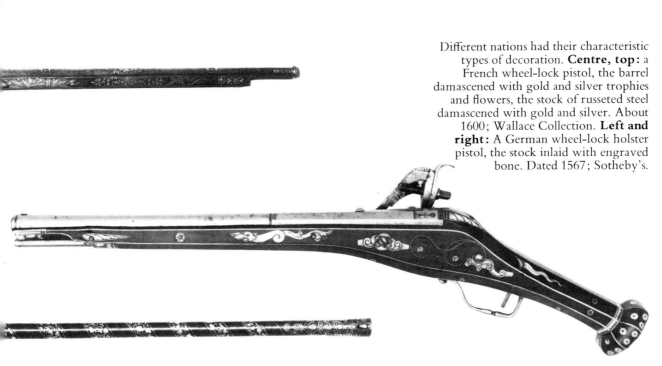

Different nations had their characteristic types of decoration. **Centre, top:** a French wheel-lock pistol, the barrel damascened with gold and silver trophies and flowers, the stock of russeted steel damascened with gold and silver. About 1600; Wallace Collection. **Left and right:** A German wheel-lock holster pistol, the stock inlaid with engraved bone. Dated 1567; Sotheby's.

comparatively low relief so as not to weaken the walls of the barrel.

By the second half of the 16th century, the stocks of many luxurious firearms were inlaid with elaborately interlaced patterns involving grotesques, and were often fitted with mounts of gilt and engraved bronze. Although German and Italian influences were then paramount, certain other national characteristics can be distinguished in the decoration of firearms, particularly towards the end of the century. French wheel-locks, for example, can be readily distinguished by their individual lock construction. A small group of long wheel-lock pistols with iron stocks, damascened in gold and silver, and probably made in France, has been identified. One of the characteristics of French decoration is the method of using gold and silver for ornament. French craftsmen often overlaid the decoration so that it stood in relief above the surface, finishing it off with chiselling and chasing.

The wooden stocks of 16th and 17th century wheel-locks were the ideal medium for elaborate forms of decoration. **Top:** a pair of wheel-lock holster pistols with walnut stocks inlaid with staghorn and ivory, after designs by Theodor de Bry. German, about 1610. **Centre and bottom:** a wheel-lock rifle with a pearwood stock set with carved ivory panels. The stock is signed behind the barrel with the monogram of Johann Michael Maucher of Schwäbisch-Gmund. South German, about 1670. Both Victoria and Albert Museum.

Facing page, top to bottom: A wheel-lock rifle, the walnut stock applied with carved ebony and staghorn panels, probably by Peter Opel of Regensburg; South German, about 1600. Detail of the rifle showing Turkish warriors on the underside, possibly from engravings by Jost Amman. A pair of flintlock pistols, the stocks inlaid with pierced brass and steel mounts, signed 'Filippus Spinodus fecit'; North Italian (Brescia), about 1690. A snaphance holster-pistol, the walnut stock inlaid with mounts of pierced iron, the barrels signed 'Lazarino Cominazzo'; Brescia, about 1650. All Victoria and Albert Museum.

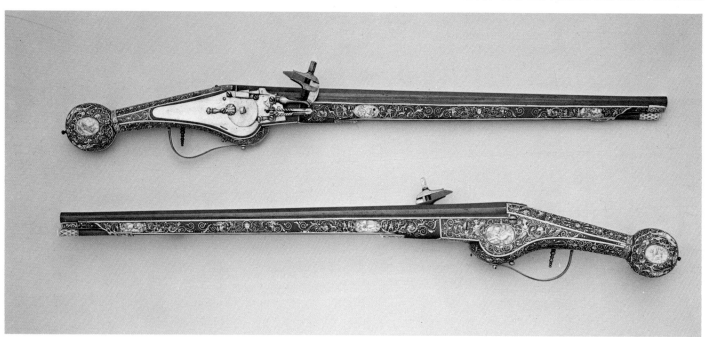

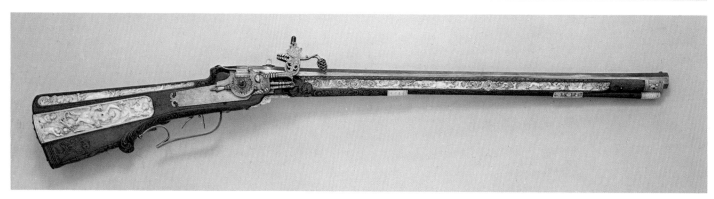

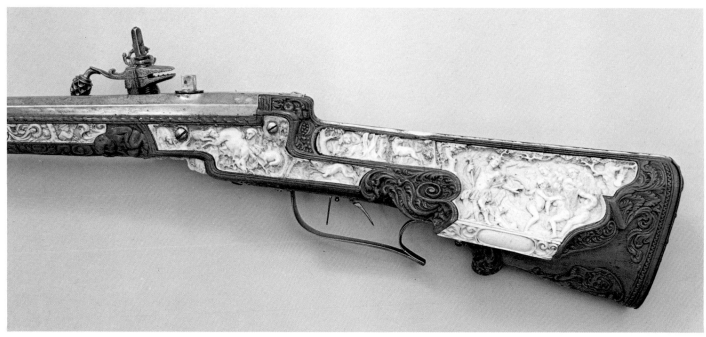

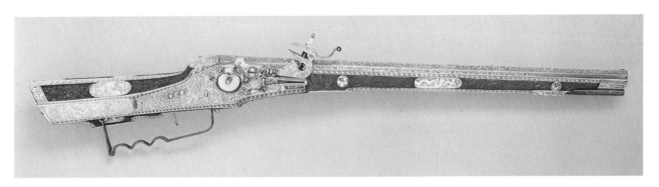

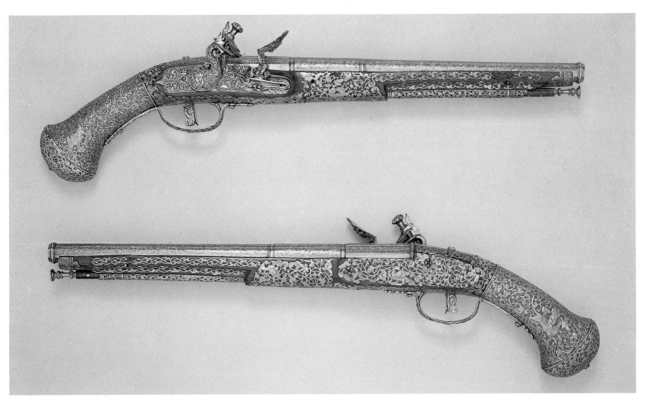

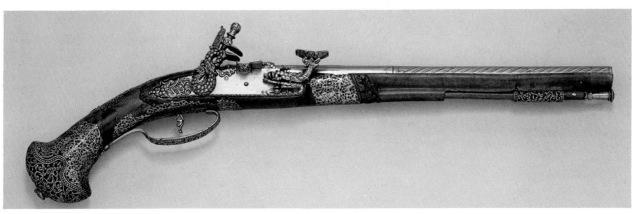

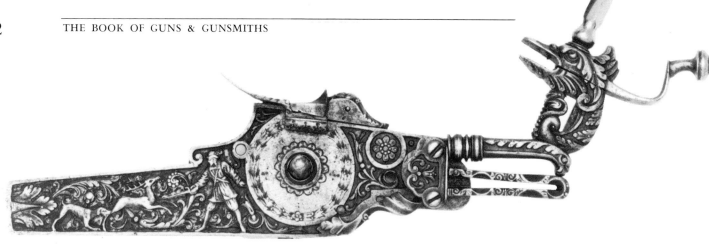

At the end of the century, a workshop was established in Munich, linked to the Bavarian court. This particular concern specialised in the production of beautifully chiselled steel-work and produced a number of finely decorated firearms. Three artists, in particular, are associated with this school: the brothers Emanuel and Daniel Sadeler and, at a later date, Caspar Spät. Their work is characterised by finely chiselled decoration executed in low relief, the designs often taken from the work of the French artist Etienne Delaune (1518–1583). The ground of the design is almost invariably gilt, the relief decoration being blued to provide a sober contrast. Two stockmakers are also associated with the Munich school: Adam Vischer and Hieronymus Borstorffer. Vischer is noted for his beautifully engraved inlay work, while Borstorffer specialized in the use of dark woods like ebony, inlaying the veneers with ivory or horn in strapwork arabesques. One of the most celebrated stockmakers working in the 17th century has not yet been named, but is known simply as the Master of the Animal Headed Scroll – his principal ornamental characteristic. A number of his works are associated with the court in Vienna of the Emperor Ferdinand III (1637–1657), and it seems reasonable to suppose that this as yet anonymous master probably worked somewhere in Austria.

One other stockmaker, working in Germany during the same century, deserves special mention. He is Johann Michael Maucher, a Swabian who worked in the last quarter of the century. He came from a family of wood-carvers, and specialized in pearwood stocks carved in high relief set with carved ivory plaques. He worked in Schwäbish-Gmund, and produced a number of presentation firearms decorated with carving as well as some ivory cups and dishes.

The 17th century also saw the growth of many different national styles. In the Low Countries, for example, Utrecht and Amsterdam soon became celebrated for their fine firearms which were exported over a wide area. Dutch gunmakers had access to native woods through their contacts in the East India trade, and many fine quality Dutch stocks are made from exotic woods. Many of the butts of Dutch pistols are carved with classical heads adorned with helmets. A workshop was operating in the Low Countries at about 1660, specializing in ivory-stocked pistols, the butts carved with the characteristic classical head. The locks of these pistols bear the signatures

Above and below: A wheel-lock from a pistol, probably made by Daniel Sadeler; chiselled iron, blued against a gilt ground. South German (Munich), about 1625; Victoria and Albert Museum.

Two pistols by Dutch gunsmiths of the 17th century. One of a pair of wheel-lock pistols, the stock of ebony, the lock engraved with scroll-work and figures and signed 'Jan Knoop Utrecht'; about 1660; Tøjhusmuseet, Copenhagen. And **(below)**, two views of a flintlock pistol with ivory stock inlaid with ebony, the lock engraved with birds and flowers, signed 'Louroux a Maastricht'; about 1660; from the Wrangel Armoury at Skokloster, Sweden.

of several gunsmiths working in Maastricht, including Jacob Kosters, Leonard Cleuter and Johan Louroux. It seems likely that the ivory stocks were also produced there. One of the most famous gunsmiths of the period, Jan Knoop, worked in Utrecht in the second half of the century. He produced a wide variety of firearms, but specialized in wheel-lock pistols, the locks based upon the characteristic French lock form.

Some of the most beautifully decorated firearms of the 17th century were produced in Italy. The manufacture of firearms was concentrated in several areas, including Brescia, Central Italy and certain parts of Southern Italy. Brescian craftsmen were extremely skilled in the working and chiselling of iron; a skill, incidentally, not only applied to firearms, but also to sword-hilts and snuff-boxes. Characteristic of firearms from this area are the elaborately chiselled and pierced steel mounts which are carefully fitted into recesses specially cut in the stocks. These mounts are usually very delicately pierced and, in spite of the intractable nature of the material they used, give the impression

of lace-work. The surfaces of these steel plates were also finely engraved. Some Brescian pistols are known in which the mounts are of brass, with the decoration treated in a similar manner. The decorative treatment was not confined simply to the stock, for some of the finest work was lavished on the lock.

After the wheel-lock had been superseded by the snaphance in about 1650, the steel-chiseller was able to devote his attention to the external parts of the lock, such as the cock and the steel. In the finest firearms these are elaborately chiselled into figures and

Many snaphances were elaborately decorated. Here we see a snaphance lock of iron chiselled with classical scenes. North Italian (Brescia), about 1675; Victoria and Albert Museum.

A barrel by Lazarino Cominazzo of
Brescia bearing his characteristic
signature on the octagonal section
adjacent to the breech of the gun.
Victoria and Albert Museum.

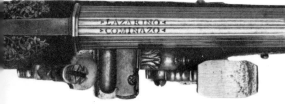

monsters. The chiselling was done in comparatively soft iron with steel tools and files. When
the work was completed, the mounts and parts
of the lock were subjected to what amounted
to a case-hardening process. They were placed
in a sealed container containing carbon producing material, such as charcoal or soot, and
heated for a long period. The case-hardened
elements were then polished and fitted to the
firearm.

Brescia was also very famous for its
barrels, especially those made by the Cominazzo
family of Gardone. In 1646, John Evelyn bought
what he described in his diary as a 'fine carbine'
from Lazarino Cominazzo, one of the most
famous makers of this family. So celebrated
were the barrels made by this family, that a
substantial number of contemporary forgeries
were produced. Genuine Cominazzo barrels
are generally of small bore, about 13mm, of
octagonal section adjacent to the breech and
changing to smooth or polygonal section after a
short distance. The forgers never quite succeeded
in copying the exact form of the signature with
its curious lettering and punched marks.

In Central and Southern Italy, although
iron was used, the decorative treatment was
rather different. The locks are decorated with
three dimensional figures consisting of rather
crudely chiselled masks and grotesques. Although the effect is very vigorous, the chiselling
lacks the refinement and subtlety of North
Italian work, and the piercings in the open-
work are usually much larger than on their
Brescian counterparts. Brescian locks are often

chiselled in low relief with figures and masks,
whereas Southern Italian craftsmen preferred
to engrave their locks.

One of the best Italian gunmakers of
the 17th century was Matteo Acqua Fresca
who worked in the town of Bargi. He produced some specially fine firearms for the Grand
Duke of Tuscany, Cosimo III, and worked in
the last quarter of the century. Like many other
Italian steel chisellers, he made not only firearms
with finely chiselled and engraved locks, but
also steel snuff-boxes.

It is generally accepted that the finest
European gunmakers of the 17th century –

particularly in the second half – came from
France. One of the noticeable features of the
French gun trade at this period is the prolifera-
tion of pattern books containing engraved
designs for the several parts of a gun or pistol.
In the middle of the century, engraving was a
particularly popular decorative treatment in
France, and the decorative schemes on a number
of surviving firearms can be traced back to
designs from particular pattern-books. Some of
the most important and influential design books
were by Philippe Daubigny (c.1635), François
Marcou (c.1657), Jean Berain (from 1650),
L. Jaquinet (c.1660) and Claude Simonin (1685),
all of whom produced numbers of designs
especially for firearms.

A fine Brescian lock-plate, chiselled
in low relief with portraits of Leopold I
and his wife Eleanor of Pfalz-Neuburg.
About 1680; Victoria and Albert
Museum.

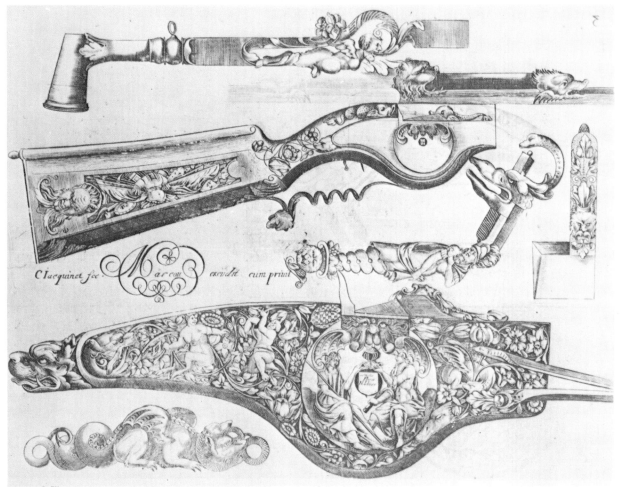

Decorative schemes for the engraving of firearms were
published in French pattern books of the 17th century.
Facing page: design for a lock by Philippe Daubigny;
Paris, 1635. **This page, top:** designs for ornamentation
on flintlock pistols by Claude Simonin; Paris, 1685.
Bottom: Designs for wheel-locks by François
Marcou; Paris, 1657. All Victoria and Albert Museum.

Designs from *Diverses Pièces d'Arque-buserie* by Nicholas Guérard. Paris, about 1700; Victoria and Albert Museum.

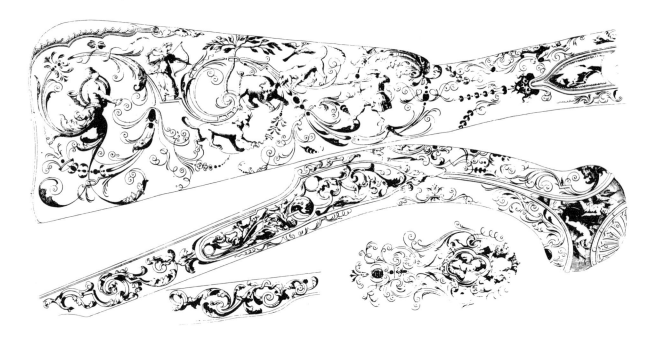

One innovation introduced by Parisian gunsmiths in mid-century, was the lockplate of concave form, a shape which was far more suitable for chiselled decoration than for engraving. From Paris this quickly spread throughout Western Europe. French gunsmiths were aware of the decorative effects produced by using fine woods for the stock of a pistol or gun. The highest quality French firearms are stocked with the best walnut showing a clear pattern. The pattern was often deliberately brought out by placing the stock in a flame so that it would charr slightly, thus heightening the contrast between the light and dark areas of the wood.

One of the reasons for the prominence of France was the substantial patronage provided by the French crown. The very finest gunmakers were given the privilege of working in the Palais du Louvre, in one of the workshops established there by Henri IV in 1608. This privilege was known as 'logement'. It meant that they were free from the regulations of the guilds and had certain exemptions from taxes or military service. Craftsmen who were granted 'logement' worked almost exclusively for the French court. This system of patronage enabled the highest standards to be maintained, both in technical achievement and ornamental skill. The names of the French gunmakers granted 'logement' in the 17th century include the finest artists in the field.

The list includes Marin le Bourgeoys, François Duclos and Bertrand Piraube. Duclos worked closely with Thomas Picquot who in 1638 produced a design book dedicated to Louis XIII. A pair of wheel-lock pistols signed by Duclos, and probably decorated by Thomas Picquot, is preserved in the Metropolitan Museum, New York. Piraube made a substantial number of presentation firearms, many of which still survive. One of his most magnificent creations was a flint-lock fowling piece with a silver-gilt barrel, probably presented by Louis XIV to the Duke of Richmond and Gordon in about 1680. Piraube is also thought to have been responsible for the re-introduction of the flat lock-plate in place of the rounded form.

Other important French gunmakers include the two who held the position of Arque-busiers Ordinaires du Roi, Thuraine and Adriaen Reynier, known as Le Hollandois. Thuraine worked with his son on a number of presentation pieces for Louis XIV. The engraver Jacquinet took many of his designs from firearms made by these two masters and it seems that Jacquinet himself also engraved the ornament on many of their firearms.

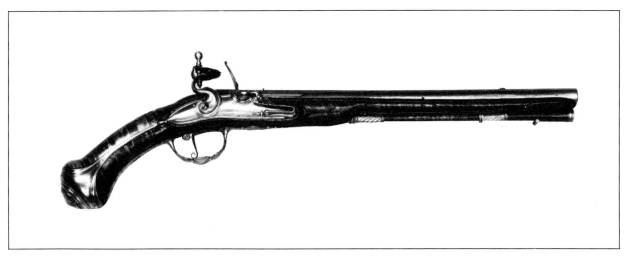

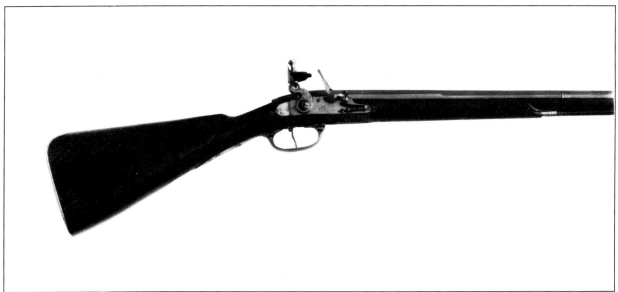

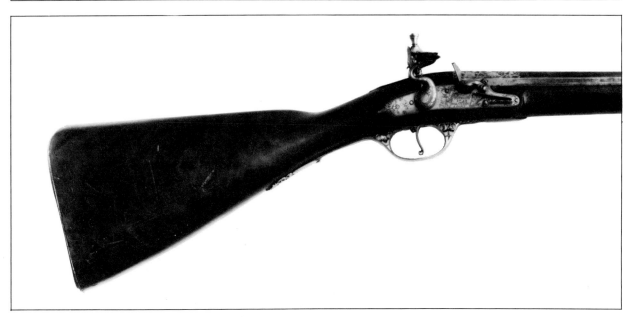

The use of fine wooden stocks, often treated to bring out the grain, was a feature of French firearms. **Top:** a flintlock with walnut stock, the lock signed 'Le Lorain a Valence'. French, about 1700; Victoria and Albert Museum. This gun also shows the concave lock-plate introduced in the mid-17th century. **Centre and bottom:** two flintlock fowling pieces with plain wooden stocks, signed 'Thuraine et Le Holandois a Paris'. Late 17th century; Tøjhusmuseet, Copenhagen.

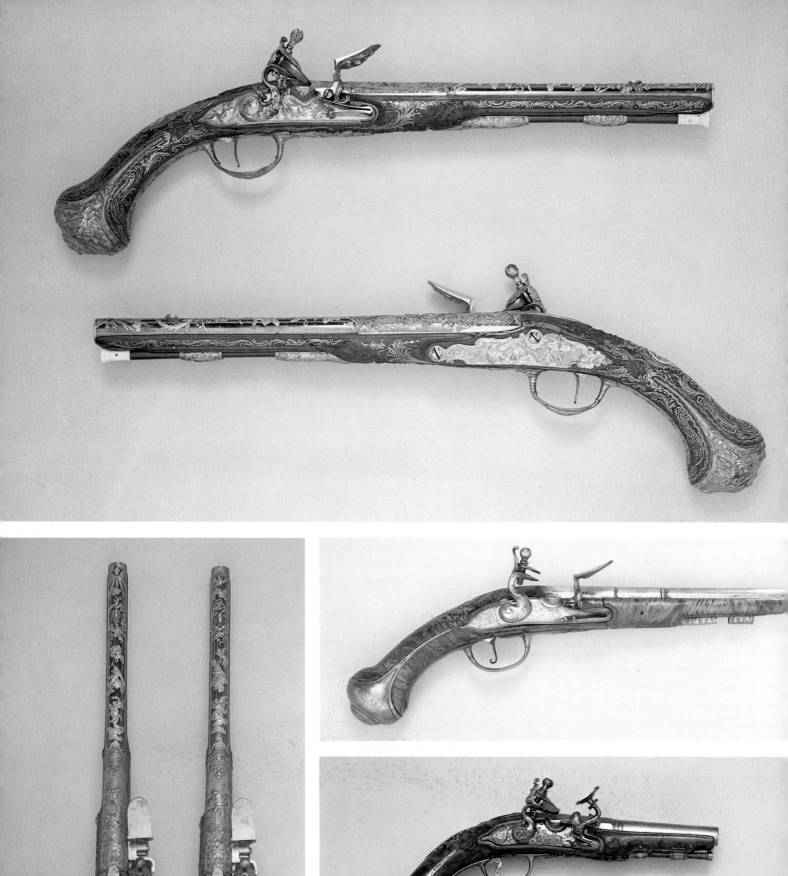
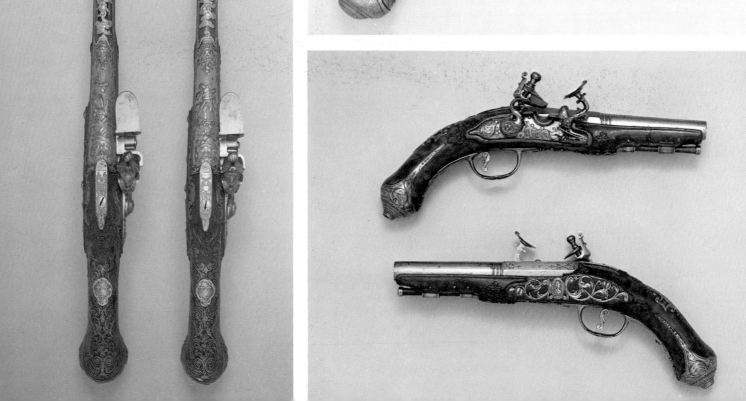

Before leaving the 17th century, something should be said about the art of the gunmaker in England. Many English firearms,
particularly of the early part of the century,
are surprisingly well-decorated. The stocks were
inlaid with a combination of mother of pearl
discs and bone plaques, often linked by horn
tendrils, and the barrels were finely chiselled
and damascened in gold and silver. Most of
the English guns and pistols of the Civil War
period are quite plain. However, at least one
dog-lock pistol, dating from 1650, has a silver
butt plate, elaborately pierced and engraved
with a floral pattern and a lock decorated with
engraved tulips. In the latter part of the century,
English guns and pistols followed French
fashions. The Revocation of the Edict of
Nantes, in 1685, had a very beneficial effect on
the English gun trade, for some of the best
French gunmakers came to live and work in
England. Their superb work encouraged a
generally higher standard among other English

makers, and laid the foundations of traditions
carried on by later makers. The most important
Huguenot gunsmiths working in England
include Pierre Monlong, who was Gunmaker
in Ordinary to William III, and Pierre Gruché,
and associated with them is a Swiss gunmaker,
Jacques Gorgo, who specialized in repeating
revolvers.

France continued to dominate European
gunmaking until the middle of the 18th century.
The introduction of the rococo style gave ample
scope to makers, such as La Roche, who
produced some magnificent work in this style
for Louis XV, including a superb pair of pistols
with chiselled steel mounts in low relief against
a gold background. In Italy, the use of chiselled
steel mounts continued to be fashionable,
some particularly fine work being done at
Anghiari by the Guardiani family. These late-
18th century snaphance pistols present a curiously archaic appearance when set against
English and French pistols of the same period.

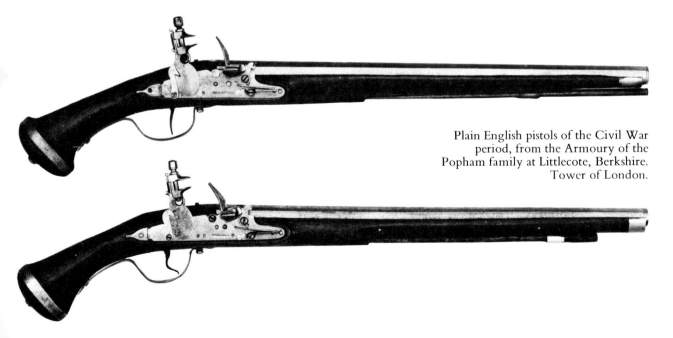

Nicholas Noel Boutet (1761–1833)

One of the most important French gun-making enterprises of this time was that established in 1792 at Versailles, under the artistic direction of Nicolas Noel Boutet. This factory, staffed with workmen from outside France, and mainly from Liège, not only manufactured a large number of military firearms, but had a special workshop for the production of luxurious presentation arms. From 1794 to 1818, Boutet specialized in these beautifully-decorated firearms. One of the distinguishing characteristics of nearly all Boutet's productions is the excellent design and finish. As most of these firearms were designed for presentation, no expense was spared and nearly all have lavish inlays in gold and silver. Not only did Boutet sign himself as 'Directeur artiste', he also had his own goldsmith's mark. Boutet was particularly patronised by the Emperor Napoleon, for whom he produced some of his finest garnitures. His fortunes rapidly declined after his workshop was sacked by the Prussians after Waterloo.

Throughout the 18th century, Spanish gunmakers exported their barrels to other countries but stoutly maintained their own national forms such as the characteristic 'Madrid'

Spanish gunmakers of the 18th century produced a characteristic form of flintlock known as the 'Madrid' lock. This example is chiselled with a matt gold ground and signed 'G. el Algora'. About 1750; Victoria and Albert Museum.

lock. This was really a development of the miquelet. Two sears operated through the lock-plate, one on an extension on the breast of the cock gave half-cock, the other on an extension on the back of the cock, gave full-cock. The top-jaw screw was also in the form of an open ring. Important Spanish gunmakers include Nicolas Bis who worked for the Spanish crown in the first quarter of the century and Diego Ventura who made guns for Charles VI of Spain.

Some fine firearms were also made in Russia during this period at the arms factory in Tula. The factory was established by Peter the Great in 1705, but the best work was done in the reign of Princess Elizabeth, between 1741 and 1762. Tula makers used a distinctive form of floral inlay in gold on a blued steel ground. The factory made not only firearms, but also furniture and candlesticks, all from steel inlaid with gold.

One of the most productive 18th century centres of firearms manufacture was the city of Liège. Predictably, in the early part of the century, the styles follow very closely those already existing in France. Makers apparently had access to French patternbooks, particularly those of Claude Simonin, and much of their work reflects his influence. Several Liège pistols are fitted with mounts of gilt-brass, perhaps due to the influence of the important brass-founding trade which had flourished in Liège from the Middle Ages. Liège makers were not above drawing on the reputation of other

A Flemish pistol with rifled barrel and engraved silver butt showing English influence. On the butt are the arms of Count Bethlen de Bethlen of Hungary. The lock is signed 'Devillers a Liege'. About 1725; Victoria and Albert Museum.

centres to sell their firearms. There are a number of pistols inscribed 'Segalas' and 'London'. It is almost certain that these were, in fact, made in Liège. Celebrated Liège makers, such as I. Devillers also seem to have been influenced by the London market, for a pair of silver-butted pistols by this maker is obviously copied from contemporary English styles.

As early as the 16th century, Scotland had established its own manufacturing traditions and styles. The stocks of the earliest Scottish pistols were of two forms, either shaped like a fishtail or in the form of a lemon. The heart-butted form, and the ram's head form, with the butt terminating in two inwards curving scrolls, developed in the 17th century. Scottish pistols are distinguished by their use of brass or iron for the stock, and by the extensive use of engraved and inlaid 'Celtic' motifs. The ram's horn form continued to be popular throughout the 18th century. Long guns of Scottish origin are exceptionally rare. However, the few that have survived, principally from the 17th century, have long, narrow stocks, curving in a gentle 'S' towards the butt end.

The decoration consists of engraved silver plates let into the stock. There were several towns and villages specializing in firearms, the most important being Dundee,

Doune, Leith and Edinburgh. The best known gunmaking families include the Cadells, Lowes, Murdochs and Campbells.

In addition to the finer firearms, gunmakers also produced a very large number of plain but serviceable military firearms. These were usually of the simplest design, with plain mounts of iron or brass. One of the best known English military longarms of the 18th century was the Brown Bess which, in its various forms, was the basic military weapon for the British Army for 100 years from the 1730s. The name Brown Bess stems from Anglo-German, the colour referring either to the barrel or, more probably, to the stock. The correct name for the Brown Bess is the Long Land musket, and the earliest examples date from about 1725–30.

These early patterns have a barrel just under four feet long, a wooden rammer, attachments on the trigger guard and muzzle-end of the stock for a sling, and a drooping rounded lock-plate. The earliest patterns tended to have iron furniture but, after 1730, brass became more common. Throughout its long history, the Brown Bess was made in a number of patterns. Some, such as the Short Land pattern, produced after 1740, had a slightly shorter barrel, and certain patterns were fitted with iron rammers.

The Brown Bess was the British Army's standard weapon for 100 years. This is an early example dated about 1730. Tower of London.

Top: a pair of flintlock pistols from the Boutet factory. The barrels are signed in gold 'Boutet a Versaille', and the lock is also engraved with the maker's name. About 1820; Victoria and Albert Museum. **Bottom:** a garniture consisting of a pair of flintlock pocket pistols, a pair of rifled flintlock carriage pistols, a rifled flintlock carbine and a sword with a silver-gilt hilt, all produced by the Boutet factory. Presented to Napoleon I in 1797 by the French Republic. Christies.

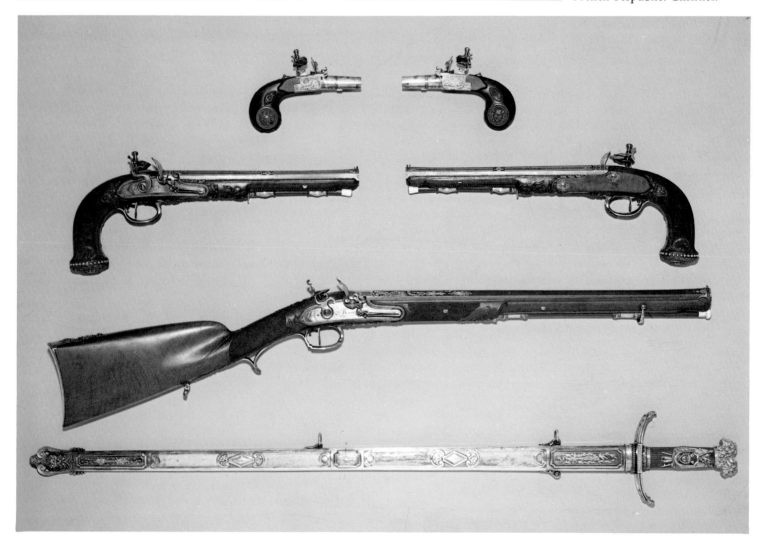

An example of the fine work produced by Russian gunsmiths at Tula in the 18th century is this flintlock fowling piece with steel mounts encrusted with gold. The lock is signed 'A. Leontiew'. About 1778; Victoria and Albert Museum.

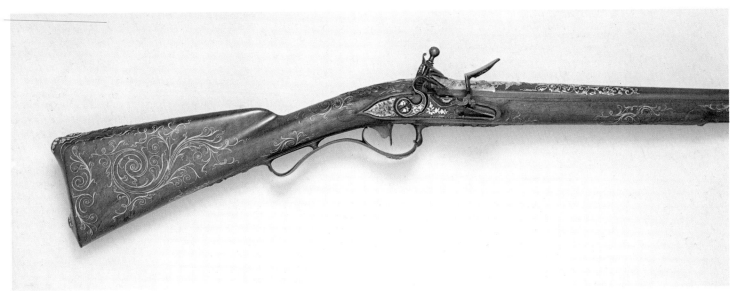

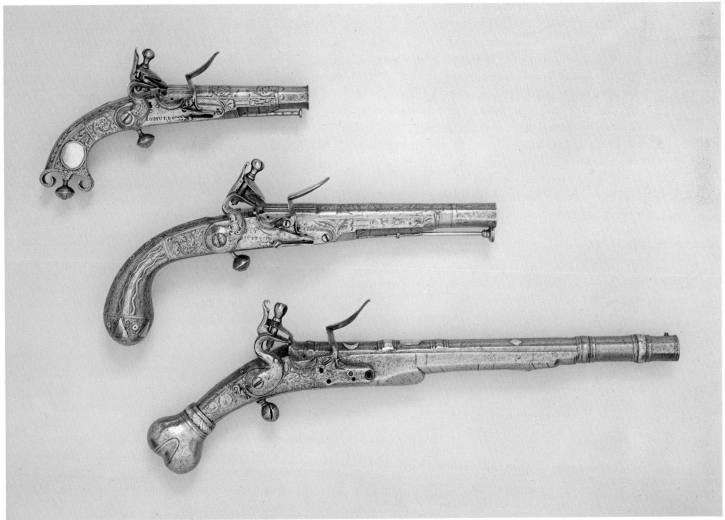

A trio of Scottish flintlock pistols with characteristically shaped iron butts, engraved and inlaid with silver. Each is signed with the name of the maker. **Top to bottom:** 'I O Murdoch', Doune, about 1760; 'T Murdoch', Leith, about 1775; 'I A McKenzie', Dundee, about 1710. Victoria and Albert Museum.

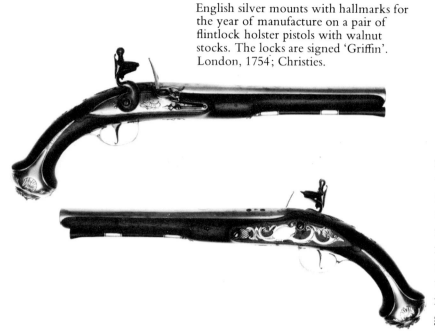

English silver mounts with hallmarks for the year of manufacture on a pair of flintlock holster pistols with walnut stocks. The locks are signed 'Griffin'. London, 1754; Christies.

In addition to muskets, a large number of pistols were made for military use, the form of their locks and brass furniture deriving from those found on the muskets. The Board of Ordnance, in the second quarter of the 18th century, introduced certain patterns of musket and pistol, especially for use by the Navy. 'Sea Service' muskets usually had brass mounts with a flat butt-plate for safe storage, and easy loading on a heaving deck. Wooden rammers were also used on Sea Service muskets as they were not usually corroded by salt water like the iron ones. These military weapons were mass-produced in two main centres, Birmingham and London. Many are marked with the word Tower, and were produced in the workshops established in the Tower of London, and on Tower Wharf, which at peak periods employed nearly 100 workmen.

Throughout the 18th century, guns and pistols were decorated with precious metals. A decorative technique, which had been used much earlier on the Continent, was the inlaying into the stock of silver wire in scroll-work. A

number of English pistols are decorated in this way. Another method of ornamenting the stock was by using plates of silver cast, or chased with the required design and setting them into recesses cut into the stock. The gunmaker did not make the mounts himself, but bought them from small-workers in London and Birmingham who supplied them in sets. These silver mounts included a butt-cap, often in the form of a grotesque mask, a side-plate and an escutcheon on the stock for the owner's initials or arms. All English silver mounts should, in theory, be stamped with a full set of hall-marks. In practice, there are a substantial number of silver mounted pistols and guns which are not marked. For example, the lavish silver mounts on the air-gun made by Kolbe for George II, are unmarked.

Some of the best-known makers of silver mounts in the 18th century were Jeremiah Ashley and John King, who supplied mounts to the London trade, and at a later period, Moses Brent, who made mounts for such prominent makers as Ezekiel Baker and Joseph Manton. English gunmakers of the late 18th century turned away from the lavish decoration used by their continental contemporaries. A good pistol or gun by the best English makers, such as Egg or Manton, was the absolute antithesis of the productions of French makers like La Roche. Any decoration was usually limited to small areas of engraving on plain blued mounts, a beautifully calligraphed signature embellished the lock plate. The plain stock was chequered, usually any gold or silver was limited to small areas on the stock and the barrel. In short, English firearms possessed all the merits of fine craftsmanship and style that make English furniture of the period so much admired.

When firearms were first introduced gunpowder was carried in a leather bag. Powder horns and flasks were apparently first introduced in the early 16th century. At first, they

A flintlock pistol by Durs Egg with chequered stock and the maker's name engraved on the lock-plate. London, about 1800; Christies.

Accessories such as powder flasks and cartridge boxes were often elaborately decorated. These examples are, (**left**) a priming flask of painted enamel mounted in gilt brass; German, about 1660. And a cartridge box of embossed iron; German, about 1550. Both Victoria and Albert Museum.

were simply cow-horns flattened and plugged at each end, but by the middle of the 16th century, some very elaborately decorated examples were fitted with metal mounts. Smaller flasks were made specially for priming powder, usually from metal. Powder-flasks were made from a variety of materials, brass, leather, wood and sometimes silver. In the late 18th century, pear-shaped flasks of stamped metal were introduced which quickly replaced the earlier, more elaborate type of container.

Some of the most individual powder-horns were made in Scotland, in the area of Aberdeen, and are engraved with 'Celtic' decoration and traditional motifs.

A number of powder-horns, made in America, were decorated in scrimshaw work, with a variety of designs including maps and patriotic mottoes. There were also other methods of carrying powder. In the mid-16th century, it was convenient to have the powder made up into charges ready for use. These charges,

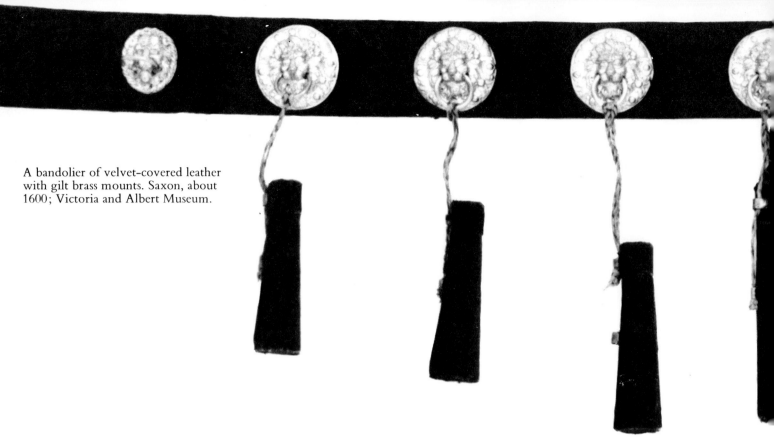

A bandolier of velvet-covered leather
with gilt brass mounts. Saxon, about
1600; Victoria and Albert Museum.

A powder flask of staghorn mounted in
silver gilt, carved with scenes depicting
Adam and Eve, and with the arms of
the zu Welsperg family of Tyrol. South
German, about 1550; Victoria and
Albert Museum.

contained in a paper cartridge, were often
carried in a specially-designed portable box
fitted with tubular openings. Powder-charges
were also carried on a strap or belt, known as
a bandolier. The charges were kept in tubes
suspended from the belt, usually of wood or
pewter, and were fitted with caps to keep them
dry. The wearing of a bandolier involved a
certain amount of risk, as there was a real danger
that the charges would go off in the action of
firing. They were discarded in the 17th century
by most European armies, but continued in
favour in Turkey, and those countries under
Turkish influence until the 19th century.

Although oriental gunmakers have always been extremely conservative in their
attitudes to mechanical developments, the wheel-
lock was completely ignored in favour of
the matchlock, the miquelet and the flintlock.
In those Eastern countries such as Turkey,
which had close contacts with Europe, the
miquelet lock was adopted in the 17th century
and continued to be used until very recently.
However, in both the Near and Far East, the
matchlock has always been the most widely used
type. In India and Persia, the form of matchlock
known as a tricker-lock was popular.

In Japan, firearms were first introduced
by the Portuguese in the 16th century. Japanese
gunmakers adopted the snap-matchlock, usually

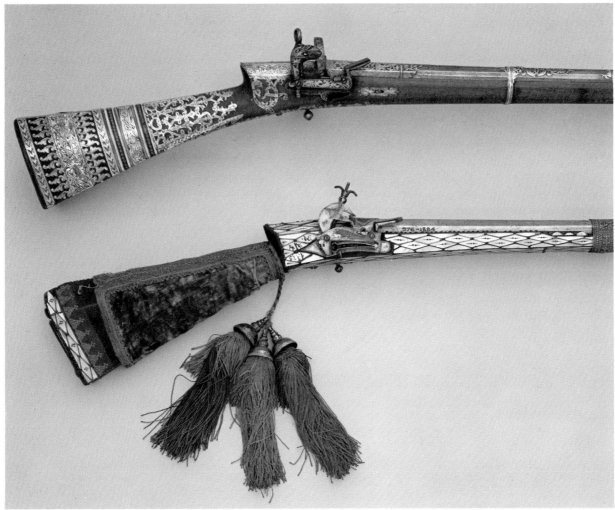

Two Turkish flintlock guns with characteristic 'stepped'
stocks. The upper gun dates from the 18th century and
has the lock and barrel overlaid with gold and the stock
inlaid with engraved silver. The second dates from the
late 17th century and has the stock overlaid with
mother of pearl, the butt covered in embroidered
velvet; the barrel is European, inscribed 'Lazarino
Cominaz'. Victoria and Albert Museum.

This Turkish pistol dating from the 1830s is covered with filigree silver set with coral, and fitted with a percussion lock. Victoria and Albert Museum.

made of brass, for their firearms and continued to use them until the 19th century, virtually ignoring all other forms of lock. The favourite lock in North Africa was the snaphance, which the gunsmiths almost certainly copied from 17th century models produced in England and the Low Countries. Each country had its own individual form of stock. Turkish guns are usually fitted with square sectioned, 'stepped', stocks, often set with ivory plaques. The Afghan stock, used in Sind, is sharply down curving and spreads at the butt end.

In most Oriental firearms, the barrels are attached to the stock by metal bands. Oriental barrels were often made of watered steel, the finest examples being heavily encrusted with gold and silver. Japanese barrels which, like all their metalwork, are very well made, are usually very heavy and are often decorated with gold and silver inlays on a blued ground. Like many swords from Japan, they are signed by the maker with the province in which he worked. Some of the finest barrels were the work of swordsmiths. The 16th century swordsmith, Noda Hankei, is said to have made both gun barrels and swords until one day he cut one of his own barrels in half with one of his swords. He then sensibly, decided that he should stick to swords.

A large number of firearms were made in the Balkans. Usually fitted with miquelet or flintlocks, the stocks, particularly of the pistols, are completely covered with silver and sometimes set with coral. After the introduction of the percussion system, a number of oriental firearms, dating from the 1830s, were fitted with percussion locks. The locks seem to have been imported–particularly from England by Turkish gunmakers who mounted them up in lavishly decorated stocks.

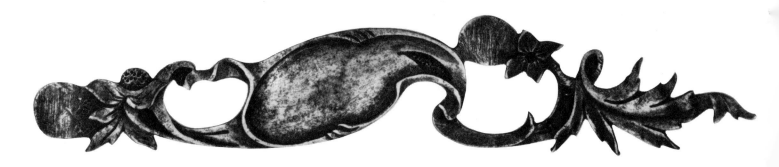

Above: an unfinished side-plate from a pistol, not yet drilled for the screws to attach it to the stock. English, about 1760. **Facing page:** the title page from a book of designs by Jean Berain. Paris, 1659. Both Victoria and Albert Museum.

DIVERSES · PIECES
ires
Vtile pour les Arquebuzieres
Nouuellement Inuentés et
Grauss par Jean Berain
le Jeune et ce Vendent
chéz l'auteur a Paris
Auec Priuilege du
Roy 1659

Chapter Seven

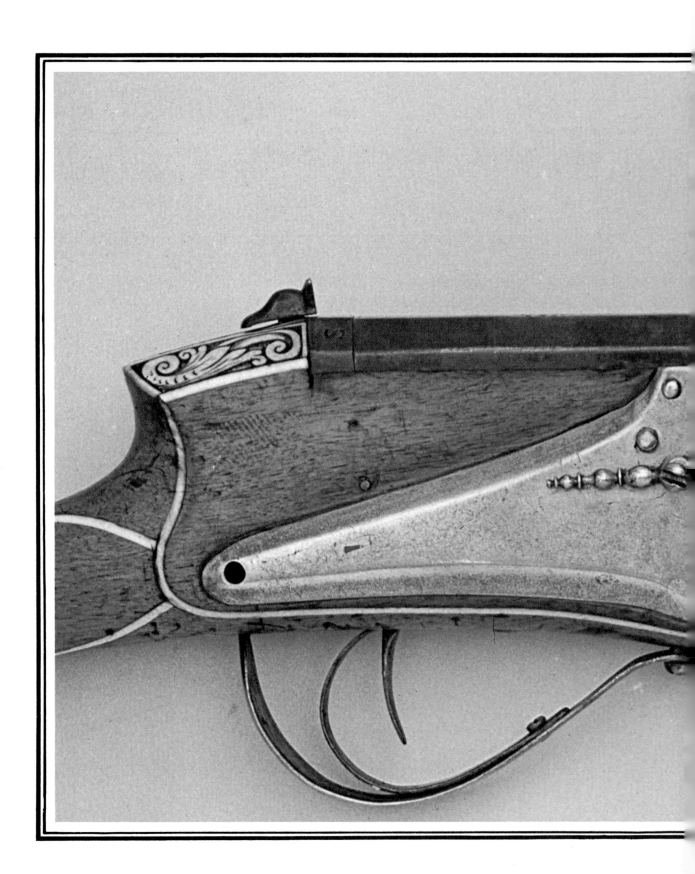

Rifling and the Breech-loading System

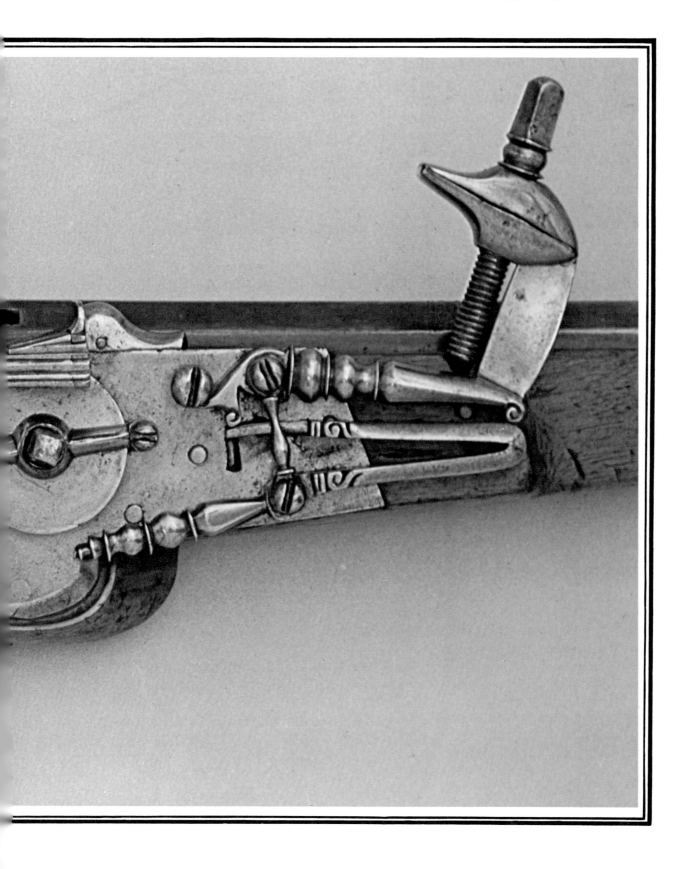

One of the earliest rifled guns which
survives is this German wheel-lock by
Ruhr, the barrel of which is dated 1542.
The stock dates from about 1640.
Tøjhusmuseet, Copenhagen.

A RIFLE can be defined as a gun with the inside
of the barrel cut with a series of spiral grooves
to make the bullet spin when it emerges from
the muzzle. It had been noticed as early as the
15th century that, if the feathers on arrows and
the flights on crossbow bolts were arranged in
a certain way, they would revolve in flight and
would fly much straighter. The earliest type
of rifling consists of straight grooves and a
plausible theory suggests that initially the
grooves served only to collect the burnt powder
from previous shots – allowing the gun to be
reloaded with ease, even after it had been fired
several times.

According to some authorities, the invention of rifling was made in the 15th century
by an armourer of Nuremberg called August
Kotter. Others have put forward the name of
Gaspard Kollner, a Viennese gunmaker also of
the 15th century. However, there has never
been any real proof to back either claim. Some
authorities recognize as the earliest rifle a hand-
gun formerly in the Meyrick Collection at
Goodrich Court, Herefordshire. On the side of
the stock, close to the breech, is painted a

heraldic shield bearing an eagle known to have
been used by the Emperor Maximilian I between
1493 and 1508. Unfortunately, the lock is
missing, but it was almost certainly originally
fitted with a match-lock. The barrel is the most
interesting feature of this gun, for traces of what
appears to be rifling have been detected at the
muzzle. However, the gun is so badly corroded
that the grooves cannot be traced all the way
down the barrel. It is, of course, almost 50
years earlier than any other known early rifle
which, in itself, is rather suspicious. Its claim
to be the earliest rifle must, therefore, be viewed
with caution.

If, on the other hand, the barrel of this
gun was rifled, it does support the theory that
rifles may have been a German invention. By
the middle of the 16th century, rifles for use in
sport were well established. Two important
dated examples survive from this period, one
a German wheel-lock rifle, dated 1542, in the
Tøjhusmuseet in Copenhagen, which is the
earliest definitely rifled gun, and a detached
barrel, dated 1547, from the Rotunda at Woolwich. As far as can be ascertained, the rifle was
used in the 16th century almost exclusively for
sport, or for shooting at targets. However, in
the early 17th century, Danish troops were
using rifles as military weapons. In Germany,
and in particular in England during the Civil
War, both guns and pistols with rifled barrels
were known. There is a well-known story of

Previous page: The lock of a German
breech-loading wheel-lock pistol in the
Victoria and Albert Museum (see pages
118–119).

The successful performance of the rifle
during the American War of Independence was a contributing factor in its
general adoption. This scene from the
Battle of Bunker Hill in 1775 is an
engraving after the painting by John
Turnbull.

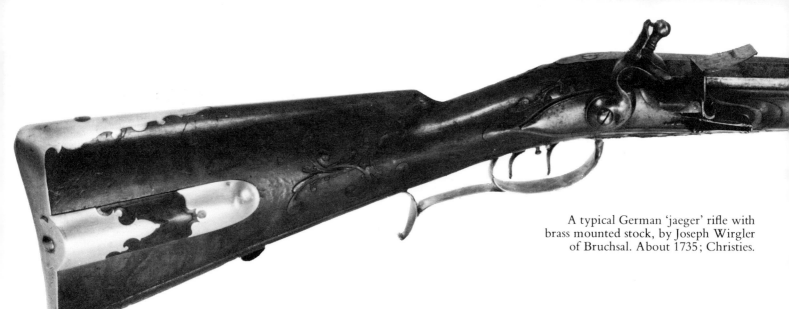

A typical German 'jaeger' rifle with brass mounted stock, by Joseph Wirgler of Bruchsal. About 1735; Christies.

Prince Rupert, who hit the weathercock of St Mary's Church, Stamford, with a shot from a rifled horseman's pistol. His uncle, Charles I, declared that the shot was a fluke, whereupon the Prince coolly drew the other pistol and repeated the feat. Two pistols signed by Harman Barne, supposedly the ones which the prince used on this occasion, are preserved in a private collection. Although the French were issued with a small number of rifles in the 17th and early 18th centuries, it was not until after 1750 that the military importance of the rifle first began fully to be appreciated and put to practical use. It has been suggested that one of the main reasons for the general adoption of the rifle was its successful performance during the American War of Independence, where the so-called Kentucky rifle was used to great effect. The rifle had always been a favourite firearm in Germany and in those countries under Germanic influence, such as Austria and Bohemia. There, the gunsmiths had developed a special flintlock rifle designed for sport known to collectors as a 'jæger' rifle. These rifles have a substantial butt

By the Napoleonic era, the military importance of the rifle was beginning to be appreciated by European Armies. This scene from the Battle of the Pyrenees, July 28th 1813, is an aquatint from a painting by W. Heath.

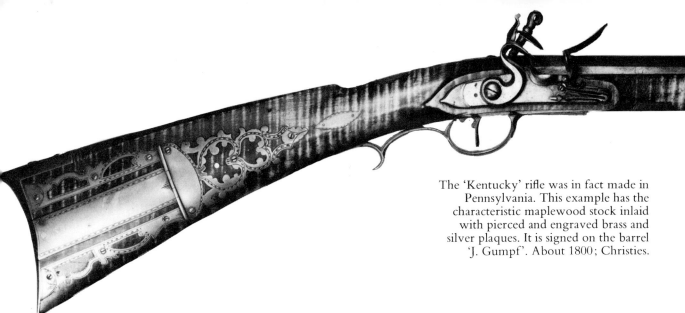

The 'Kentucky' rifle was in fact made in Pennsylvania. This example has the characteristic maplewood stock inlaid with pierced and engraved brass and silver plaques. It is signed on the barrel 'J. Gumpf'. About 1800; Christies.

and heavy octagonal barrels which are generally fairly short. Makers such as the Kuchenreuter family, of Regensburg, produced some excellent examples.

When Swiss and German immigrants arrived in America in the early part of the 18th century, they carried with them their rifles and their skill in making them. The Kentucky rifle was, in fact made in Pennsylvania, particularly in York, Lancaster, and Berkshire counties. The local craftsmen made the stocks and barrels, but the flintlocks were imported, first from Germany and later from Birmingham. In its heyday, the Kentucky rifle had a number of recognizable characteristics, an octagonal barrel of about 40 inches, a maple-wood stock, a brass patch-box, brass mounts, and some light relief carving on the stock. The first Kentucky rifles were made for the Revolutionary War, and whole dynasties of specialist gunsmiths are known. This rifle and its users gained a formidable reputation. Describing an incident in the war, Major Hanger, of Tarleton's Legion, wrote, 'I never in my life saw better rifles (or

This impression of an American gunsmith's shop from a painting by Gayle P. Hoskins contains what are clearly a number of Kentucky rifles.

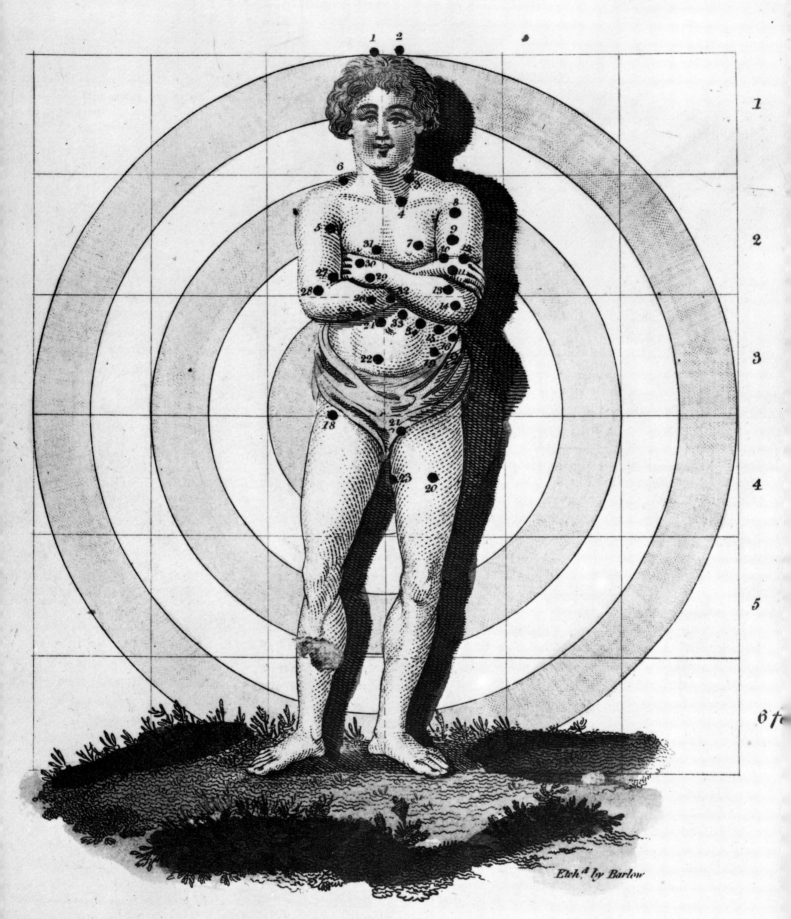

34 Shot at 100 Yards.

Rifle Made and Shot by Ezekiel Baker.

Published by E. Baker Gun-maker No 24 White Chapel Road, opposite the Church from Little Alie Street.

One of the first British rifles to be generally issued was
designed by the English gunsmith Ezekiel Baker.
Below: a Baker rifle with plain stock and brass
mounts, bearing the cypher of George III on the lock.
Facing page: A rifle target from *Baker's Practice*,
published by the maker. Both Tower of London.

men who shot better) than those made in
America'. He went on to describe how, at a
range of 400 yards, a rifleman in prone position
shot the horse of a bugler who was standing
some distance behind the major and Colonel
Tarleton, who were observing an American
position. Rifles were made in Pennsylvania
until well into the 19th century.

The Ferguson rifle, designed in 1774,
was the first English breech-loading rifle made
for military use. It was based on a breech-loading
action first developed by the Parisian gunmaker,
Isaac de la Chaumette, in the early 18th century.
Patrick Ferguson organised the manufacture
of 100 of these rifles, and a detachment of a
hundred N.C.O.'s and men used them in the
American war. A number of Ferguson rifles
were made for presentation as well as military
versions by Durs Egg, one of the best London
gunsmiths of the 18th century.

Ezekiel Baker designed a rifle with seven-
groove rifling which was adopted in 1800 after
extensive tests, and was the first British rifle to
be generally issued. Like the Kentucky, it was

based on the German 'jæger' rifle. It had a brass
patch box in the butt, was stocked to the
muzzle and had a trigger-guard shaped like an
elongated 'S', giving a good grip. It was replaced
in 1838 by the percussion Brunswick rifle,
designed by George Lovell. Ezekiel Baker
was at one time apprenticed to Henry Nock,
and after the success of his rifle, was patronized
by the Prince Regent – an avid collector and
connoisseur of firearms.

Another contributor to the development
of the rifle was a French Captain, Delvigne who,
in 1826, produced a design in which the powder
chamber was smaller than the barrel. The ball
was hammered into the chamber by means of an
iron rammer expanding the ball into rifled
grooves. In spite of its disadvantages, this rifle
enjoyed considerable success in service with the
French – particularly in Algeria.

Several of these rifles are breechloaders.
Gunsmiths had made various experiments with
such guns and a number of cannon with separate
breeches have survived. This system of loading
was first applied to smaller firearms, probably

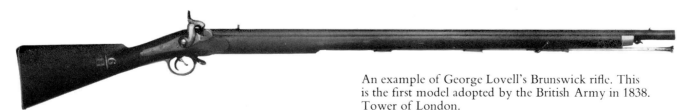

An example of George Lovell's Brunswick rifle. This
is the first model adopted by the British Army in 1838.
Tower of London.

Far left: an early example of a breech-loading gun, a carbine from the armoury of King Henry VIII. The barrel is chiselled with the monogram H R and the date. English, 1537; Tower of London.

Left: the German breech-loading wheel-lock pistol in the Victoria and Albert Museum. Here we see how the breech is hinged at the side, permitting an iron cartridge to be inserted. About 1600.

in the 16th century, for some of the earliest examples belonged to Henry VIII. Two guns from his armoury are preserved in the Tower of London. One of these is dated 1537 on the barrel. The initials W. H. stamped on the breech-block suggest that it may have been made by William Hunt, who had the title of Keeper of the King's Handguns and Demy-Hawks. Both are wheel-locks, though the original locks have been removed. The breech on both guns has a small hinged trap which can be opened so that an iron tube holding the charge can be placed in the barrel. Also associated with Henry VIII are a group of shields, probably made by Giovanni Battista of Ravenna,

between 1544 and 1547. These shields are of iron with a lining of wood. Through the centre is inserted a pistol barrel operated from behind by a matchlock mechanism. As with the other guns, a separate iron tube contains the charge, the breech is pivoted to allow the charge to be inserted and, when returned to its usual position, is held in place by an iron latch.

The breech-loading system, in which a separate tube for the charge is employed, was also popular in the 17th century. A German wheel-lock pistol in the Victoria and Albert Museum, dating from about 1600, has part of the barrel on a hinge, secured by a sprung catch at the back.

A shield combined with a breech-loading matchlock pistol, probably supplied by Giovanni Battista of Ravenna to Henry VIII and mentioned in an inventory of 1547. Victoria and Albert Museum.

A flintlock breech-loading rifle on the Crespi system by Durs Egg. This experimental version for cavalry use has a spear bayonet attached to the muzzle. English, about 1785. Tower of London.

Some gunsmiths found different solutions to the problem of breech-loading. A gun by John Bicknell who made guns for Charles II, which is now in the Tower of London, is fitted with a breech that tips up when the extended trigger-guard is moved downward. A variation on this system was developed by Giuseppe Crespi, of Milan, in 1770. The breech was secured by means of a lever which caught on two catches on the side. A carbine based on this system was used by Austrian cavalry. In the Tower of London is a flintlock carbine made by Durs Egg employing the breech-loading system. Egg produced a number of these carbines in 1785 for the Master General of the Ordnance, to be issued to the Light Dragoons. It is thought that this is one of them.

The Crespi system had the same disadvantage of all breech-loaders – it was practically impossible to get a gas-tight seal between chamber and barrel. It was a loading system that continued in popularity well into the 19th century, and in 1817 the U.S. army adopted a breech-loader, patented by John Hall and William Thornton, which employed the same idea. A number of ingenious attempts were made to solve the problem of leakage from the join. In 1817, a Frenchman named Sartoris patented a breech-loader on the Crespi system, which had a partial screw thread on the end of the chamber. By turning a folding lever, the barrel could be rotated and separated from the chamber.

One of the most successful breech-loading systems was that patented by Isaac de la Chaumette in 1721. In the words of the patent, firearms 'were charged by the breech through the barrel'. A screw-plug attached to the trigger-guard passed vertically through the breech. The thread of the screw was made very steep, so that a 360 degree turn of the trigger-guard lowered the plug, allowing the charge to be loaded into the aperture. A few guns and some pistols were made using this system, one by

A breech-loading flintlock rifle made at Harper's Ferry in the U.S. in 1838, with the John Hall breech action. Tower of London.

the Frenchman Bidet, for King George I, and another by the English gunmakers, Barbar and Clarkson. This system was adopted by Captain Patrick Ferguson for his splendid rifle, patented in 1776. Ferguson's improvements to La Chaumette's invention were principally limited to the design of the screw-plug. He introduced channels, and an aperture for holding grease on the screw, so that it would not foul up during frequent use. Experiments with the Ferguson have shown that the best results are obtained by leaving the breech-plug open after shooting.

An ancestor of the modern cartridge firearm was invented by an enterprising Swiss technician, Samuel Johannes Pauly (1766–1820). As an inventor, Pauly was not only interested in guns, but also in airships. In Paris, in 1812, Pauly patented a breech-loading gun which used a self-obturating brass cartridge containing fulminate in a recess in the base. It worked on the centre-fire principle, where a pin strikes the central part of the base of the cartridge, which is made especially soft. It was also a breech-loader. It used all the technical principles of the modern firearm, and was years ahead of its time. The breech-loading systems described in the patent either involve the barrel being 'broken', as on a modern shot-gun, or the breech-block being lifted up to allow the gun to be loaded. In terms of performance, Pauly's gun was phenomenal, he fired 22 shots in two minutes in one demonstration. However, Napoleon was not very impressed and, although a number of shotguns and pistols were made, they did not achieve the success that the invention deserved. A seven-barrelled volley gun, patented by Pauly in 1814, is preserved in the Tower of London.

Other inventions by Pauly included a device to set off the main charge in a gun by air heated by compression, a patent for a waterproof fabric for an airship, called the Dolphin, and a mortar firing explosive shells. Hardly any success followed these projects, the Dolphin

A double-barrelled breechloading gun
on the Pauly system, by A. Renette.
French, about 1812; Tower of London.

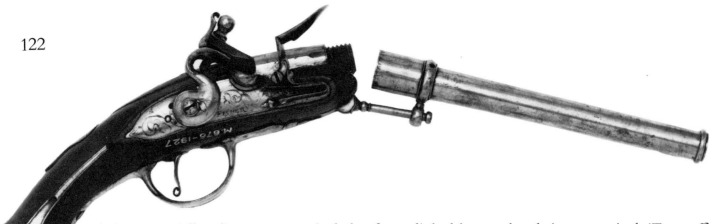

being especially disastrous, particularly for Durs Egg, who became involved in the venture and lost £10,000 on it. Pauly died in obscurity, probably in 1820.

A breech-loading system, probably developed on the Continent in the first half of the 17th century, used a 'turn-off' barrel. A wheel-lock gun by Michael Gull, of Vienna, dating from 1650, is an example. The barrel was unscrewed just in front of the breech, allowing the charge to be loaded. The ball was often made slightly larger than the bore of the barrel, and the tighter fit increased its velocity. 'Turn-off' pistols were particularly popular in England, some of the earliest examples being made by Harman Barne. Carbines were also made using this system. In order to prevent the unscrewed barrel from being separated from its breech, it was often

linked by a rod and ring, or swivel. 'Turn-off' barrels were particularly suitable for rifling and also deliberately bored to take a heavier charge. Although loading took much longer, it could also be done much more precisely. Some English guns with 'turn-off' barrels have small lugs on the side of the barrel which were intended to provide a grip for a wrench or spanner.

From the earliest period, gunsmiths had tried to make guns more effective. One method was to improve the fire-power of a gun by grouping together a number of barrels. The earliest multi-barrelled guns are known as ribaudequins or organs, due to their similarity to organ pipes. The barrels were set side by side, or in a group of three or four, held together by iron bands. They were set off by a slow match, or a powder train. A number of 15th and

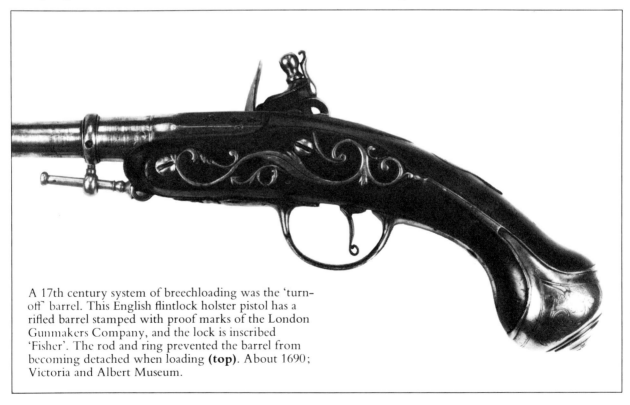

A 17th century system of breechloading was the 'turn-off' barrel. This English flintlock holster pistol has a rifled barrel stamped with proof marks of the London Gunmakers Company, and the lock is inscribed 'Fisher'. The rod and ring prevented the barrel from becoming detached when loading **(top)**. About 1690; Victoria and Albert Museum.

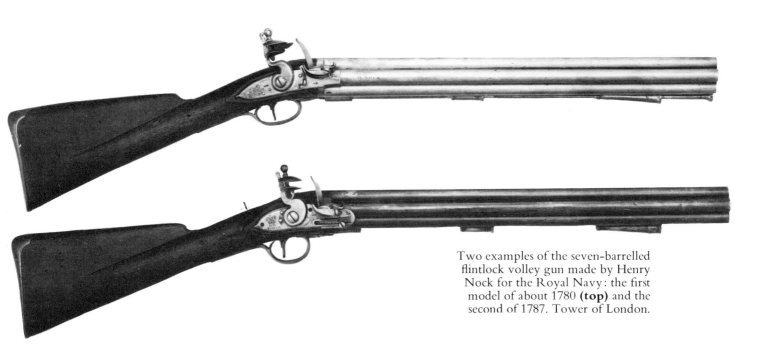

Two examples of the seven-barrelled flintlock volley gun made by Henry Nock for the Royal Navy: the first model of about 1780 (**top**) and the second of 1787. Tower of London.

16th century manuscripts depict these devices fitted into a small wagon or cart. The direct descendants of these were the seven-barrelled volley guns, of the type Henry Nock manufactured for the Royal Navy in the latter part of the 18th century.

Another comparatively early repeating system, the principle of which was known by the late 16th century, is the 'Roman candle system', in which a number of charges were loaded into the same barrel and ignited by a series of touch-holes, or when each charge ignited its neighbour by means of a special type of loading.

During the 17th century, a number of experiments were made by gunsmiths trying to devise a method of making a gun hold enough ammunition for several shots, thus avoiding the long delay caused by continual reloading. One of the earliest magazine repeaters was invented in about 1640, by the German gunsmith Peter Kalthoff. The Kalthoff family originally came from Solingen, in Germany. Three members of the family made valuable contributions to the development of firearms. Peter was granted a monopoly by the States

General in 1641 for his magazine repeater. His brother Mattias also produced repeaters, and a number of their magazine rifles are preserved in the Tøjhusmuseet, Copenhagen. Caspar Kalthoff worked in England from 1654 and was encouraged by the Earl of Worcester. In the Kalthoff system, the trigger-guard can be moved through 180 degrees, this moves a breech-block from left to right, placing a ball in the aperture at the back of the barrel.

A powder measure is linked to the trigger-guard which, when moved, conveys powder from a magazine behind the lock to an aperture in front, connected to the breech. This allows powder to fall into the chamber. When the trigger-guard is returned to its usual position, the breech-block and the loaded chamber return to their position behind the ball. At the same time, the pan is primed, the pan-cover shut, and the gun is closed. Harman Barne made firearms based on this system, and the Klett family, in Salzburg, produced a slightly improved model. By incorporating two vertically rotating breech-blocks, one for ball and one for powder, the awkward trigger-guard loader could be dispensed with.

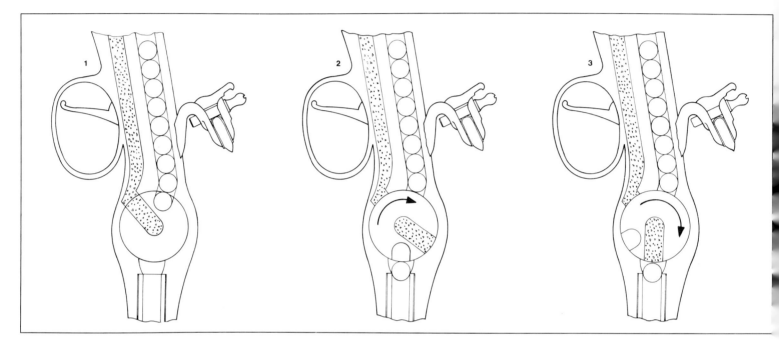

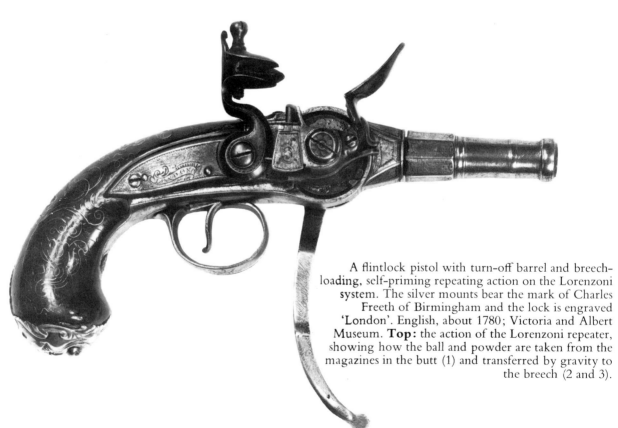

A flintlock pistol with turn-off barrel and breech-loading, self-priming repeating action on the Lorenzoni system. The silver mounts bear the mark of Charles Freeth of Birmingham and the lock is engraved 'London'. English, about 1780; Victoria and Albert Museum. **Top:** the action of the Lorenzoni repeater, showing how the ball and powder are taken from the magazines in the butt (1) and transferred by gravity to the breech (2 and 3).

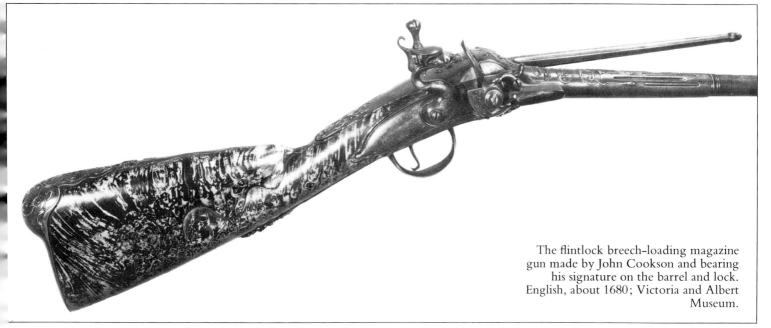

The flintlock breech-loading magazine gun made by John Cookson and bearing his signature on the barrel and lock. English, about 1680; Victoria and Albert Museum.

Another magazine-repeater was invented in Florence in about 1650, possibly, though there are other candidates, by a gunmaker called Michele Lorenzoni. In the butt of the gun were two magazines for powder and for ball, as well as a priming magazine attached to the lock. The gun was held with the barrel upwards and a lever attached to the left side of the breech-block was pulled back. This aligned two apertures in the breech with the two magazines in the butt. The barrel was then pointed downwards and ball and powder fell by gravity into the breech and were carried to the chamber by returning the lever to its usual position. As with the Kalthoff system, the action of the lever also cocked the gun and primed the pan. English makers produced a few guns based on this system. One, now in the Victoria and Albert Museum, is signed by the mysterious John Cookson, about whom

virtually nothing is known. This gun has finely chiselled steel furniture and dates from about 1680–90. It is possible that there is some connection between this maker and the John Cookson of Boston, Massachusetts, who advertised himself in 1756 as selling flintlock repeaters of the same type.

Apart from gunpowder, other methods of driving a projectile were devised. One method was to use compressed air and several early air guns have survived. These can be divided into two types: those which operate by means of a spring-operated plunger, and those containing a reservoir which has to be pumped full of air. The earliest examples are of the latter type. The earliest is in the Livrustkammaren, Stockholm, and is dated 1644. It is signed by Hans Köler, of Kitzing. A valve was opened and closed by a spring-mechanism which had to be cocked each time and let out

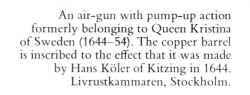

An air-gun with pump-up action formerly belonging to Queen Kristina of Sweden (1644–54). The copper barrel is inscribed to the effect that it was made by Hans Köler of Kitzing in 1644. Livrustkammaren, Stockholm.

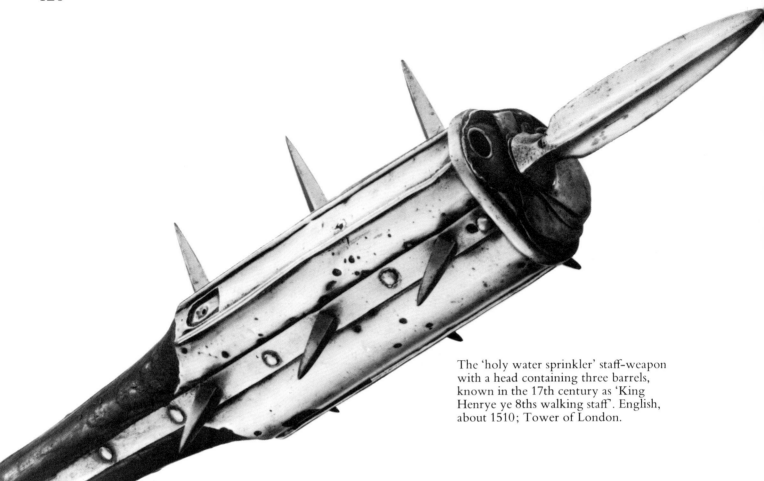

The 'holy water sprinkler' staff-weapon with a head containing three barrels, known in the 17th century as 'King Henrye ye 8ths walking staff'. English, about 1510; Tower of London.

enough air to propel the bullet. Some splendid air-guns were signed by the German J. G. Kolbe, who specialized in the chiselling of iron, and was also a talented engraver. A fine air-gun of his which is fitted with a dummy flintlock is now in the Victoria and Albert Museum. It was made in about 1735, probably for George II, and is decorated with inlay and chased silver mounts.

In the early 19th century, George Wallis, of Hull made air-guns which provide a fine contrast with Kolbe's, being absolutely plain with a long barrel. The reservoir is separate from the gun, and consists of a spherical ball which was pumped up then screwed underneath the breech. Some air-guns were issued for military use. Girandoni, a gunmaker in the Tyrol, designed an air-rifle with a separate reservoir in 1779. A number of these were issued to troops fighting for Leopold of Austria in Holland, and on the Rhine, in the late 18th century. These air-guns seem to have been regarded with particular dread by the French troops, and one account relates that any soldier found with one was immediately hanged. Air-guns operated by springs, although found at an earlier date, did not really become popular until the 19th century, and it is this type of mechanism which powers the modern air-rifle.

Revolvers fall readily into two groups: those with revolving barrels and those with revolving cylinders. With the first category, a number of loaded barrels are rotated, usually by hand, to align them with a fixed chamber. The alternative system employs several chambers each loaded with a charge which can be rotated on a central rod to bring them in line with a single fixed barrel. Guns with revolving barrels were known in the early 16th century. The Tower of London has a splendid combination weapon, which consists of a staff with a spiked head in which are fitted three pistol barrels. This has a cover to protect the barrels from the rain, and dates from the second quarter of the 16th century. Associated with Henry VIII, it was described in 17th century inventories as 'King Henry ye 8ths walking staff'.

The earliest revolvers had multiple
barrels revolved by hand. This three-
barrel snap-matchlock pistol is from the
Palazzo Ducale in Venice, and dates
from about 1540. An exploded
view is shown below.

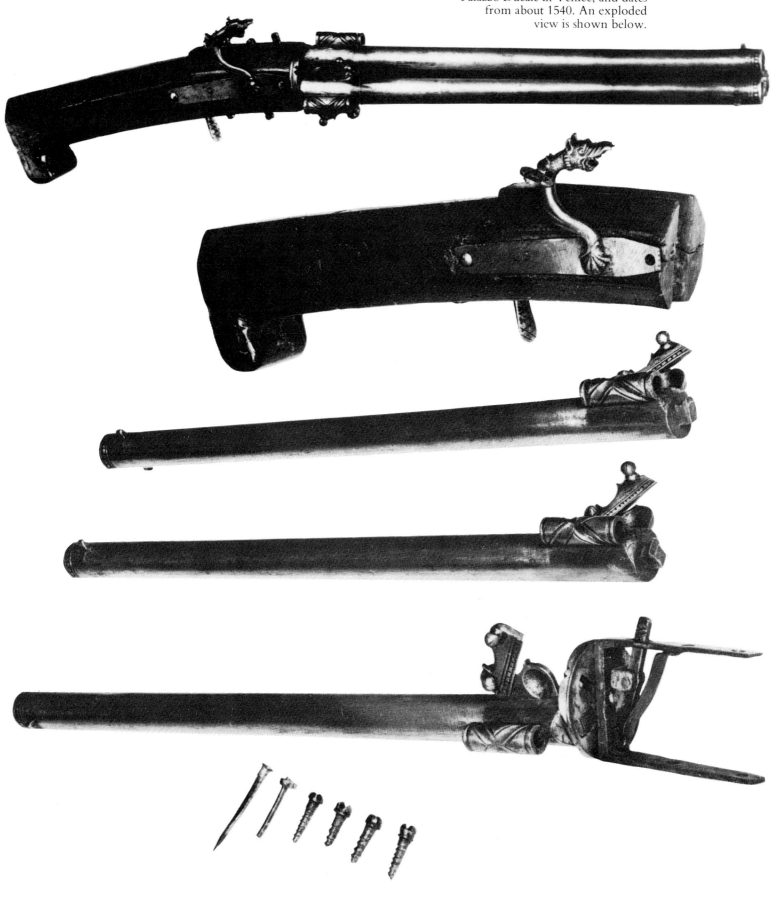

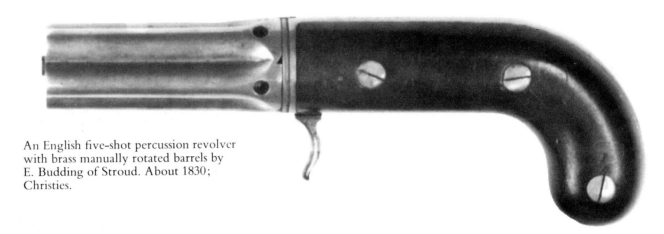

An English five-shot percussion revolver
with brass manually rotated barrels by
E. Budding of Stroud. About 1830;
Christies.

In the Palazzo Ducale, in Venice, is a three-barrelled matchlock described in an inventory of 1548, but probably of even earlier date. A unit of barrels from a matchlock revolver, possibly contemporary with the Venice example, is preserved in Oxford in the Ashmolean Museum. During the 17th century, a type of revolver was developed on the Continent known as the Wender type. The name comes from the German word for turning. Both guns and pistols using this system survive, but it is more usually found on handguns.

A Wender revolver usually has two barrels, which can be brought into line with the fixed breech by depressing the trigger guard. In the late 18th century, a type of revolver was developed which, due to its similarity to contemporary pepper-pots, was known as a pepperbox. The earliest examples have manually operated revolving barrels, but after 1830 the barrel automatically revolved as the pistol was cocked. The first patent for a single-action pepperbox was taken out in 1836 by the Darling brothers of America.

The alternative revolver system, in which the cylinder moves and the barrel remains fixed, appears to have already been known in the mid-16th century. A number of German wheel-lock revolvers have survived, including an important snaphance revolver, dated 1597, by Hans Stopler of Nuremberg, now in the Tøjhusmuseet, Copenhagen. Like the breech-loader, one of the difficulties facing the makers of revolvers was to design a gas-tight seal. The Swiss gunmaker, Jacques Gorgo, who worked in London at the end of the 17th century, made a series of revolving guns and pistols. These had two chambers aligning on a single barrel, but fired by separate flintlocks.

An important revolving snaphance, attributed to John Dafte and now in the Tower of London, incorporates a principle which was to be employed much later by Samuel Colt. Made in about 1680, this revolver with brass fittings has a cylinder which is revolved automatically when the pistol is cocked. A lever pushes up against a ratchet on the cylinder and moves it round one turn.

The revolver by Hans Stopler of
Nuremberg in the Tøjhusmuseet,
Copenhagen. Dated 1597.

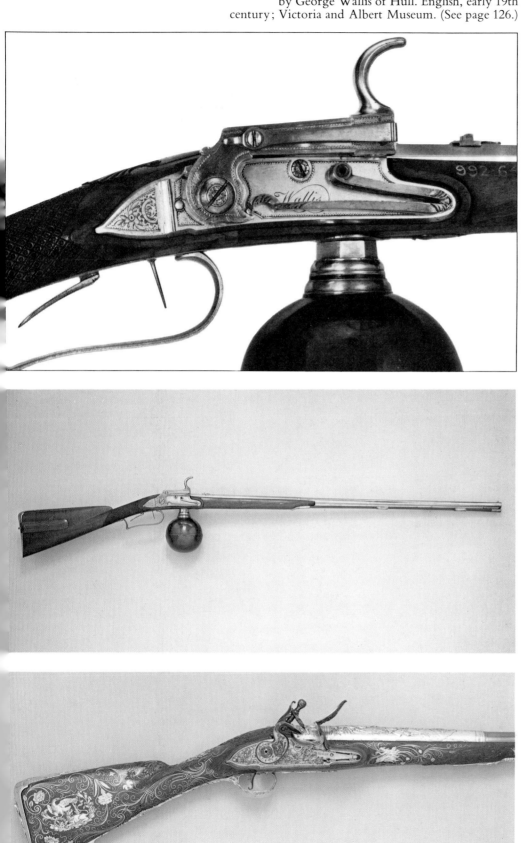

Below and centre: an air-gun with spherical reservoir, plain stock and engraved steel mounts, by George Wallis of Hull. English, early 19th century; Victoria and Albert Museum. (See page 126.)

KOLBE
FECIT
LONDINI

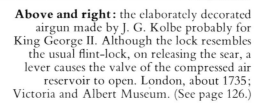

Above and right: the elaborately decorated airgun made by J. G. Kolbe probably for King George II. Although the lock resembles the usual flint-lock, on releasing the sear, a lever causes the valve of the compressed air reservoir to open. London, about 1735; Victoria and Albert Museum. (See page 126.)

James Puckle (1667?–1724), from the title page of his book *The Club, or A Gray Cap for a Green Head. A Dialogue Between a Father and Son.* London, 1824.

A revolver which has enjoyed much novelty value for many years, because of the inscription it bears, is the gun by James Puckle. His gun, patented in 1718, was a large revolver mounted on a tripod. Fitted to it were interchangeable cylinders holding a variety of charges which were rotated by hand. Every chamber had a cone-shaped projection which fitted into a recess in the breech. Contemporary newspaper accounts describe it as firing '63 times in seven minutes'. One is now in the Tower of London, and the inscription on this gun says it can be loaded with 'round bullets for Christians, but square bullets for Turks'.

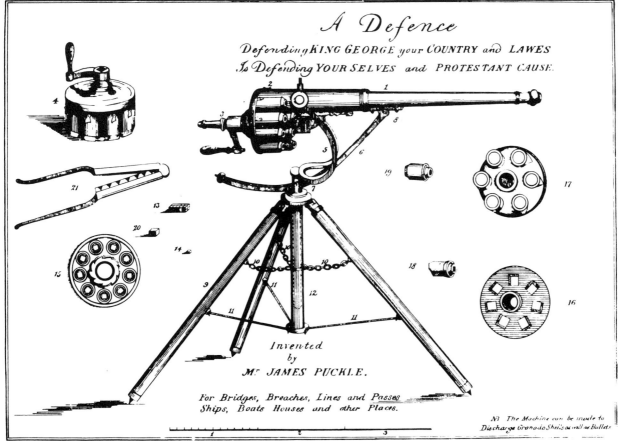

The revolving gun patented by James Puckle in 1718 and the printed patent card for his invention. Both Tower of London.

One of the ancestors of the modern revolver, a flintlock
revolver with five chambers and a manually operated
cylinder, patented by E. H. Collier in 1818. **Top:** the
first model, with ratchet-operated primer and internal
cock, the lock-plate signed 'E.H. Collier Patent No.
23'. English, about 1819. **Bottom:** Collier's second
model with improvements including an external cock and
fluted cylinder, signed on the barrel 'E.H. Collier 14
London'. About 1820. Both Victoria and Albert
Museum.

A typical combination weapon:
a combined hunting-sword and flintlock
pistol with mounts of engraved iron;
English, about 1750; Victoria and
Albert Museum.

One of the direct ancestors of the modern revolver was patented by Captain Artemus Wheeler, of Concord, Massachusetts, in 1818. A flintlock, it was described as 'a gun to discharge seven or more times'. One of his associates, Elisha Haydon Collier, patented an improved version of the same revolver later that year. He almost certainly stole Wheeler's idea. Collier's patent was recognized, and a number of revolvers bearing his name were made in London. In the first model Collier made, in 1819, the cylinder was turned by a spring and escapement as the pistol was cocked. In the second model, the fluted cylinder was rotated by hand. Collier succeeded in producing a comparatively gas-tight joint between barrel and cylinder, by using a wedge which was moved forward when the cock fell. Both models are in the Victoria and Albert Museum.

Throughout their history, firearms have often been combined with other weapons, not only as novelties for the enthusiast, but also to provide a secondary weapon should the first one fail. The more common combinations are usually with staff-weapons, or maces and axes, where the long shaft provides a convenient seating for the barrel. We have seen that some of the most important early wheel-locks are to be found on crossbows. In the 18th century there was a vogue for combining pistols with hunting swords. It is thought that these were designed to give the coup-de-grace to a wounded animal. Pistols are found combined with the most unlikely objects, including purses – as the famous sporran from Sir Walter Scott's collection at Abottsford demonstrates. There are also some keys, perhaps for prison warders, which can be used as pistols.

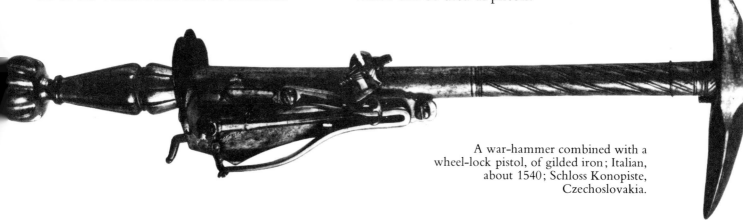

A war-hammer combined with a
wheel-lock pistol, of gilded iron; Italian,
about 1540; Schloss Konopiste,
Czechoslovakia.

The origins of the Mauser company go
back to the Royal Württemberg Rifle
Factory at Oberndorf, shown opposite.
Founded in 1811, the factory was taken over
by Peter Paul Mauser and his brother
Wilhelm in 1871. The company prospered
through contracts with the German armed
forces and grew into one of the great names
of modern small-arms manufacture.

Part Two

Modern Small Arms

Chapter Eight

The Rifle

Nicholas von Dreyse (1787–1867) was
the father of the modern rifle. His
Needle Gun **(facing page)** was the first
to use the bolt as a breech-closing device.

Previous page: The transition from
muzzle-loading musket to bolt-action
magazine rifle: a heavily armed fur-
trapper of the *ancien régime* and a
French soldier of the line in the 1880s
flank a Montenegrin soldier of the
First World War.

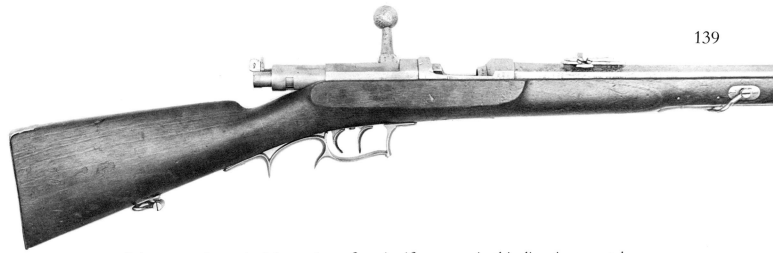

THE ARRIVAL of the percussion principle made little significant difference to the rifle for some years; the normal reaction was simply to take the same basic design which already existed, remove the flint ignition system, and re-design the breech end to take a percussion cap. However, in the early years of the 19th century a good deal of work went into improvement of the bullet. Rifling was now fairly commonplace, but it was soon apparent that the normal spherical ball was not a good projectile to fire from a rifled barrel, and gradually the bullet changed to a pointed and cylindrical form.

At the same time, efforts were made to shape the rear end of the bullet to improve its sealing qualities and utilise the propelling gas to its maximum. The difficulty was that the bullet had to be easily loaded from the muzzle and yet be capable of expanding so that it would 'set up' into the rifling when fired, sealing the gas and gripping the grooves well enough to pick up spin. Probably the most effective and best-known was the Minie bullet, which contained a wooden plug in its hollow base: the explosion of the cartridge forced the plug into the bullet and thus expanded the bullet base into the rifling. Minie bullets were widely adopted and remained in use until the late 1860s, being particularly prominent in the American Civil War.

But the only real solution was to do away with muzzle loading and load the rifle through the breech so that the bullet could be made an 'interference fit' in the rifling. The first significant step in this direction was taken in 1840 when the Prussian Army adopted the 'Needle Gun' of Nicholas von Dreyse, a weapon to which practically every modern rifle owes its ancestry.

The Needle Gun pioneered the use of the bolt as a breech-closing device. A mechanism derived from the domestic door bolt, this bolt was carried at the rear end of the barrel and contained a long, spring-propelled firing needle. The soldier first drew back the needle, together with its spring and a tubular casing which was a sliding fit within the bolt. He then grasped the bolt handle, turned it up through 90°, and pulled back, opening the bolt and exposing the rifle breech. After this, he inserted a lead bullet with a paper cartridge attached to its end. The bolt was then closed and the handle turned down to lock it, after which the needle casing was thrust into the hollow bolt until retained by a spring catch. Thrusting in the case also compressed the needle spring and held it against a catch, or 'sear', attached to the trigger. On pulling the trigger the needle was released, to pierce the paper cartridge, pass completely through the black-powder filling, and impinge against a fulminate cap at the front end of the cartridge. This cap was thus nipped between the needle and the solid base of the bullet and ignited, in turn firing the cartridge. The face of the bolt was chamfered and hollowed out so that it fitted tightly around the rear end of the barrel and sealed the joint against possible escape of gas.

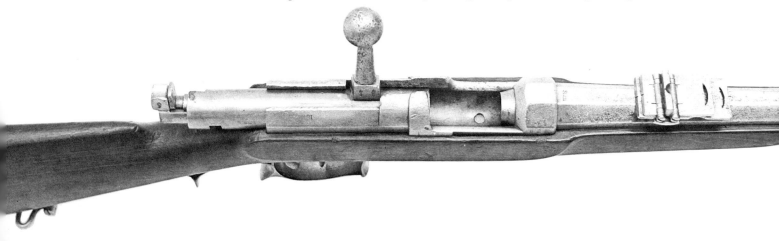

Taken all in all, it was a cumbersome device, but it was a good deal easier in use than the long rigmarole of muzzle-loading and, with this weapon and the improved tactics which it permitted, the Prussian Army was to make short work of its opponents for the next 30 years.

The French, apprehensive of this weapon, encouraged inventors to produce something comparable, and Antoine Chassepot, a foreman in the French Artillery Arsenal, produced a design which was adopted as the 'Fusil Mle 1866'. This made some substantial improvements over the Needle Gun, for the needle unit was now a fixture inside the bolt and was automatically cocked as the bolt was closed. Sealing of the breech was done by an india-rubber plug on the head of the bolt which entered tightly into the breech behind the cartridge, and a special cartridge was designed which carried its ignition cap on the base so that the needle no longer had to pass through the powder in order to fire it. Following the example of the Needle Gun and the Chassepot, numerous 'needle-fire' rifles were produced on the Continent, and the Italian, Austrian and Russian armies adopted this type of weapon.

Some nations were naturally reluctant to jettison vast stocks of muzzle-loading weapons and sought methods of converting them to breech-loading systems. Most adopted similar solutions – cutting away the breech and inserting a hinged unit carrying a chamber and a nipple for the percussion cap. By lifting the unit, a prepared cartridge could be inserted into the chamber; after closing it, a cap went on to the nipple and the weapon was ready. As a means of using up old stocks of weapons at a low cost, these systems served their purpose, but the numerous joints and opportunities for gas escape prevented them from being very efficient.

When the metallic cartridge became more common in the 1860s, similar conversions were made in order, once again, to save the considerable investments which the massive stands of arms represented. These devices, such as the British Snider and the American 'Trap-door Springfield', were little more efficient than the percussion conversions, and the obvious thing to do was to go back to first principles and design fresh rifles. In this case, it meant going back to von Dreyse's needle gun and that is precisely how the most famous name in the rifle world got its start.

Peter Paul Mauser was born in 1838, and became a gunsmith at the Royal Württemberg Rifle Factory. His elder brother Wilhelm pursued a similar career, and between them they set about redesigning the needle gun to take a metallic cartridge. By 1867, they had perfected a design but failed to raise any military interest in it; the Prussians had just defeated the Danes and Austrians in short and decisive wars and were happy that their needle gun was all they required. The Austrians had already decided on a design to adopt and were not interested in anything new; and the story was much the same throughout Europe.

At this point, a strange piece of chicanery occurred. American historians have frequently stressed the fact that Mauser's original rifle patents were taken out in the U.S.A. and this appears to credit America with the invention of the Mauser rifle. It is, perhaps, impertinent to point out that Colt took out his first revolver patents in England, although the English have never claimed the Colt as their own. The fact is that the Mauser brothers, anxiously seeking backing for their invention, were approached by one Samuel Norris, an itinerant salesman then travelling Europe on behalf of the Remington company.

Norris thought he had a chance of selling the Mauser design to the French so that they could convert their Chassepot rifles – which only

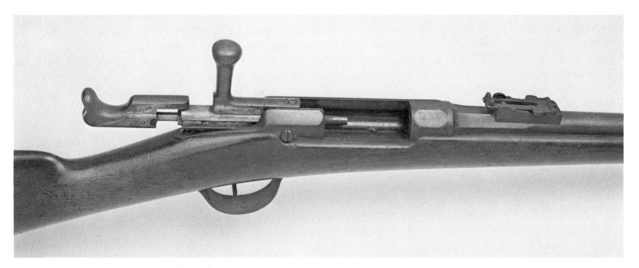

Antoine Chassepot's rifle with the bolt open.

The Mauser rifle adopted by the Prussian Army
in 1871. This model was made in 1880.

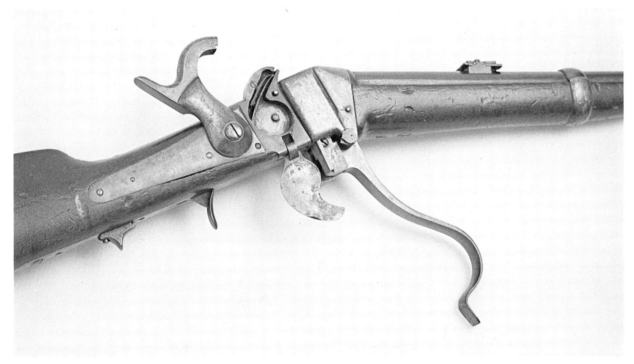

One of several variants of the Sharps
breech-loading rifle, with the operating
lever lowered and a separate chamber
for the primer.

Peter Paul Mauser (1838–1914) and his brother Wilhelm (1834–1882).

shows how little he knew of French military psychology of the period – and he bound the Mauser brothers by a dubious contract, in return for which he took out the American patent. In the event, the French declined the offer, and Norris forthwith abandoned the Mausers. He voided the contract by simply failing to make a stipulated annual payment of $1,000 and, in the process, lost himself a fortune.

Thrown back on their own resources, the Mauser brothers managed to rouse the interest of the Prussian Army and in the following year, 1871, the Prussians adopted Mauser's design as their rifle of 1871. The Mauser system had arrived.

The basic changes that the Mauser brothers made to the Dreyse mechanism were, firstly, that the striker was automatically with-drawn into the bolt and cocked as soon as the bolt began to open. This prevented the danger of inadvertently closing the bolt with the striker, or needle, protruding past the bolt head and accidentally firing the cartridge in the chamber. Secondly, an automatic extractor was fitted to the bolt to remove the empty cartridge case. Thirdly, the bolt head was a separate unit. Finally, the opening action of the bolt worked against a cam surface in the rifle body to exert a powerful 'primary extraction' pull, and unseat an expanded case. All these features were original, and all became necessary features in any bolt action which followed.

There were other ways of closing a breech apart from using a reciprocating bolt, and in the United States it was these systems which predominated. In 1853, Christian Sharps

A Sharps breechloading carbine derived
from the rifle of 1853.

introduced a rifle with a vertically-sliding breech block opened by a lever beneath the butt-stock. Pressing down on this lever lowered the block in mortised guides in the body of the rifle and allowed a prepared paper cartridge to be loaded. As the lever was pulled back up, so the block rose and the sharp front edge sliced the end off the paper cartridge, exposing the black powder to a vent bored through the block. A percussion cap went on to the outer end of this vent and was struck by an external hammer. As metallic cartridges supplanted paper ones, so the mechanism was modified, an extractor being fitted and a firing pin in the block replacing the vent and nipple.

Another system, destined to become more famous, was originated by a Bostonian, James Peabody, in 1862. Breech closing was again done by a block, but one which lay behind the breech and was hinged at the end away from the breech opening. It was actuated by a lever

below the butt-stock. As the lever was dropped, so the front end was lowered so that the upper surface of the block formed a convenient ramp down which a cartridge could be slid to enter the chamber. Again, the ignition system consisted of a nipple and vent in the block and an external hammer. This was later changed to a firing pin, with the external hammer being retained. The Peabody rifle proved fairly popular and specimens found their way to Europe, where the basic idea was considerably changed by native inventors. The most efficient of these modifications was that of Martini, a Swiss, who did away with the external hammer and placed a firing pin inside the breech block, controlled directly by the trigger. This action was adopted by the British Army and, when allied to a barrel rifled according to the ideas of Alexander Henry, a Scots gunsmith, produced the successful Martini-Henry service rifle of 1869. The Martini action is still widely used

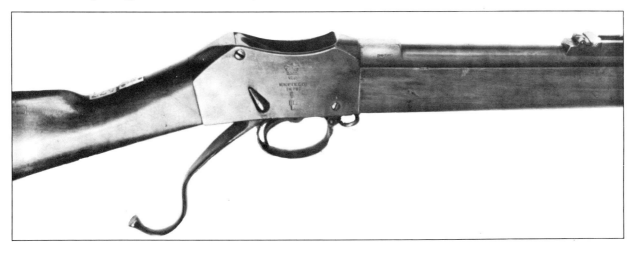

The lever action Martini-Henry was the
British Army's standard rifle until the
introduction of the bolt-action
Lee-Metford.

Facing page: British soldiers armed
with the Martini-Henry rifle at the
battle of Tel-El-Kebir, Egypt,
September 1882.

for target rifles, for it is simple and robust, and because the integral firing pin has an extremely short travel which, in turn, leads to a short 'lock time', the time elapsing between pressing the trigger and firing the cartridge. As may be imagined, a short lock time is of great value in competitive shooting since it reduces the time in which the aim can waver.

So far the rifle had been strictly a single shot weapon, which had to be re-loaded after every shot. Since the revolving pistol was now common, it was only a matter of time before rifles were demanded which had the same facility for repeating fire. The revolver system was an obvious choice, and since 1840 Samuel Colt had manufactured rifles which were little more than enlarged versions of his revolvers. They were never very successful. Being intended for long range firing, they used powerful charges and they showed a distressing propensity to 'flash over', the flame from the fired chamber igniting the powder in the other chambers, so that the entire contents of the cylinder exploded at once. Other American and European makers also examined a revolving rifle, but even when the metallic cartridge came along this type of arm never achieved a great degree of popularity.

The first repeating rifle to be successful was the American Spencer of 1860. This used a down-and-back swinging breechblock operated by an under-lever, together with an external hammer. A tube in the rifle butt carried nine ·56 cartridges and operation of the lever opened the breech, collected a cartridge from the tube, rammed it into the chamber and closed the breech again. Almost 250,000 Spencer carbines were bought by the Union Army during the American Civil War, and numbers were also used by the French Army in the war of 1870–71.

A more enduring design was that developed by Benjamin T. Henry. He had made considerable improvements on a lever-action rifle

The Spencer repeating carbine (leaning against the drums) was widely used by the Union Army in the American Civil War. The Unionist NCO is holding a U.S. rifle-musket, Model 1861.

Facing page: the legendary Annie Oakley poses with her Winchester rifle.

known as the 'Volcanic' in about 1850, but lacking the means to produce the modified weapon, he sold the idea to Smith and Wesson, who proceeded to manufacture it. They promoted both the rifle and a similar pistol, but in 1857 decided to pursue other ideas and sold out to Oliver Winchester. He formed the 'New Haven Arms Company' and hired Henry to be his factory manager. (Winchester himself knew nothing about the mechanics of firearms, but was a good businessman.) Henry's repeating rifle used

a tube beneath the barrel to carry the cartridges. The breech was closed by a reciprocating block operated by an under-lever. As this lever went down, the bolt was drawn back and in this movement contacted the hammer and cocked it. A 'lifter' collected a cartridge from the rear end of the tube, and as the under-lever was brought back up, so the lifter carried the cartridge up to the breech and the bolt was driven back to chamber it and then lock behind it. The Henry was used in the Civil War by both

Colour bearers of the 7th Illinois Infantry, Union Army, armed with Henry repeating rifles.

BUFFALO BILL'S WILD WEST
CONGRESS, ROUGH RIDERS OF THE WORLD.

MISS ANNIE OAKLEY,
THE PEERLESS LADY WING-SHOT.

During the American Civil War, the repeating rifle gradually replaced the musket as the standard military weapon. **Facing page, top to bottom:** the Battle of Chattanooga, 23–25 November 1863; the Assault on Fort Sanders, 29 November 1863; the Battle of Franklin, 30 November 1864.

The modified Winchester model of 1866.

sides and acquired a good reputation. It was known to some Confederates as 'that damn Yankee rifle they load on Sunday and fire the rest of the week'.

Henry's original method of loading the magazine was to remove the front end of the tube and insert the cartridges. In 1866, this was changed to 'King's Patent' system, a hinged flap in the gun body beneath the breech into which the cartridges could be pushed and from which they passed straight into the magazine. In 1873, the Henry rifle appeared as the 'Winchester 1873 Model'. In 1886, the design was again improved by John Browning, who made the bolt-locking system stronger so that it was able to withstand the heaviest cartridges. Since that time, the Winchester company have continued to produce this type of rifle, and indeed their name is virtually synonymous with 'lever-action rifle'.

The lever-action was a very sound action, and thousands of these rifles saw military service – notably in the Russo-Turkish war in 1877, in which Turkey deployed 50,000 Winchesters and shot the Russian army to ribbons on more than one occasion. As war moved away from the standing volleys of yesteryear, the great defect of the lever-action as a military arm became apparent: it was almost impossible to operate it in the prone position without becoming exposed to enemy fire. The lever action lost its attraction for the military and it

was necessary to look for a bolt-action repeater.

The Mausers rose to the challenge by the simple expedient of adopting the under-barrel tube of the Henry rifle and marrying it to his existing bolt action. Opening the bolt allowed eight 11mm cartridges to be pushed across the lifter and into the tubular magazine; a ninth cartridge could then be placed on the lifter so that as the bolt was closed this was placed in the chamber ready to fire. Subsequent operation of the bolt ejected the spent case and brought up a fresh cartridge from the magazine.

Unfortunately, the tubular magazine has two distinct disadvantages. One is that the gradual emptying of the magazine changes the point of balance of the rifle, necessitating a shifting grip and a moving point of aim. The other is that the cartridges in the tube lie with the point of a bullet touching the percussion cap of the next cartridge, and the recoil of the weapon on firing is sometimes enough to bring them into violent contact so that the cap is fired, leading inevitably to a chain reaction in which the entire magazine contents explode. This defect was not apparent in the early days of blunt lead bullets with rounded noses, but when military calibres began to shrink and as jacketed sharp-pointed bullets appeared, trouble began and the tubular magazine was rapidly retired from military service.

In 1879, James Paris Lee, a Scots-born American, patented a 'box magazine', a vertical

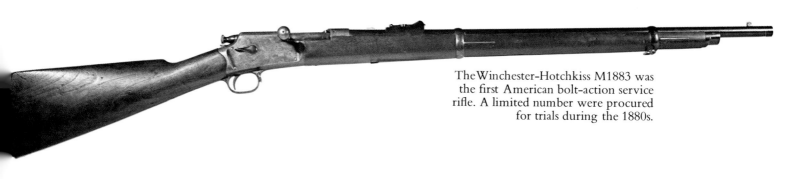

The Winchester-Hotchkiss M1883 was the first American bolt-action service rifle. A limited number were procured for trials during the 1880s.

One of the first weapons to use the Lee box magazine, the Remington Lee carbine in 7mm calibre.

metal box which fitted beneath a rifle bolt and into which a number of cartridges could be placed. As the bolt was withdrawn, so a spring beneath the cartridges forced them up until the topmost cartridge was lying in the bolt's path. As the bolt closed, so this cartridge was swept out of the magazine and into the chamber. In the same year, Antonin Spitalsky, chief foreman of the Austrian Steyr arms factory, designed a bolt action with a rotary magazine. It resembled a revolver cylinder in that it carried six cartridges and revolved. However, instead of chambers, the cylinder merely had external grooves in which the cartridges lay, and were held in place by a light metal cover, or by the stock of the rifle. As the bolt was closed, so it took the topmost round from its groove and loaded it into the chamber; as the bolt opened, the cylinder was indexed round to present a fresh round to the bolt on its closing stroke.

Lee's box magazine was more practical and a good deal easier to make, and it was adopted by the Remington company, who sold 40,000 Remington-Lee rifles and carbines to the Mexican Government in 1884. At this time, the British Army were seeking to replace the ·45 Martini-Henry single shot rifles with a small-calibre repeater. After extensive and exhaustive trials, they adopted Lee's bolt and magazine system, allying it to a barrel rifled according to

the principles of William Metford. The result was the ·303 Lee-Metford rifle, which was first announced in 1889.

The Lee bolt action has certain characteristics by which it differs from the Mauser, its principal rival in two world wars. The Lee bolt is locked into the rifle body by two lugs set about two-thirds of the bolt length back from the chamber. It cocks on the closing stroke and, owing to the shape of the lugs, there is an easy translation from the axial closing stroke to the rotary locking movement. All this adds up to an action which is undoubtedly the fastest of its type, though theoretically, due to the position of the lugs, it is less strong and less accurate than the Mauser. Theory, however, counts for little on the battlefield and, in the hands of trained soldiers, the Lee system can always deliver faster aimed fire than the Mauser. Although theorists complained when the Lee system was adopted, its subsequent career vindicated the men who selected it. When smokeless powder replaced black powder, a new rifling system – known as the 'Enfield system' from the place of its design – was substituted for the Metford patterns, and the rifle became the Lee-Enfield in 1895. With slight modifications, this was to remain the British Army's basic weapon until 1956.

During this period, Mauser had been steadily improving their design. Every year, so

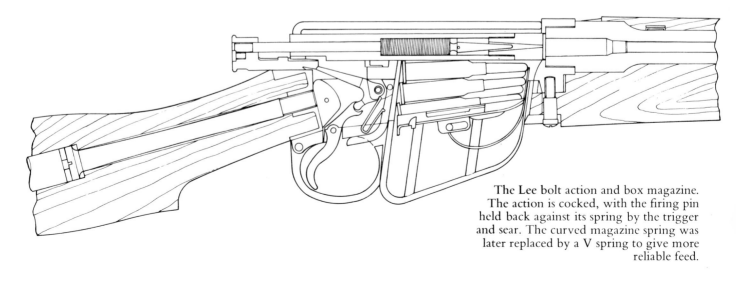

The Lee bolt action and box magazine. The action is cocked, with the firing pin held back against its spring by the trigger and sear. The curved magazine spring was later replaced by a V spring to give more reliable feed.

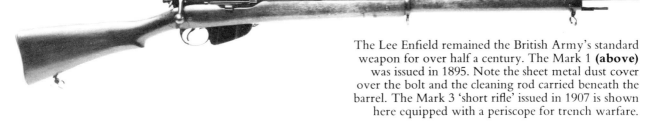

The Lee Enfield remained the British Army's standard weapon for over half a century. The Mark 1 **(above)** was issued in 1895. Note the sheet metal dust cover over the bolt and the cleaning rod carried beneath the barrel. The Mark 3 'short rifle' issued in 1907 is shown here equipped with a periscope for trench warfare.

The Lee Enfield No. 4, developed shortly before the Second World War, is shown here in action in the attack on the Odon Valley, France, July 1944.

Some of the Lee-Enfield's rivals. **Top to bottom:** the Mauser Gewehr 98, with the five-shot magazine concealed inside the stock; the U.S. Carbine M1898 with the Krag-Jorgensen bolt action; the U.S. Army's Model 1903 'short rifle', otherwise known as the Springfield.

it seemed, another nation would adopt a Mauser design and with each new adoption there was some small improvement added to the rifle. In 1893, the Spanish Army adopted a Mauser which, for the first time, used a box magazine concealed entirely within the rifle's stock. Finally, in 1898, the German Army decided upon a Mauser and introduced their 'Gewehr '98', which was the final flowering of Mauser's genius. In basic principles, it was much the same as its predecessors, but small refinements made it one of the finest military rifles of all time. Once given the German seal of approval, it was widely adopted by other countries.

In 1892, the United States Army, after conducting trials, adopted the Krag-Jorgensen rifle as their repeater, a decision which has always

defied rational explanation. The Krag was a Danish invention which used a bolt more or less based on Mauser practice, but allied it to a peculiar box magazine. This was loaded through a trap-door in the side of the rifle, and the cartridges passed underneath the bolt and up the far side, to be fed into the boltway from the left. Why such a system was adopted in place of the locally-available Lee is not known.

The Krag soon had its baptism of fire in the Spanish-American War, and the comments of the U.S. soldiers when confronted with Spanish troops armed with the latest Mauser were somewhat acid. As a result, the Americans rapidly took a second look at the rifle systems available and decided to modify the Mauser to suit their own ideas. Paying Mauser $200,000

The Arisaka Type 38, based on the Mauser, was the Japanese Army's standard weapon from 1908 to 1945.

for the privilege, they adopted the Mauser bolt and magazine and designated their rifle the 'Model 1903', though it was always known as the 'Springfield', from the armoury in which it was made.

The original Springfield was designed in 1901 with a barrel 30 inches long. This conformed with the standard practice of the period, of having two distinct shoulder arms. The major weapon was the rifle, used by infantry; the minor weapon was the carbine, a shorter version of the same weapon, but for use by cavalry, artillery and engineers, who wanted a less cumbersome weapon to carry while performing their own particular functions. This dual need was a nuisance. In the first place, it meant two distinct patterns in supply, two distinct sets of spare parts, two distinct manufacturing set-ups. There was also the ballistic problem that a cartridge optimised for use in, say, a 30-inch

rifle barrel would not be at its best in a 20-inch carbine barrel, or vice versa.

The solution to this is, of course, so obvious that one wonders why it took so long to provide a rifle of intermediate length for all troops. In the early years of the century, the same solution apparently struck the British and American armies at the same time. In 1903, both produced a 'short rifle'. The Americans shortened their Springfield to a 24-inch barrel, and the British cut their Lee-Enfield from 30 inches to 25 inches.

By the start of the First World War, the machine gun had become a standard item in all the world's armies, and it followed from this that inventors began to look again at military rifles and wonder if they could not be automatically operated in a similar manner. Indeed, inventors had been working on this since the 1890s, but not only were they having difficulties

The First World War: French soldiers are given a demonstration of the Springfield rifle at an American camp in France.

with the mechanical features of design, they were stoutly opposed by most members of the military hierarchy.

The magazine rifle itself had run into considerable opposition in its early days, the opinion being voiced that given a magazine full of ammunition the simple soldiers would blaze it all off as soon as the enemy appeared on the horizon and thus be left with nothing when he got closer. Such expenditure of ammunition would also place an intolerable strain on the supply organisation.

The same objections, but stronger, now appeared to damn the automatic rifle. If a magazine rifle could get rid of ammunition quickly, how much more quickly would an automatic do the job, and how much greater strain would be placed on the supply lines? In order not to appear too reactionary, most military departments announced that they would welcome an automatic rifle, provided it met stringent requirements – and these were pitched so strongly that even today it is unlikely that any

military rifle could match them. After a period of hesitation, the first country ever to adopt an automatic rifle was Denmark, which took a small number into Naval service in 1886. They were not entirely successful and the design, suitably modified, turned itself into the Madsen machine gun in later years with much greater success. After this chastening experience, there was no movement for a long time until the Mexican Army – who, strangely enough, were always well to the fore in adopting new types of weapon – decided to adopt the Mondragon automatic rifle. Invented by General Mondragon of the Mexican Army, this used a gas cylinder beneath the barrel, in which a piston, driven by some of the propelling gas behind the bullet, drove back the bolt to extract and re-load each shot. It was officially approved in 1908 and manufacture was contracted to a Swiss company. Some were delivered before the outbreak of war in 1914 but, after that, the remainder of the contract went to Germany and many of these rifles were used by air observers

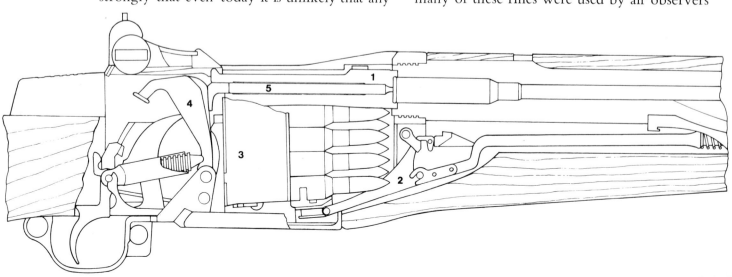

Early automatic rifle designs. **Top to bottom:** the Mexican Mondragon of 1908; the Pedersen ·276 rifle, shown with the toggle lock open; the U.S. Rifle ·30 M1, better known as the 'Garand' after its inventor. **Right:** John C. Garand (1888–1974).

in the early days of aerial warfare. A few were used in the trenches, but they did not show up well in ground combat, being prone to jamming from the mud and dirt, and this tended to colour everyone's view of automatic rifles for the remainder of the war. By and large, the First World War was fought with bolt-action magazine rifles on all sides.

After the war, the Americans began to work in earnest on an automatic rifle design. John C. Garand, in 1920, offered the army an unusual rifle in which the locking of the bolt was overcome by the set-back of the cap in the cartridge case. The whole design was considered too frail for military use, but on the strength of it, Garand was employed at Springfield Arsenal to work on an automatic rifle. At the same time, another American designer, J. D. Pedersen, produced a rifle using a toggle lock, similar to that employed in the Maxim machine gun and the Luger pistol. With it he developed a ·276 calibre cartridge, but the rifle was turned down because it needed to have its cartridges lubricated by grease or wax in order to make it function correctly, and greasy cartridges attract dust and lead to jammed mechanisms. The cartridge, though, was highly thought of, and Garand now produced a gas-operated rifle firing the ·276 round. A gas piston beneath the barrel was forced back on firing and, through the interaction of cam surfaces, turned and then opened the rifle bolt. A 'clip', or metal sheath, containing eight cartridges was dropped into the magazine and a spring-loaded 'follower arm' gradually pushed the cartridges up into the path of the bolt. When the last shot had been fired, the bolt stayed to the rear to indicate that the weapon was empty and the empty clip was ejected from the magazine.

The Garand was robust, simple and easy to maintain. In 1929, it was approved as the possible service rifle. General MacArthur, then Chief of Staff, concurred with the expert's choice, but vetoed the ·276 cartridge on the grounds that the stocks of ·30 ammunition, and the facilities for production, represented too great an asset to be discarded, so the Garand went back to the workshop to be re-designed in ·30 calibre. In 1936, it was approved as the 'Rifle M1', and the U.S. Army became the first major force to adopt an automatic rifle as its standard infantry arm.

The American adoption of the Garand spurred other nations into acceptance of the automatic rifle. The Soviet Army were the first to react, adopting a design by Simonov, also in 1936. This was also gas operated, using a cylinder and piston over the barrel to impel a 'bolt carrier' inside which the bolt was moved, locked and unlocked. However, they were premature in taking the weapon into service. It suffered from excessive recoil and was liable to stoppage from dust and dirt. Within two years, it was replaced by a different design by Tokarev. This, in turn, proved to be insufficiently robust for service life, and the bulk of the army stayed

Facing page: The Garand rifle action. The bolt (1) is driven by a gas piston. The follower (2) forces rounds from the clip (3) into the bolt's path. When the trigger is pressed the hammer (4) strikes the firing pin (5).

The Mauser Karabiner 98K was actually
a short rifle rather than a carbine. It
remained the basic weapon of the German
Army until 1945.

wedded to the Mosin-Nagant bolt action rifle,
a hangover from the days of the Tsar.

The German Army had as their standard
rifle the 'Karabiner 98K', a shortened version of
the Gewehr 98, but, as the nations of Europe
moved towards war in the late 1930s, they too
began to examine the prospect of an automatic
rifle. In 1940, the Walther company produced a
model which used a cup over the muzzle, driven
forward by the blast of the emerging gases, to
actuate a connecting rod and thus the bolt.
Several thousand were made, but it was not a
good design and was not perpetuated in service.

In the German Army there were two
distinct schools of thought on the question of a
new rifle. The traditional school merely wanted
an automatic rifle which would use the same
7·92mm cartridge which had been the service
standard since the turn of the century. Another
body of opinion began looking at the whole
question from a different angle. Analysis of
infantry actions of the First World War, indicated that it was rare for an infantry soldier to
be called upon to fire a rifle at greater ranges
than about 500 yards. Indeed, practical tests
showed that most soldiers could not distinguish
or identify targets any further away. Was it
really necessary to continue to use a powerful
cartridge which was designed to shoot accurately up to 2,000 yards, a performance based on
the sort of warfare which had been seen in
South Africa in the Boer War?

As a result of this reasoning, a new and
shorter cartridge was developed which fired a
lighter bullet – though still of 7·92mm calibre –
with a smaller cartridge case and less powerful
charge. It was still good enough to deal with

targets up to about 800 yards, but the shorter
cartridge meant a shorter bolt stroke and thus
a shorter rifle. The lighter bullet and charge
meant less recoil, easier training and a quicker
return to the aim after firing. Moreover, the
soldier could carry more ammunition. From
this starting point a completely new type of rifle
was evolved. In the first place, it was designed
with mass-production in mind, using stamped
sheet metal components, plastic instead of wood,
welding instead of screws and rivets. It was gas
operated, and in addition to being an automatic
rifle, it could be switched to full-automatic fire
so as to act as a machine gun.

Called the 'Maschinen Karabiner 42' a
few thousand were made and shipped to the
Russian front, where they immediately proved
to be popular with the troops. However, going
into production required the approval of Hitler.
Basing his opinion on his own experiences in
the trenches in 1917–18, he turned the idea down
flat, insisting that the rifle must fire the full-
sized round and be capable of shooting to 2,000
metres. The Army were aghast at this decision
and, like soldiers everywhere when confronted
with a bad decision, they agreed – and then went
away and did what they wanted. The weapon
was put into production without Hitler's
approval, and concealed in the monthly returns
by being re-christened. It was now called the
'Maschinen Pistole 43' and classed as a submachine gun. Eventually, the deception was
discovered, and Hitler threw one of his monumental rages, but when the weapon was finally
demonstrated to him he was won over and gave
it yet another name. Now it became known as
the 'Sturmgewehr 44' or the 'Assault Rifle'.

The Russian Mosin-Nagant M1891 with
1908 rear sight. A quantity of these,
manufactured by Remington, were used
by the U.S. Army as training rifles in 1917.

A postwar design, the Soviet SKS46
carbine was the first Soviet weapon
chambered for the 7·62mm short
cartridge.

U.S. troops armed with Garand rifles
land at Leyte, Philippines, October
1944. Painting by H. Charles McBarron.

The modern generation of automatic rifles.

Top to bottom: the Maschinen Karabiner 42(W), designed by Walther – a rival model was developed by the Haenel company; the Maschinen Pistole 43, developed from the Haenel MKb42 design; the Enfield EMI semi-automatic rifle in ·280 calibre; the Kalashnikov assault rifle designed for the short 7·62mm cartridge.

In the years following the war, this German development caught the imagination of many countries and several new designs of rifle were produced, using the same parameters of small cartridge and reduced performance to give a lighter weapon. In Britain, the revolutionary 'EM1' (Enfield Model 1) rifle appeared. This was developed around a short 7mm cartridge, and the layout of the weapon was unlike anything seen before. Instead of having the bolt well in front of the firer's face and a long shoulder stock, the stock was simply a flat cushion immediately behind the rifle body, so that the bolt was actually under the man's face. This meant that for a given length of barrel, the whole rifle was shorter by what would have been the length of the butt. Unfortunately, politics got into the argument. NATO standardisation was the order of the day, and NATO settled on a slightly shortened version of the American ·30 cartridge, calling it the '7·62mm NATO' cartridge and adopting the Belgian-designed Fabrique Nationale automatic rifle. The Americans modified the Garand design to produce their own rifle, firing the 7·62mm NATO cartridge.

The Russians too, appreciated the German reasoning, and produced a 7·62mm cartridge almost the same size as the wartime German round, after which they produced a gas operated assault rifle, the Kalashnikov, to go with it. This robust and simple weapon is, by now, probably the widest-distributed rifle in history, having been adopted by every Soviet satellite and supplied to every nation which has applied to the Soviets for aid.

Eventually, the short cartridge had to succeed in America and it did so by the back door. The Armalite rifle, developed as an assault rifle around a new 5·56mm cartridge, was produced speculatively and was adopted by the U.S. Air Force who required a lightweight weapon to be carried by their aircrews. It was used by American forces in Vietnam, and from this it was diffused to the U.S. Army and was finally adopted by them as standard, gradually replacing the 7·62mm NATO weapons which were generally in use in infantry divisions.

The British 4·85mm 'Individual Weapon' is of similar layout to the EM1, with a shortened stock and the magazine behind the trigger.

Chapter Nine

The Revolver

A Belgian pin-fire pepperbox revolver
in which the chambers are elongated to
provide the barrels. It has a folding trigger.

THE IDEA of using an assembly of revolving chambers is one of the oldest methods of obtaining multiple discharges. However, as with so many other mechanical notions, so long as the ammunition consisted of powder, ball and flint, it was not entirely practical. With the perfection of Forsyth's percussion system and the introduction of the percussion cap, the problem was greatly simplified and practical revolving arms began to appear.

The 'Pepperbox' revolver, in which the revolving unit comprises a number of complete barrels, had been attempted in the flintlock era and was an obvious candidate for the percussion role. The first models were hand operated, the cylinder having to be turned by the firer between each shot. By the middle 1830s, the self-cocking pepperbox was in production. This used a simple operating bar, attached to the trigger, to push up on a ratchet at the rear of the cylinder unit, thus forcing it round far enough to place a loaded barrel in line with the hammer. The hammer was, at the same time, brought to the full cock position and was then released by the final movement of the trigger. In most designs, the hammer was on top of the pistol, striking down on to the percussion cap which was arranged at right-angles to the chamber. More sophisticated designs soon appeared which had the cap nipples mounted axially on the end

of the barrel and used an internal hammer striking forwards.

It should, perhaps, be pointed out that these were the years of the 'Long Peace' and there was, in consequence, little demand for pistols in Europe. Much the same situation existed in America. The Revolution and the Frontier Wars were behind them and the opening of the West was still to come, so that even there the demand for pistols was small. Nevertheless, in 1835, as soon as he had reached his majority, Samuel Colt patented his immortal revolver. He introduced a new configuration by shortening the revolving assembly until it merely contained the chambers and then placing a barrel in front of the topmost chamber. Colt's actual patent claim (English Patent 6909 of 22 October, 1835) was for 'Improvements applicable to firearms' and detailed such matters as the method of rotating the cylinder by a pawl linked to the hammer, and a method of locking each chamber in alignment with the barrel. In 1836, he obtained a similar patent (No. 9430X) in America and, with these, effectively stifled any attempt to develop any other form of mechanical cylinder rotation and locking for several years.

Late in 1836, revolvers to Colt's design began to be made by the 'Patent Arms Mfg Co' of Paterson, New Jersey, from which location these weapons have since come to be called the 'Paterson Colts'. Owing to the lack of demand previously mentioned, the venture was not a success and the company folded in 1843. That might have been the end of Sam Colt and his revolver, but in 1847 came the Mexican War. Colt succeeded in obtaining an order for 1,000 revolvers in ·44 calibre and these were made for him by Eli Whitney's Whitneyville Armory. Colt's original design had been improved, largely on the basis of suggestions by a Captain Walker of the Texas Rangers and also by

Previous page: 'Gunfight', by Charles M. Russell.

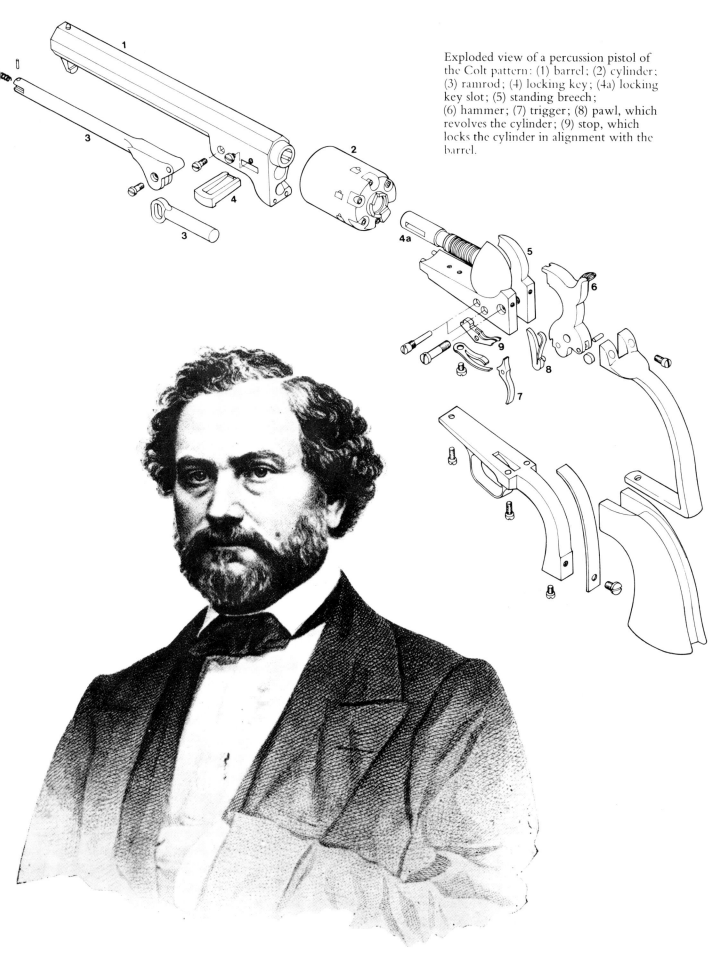

Exploded view of a percussion pistol of the Colt pattern: (1) barrel; (2) cylinder; (3) ramrod; (4) locking key; (4a) locking key slot; (5) standing breech; (6) hammer; (7) trigger; (8) pawl, which revolves the cylinder; (9) stop, which locks the cylinder in alignment with the barrel.

Samuel Colt (1814–1862), inventor of the famous Colt revolver.

success of this pistol Colt was able to finance the construction of his own factory in Hartford, Connecticut, and from then on, as the saying goes, he never looked back.

In 1851, the 'Great Exhibition of the Industry of All Nations' was held in London, and in spite of its professed theme of 'Peace and Industry', Colt displayed more than 100 revolvers of various sorts. These, together with some astute publicity by Colt, who was probably his own best salesman, caught the public eye, and suddenly the revolver business began to boom. This proved to be fortuitous for Robert Adams, an English gunsmith who, in 1851, had patented a number of firearms improvements among which was a design for a revolver. The Adams revolver was the only good design in existence, other than Colt's, and so Adams began to prosper in the wake of Colt's success.

The Adams was, in fact, a considerably better revolver than Colt's. In the first place, it used the solid frame form of construction in which the butt, frame and barrel were forged in a single unit, with a rectangular opening left for the insertion of the cylinder. This was inherently stronger than Colt's design of 'open frame' in which the barrel was a separate unit pinned to the front of the frame. Adams's second improvement was in the lock mechanism. The Colt pistol used a 'single action' lock which made it necessary to cock the hammer with the thumb and then squeeze the trigger to release the hammer and fire the pistol. The Adams revolver used a 'self-cocking' lock. Continuous pressure on the trigger would first raise the hammer to a cocked position and then, without pause, release it. This meant that for rapid firing the Adams had an advantage. On the other hand, when it came to slow and deliberate shooting the Colt mechanism was superior since it allowed a precise aim to be taken with the hammer cocked, after which a slight pressure on the trigger,

Whitney, who had considerable experience of volume manufacture of firearms. Although officially called the 'Model of 1847', these heavy revolvers are more generally known to collectors as the 'Whitneyville-Walker Colt' and they are extremely rare and valuable. From the

Above: The English gunsmith Robert Adams loading the revolver of HRH the Prince Consort. From *The Revolver*, by Patrick Edward Dove.

A typical Adams solid-frame revolver –
a cartridge-loading ·45 of 1872.

which would not disturb the aim, fired the shot. By that time, though, a third system was making an appearance, in which the hammer could be operated in either fashion. Known as the 'double action' lock, it has since become the normal pattern, but diligent research has failed to identify who invented it.

Adams and Colt between them, with their comprehensive patents, dominated the revolver field for some years. It was not until the Colt patent expired in 1857, and the Adams in 1865, that revolver manufacture became commonplace in the U.S.A. and Britain. Among those who awaited this freedom were two Americans, Horace Smith and Daniel B. Wesson. They combined in 1852, to manufacture a totally different type of pistol, aiming to evade the Colt master patent. They developed a magazine pistol in which a tube beneath the barrel contained the supply of cartridges. They abandoned the cap, powder and ball combination and used a self-contained round, which they called the 'Volcanic' bullet. In essence, it improved on an earlier, unsuccessful, design by Walter Hunt, the rights to which had been bought up by Smith and Wesson. The lead bullet had a hollow base in which a charge of powder was retained by a cork, in the centre of which was a fulminate cap. The pistol was

operated by a lever beneath the body, and pressing down this lever opened the breech and lifted a bullet from the magazine. Raising the lever loaded the bullet into the chamber, closed the breech and returned the lifter, after which pressure on the trigger dropped the hammer to fire the round.

While Smith and Wesson made a success of this, they were not entirely satisfied and they continued to work on the bullet until they evolved something entirely different: the rimfire metallic cartridge. The bullet was seated in a tubular copper case with an upstanding rim into which a fulminate composition was pressed. The remainder of the case carried a gunpowder charge. With this perfected, they began to design a revolver and, in the course of their preparation they discovered that Rollin White, a Colt employee, had taken out a patent (U.S. 12648 of of 1855) which covered a revolver employing a form of magazine for rapid reloading and priming the cylinder. More or less as an afterthought, White had claimed novelty for 'extending the chambers through the rear of the cylinder for the purpose of loading them at the breech from behind and not, as was the case in percussion revolvers, 'blind' at the rear end.

Smith and Wesson managed to obtain an exclusive license to this feature from White, and their terms gave White a royalty of 25 cents on every revolver sold, but also gave him the responsibility of protecting the patent. With this security, Smith and Wesson produced their first cartridge pistol, in ·22 calibre, in 1857. The patent remained in force until 1869 and Smith and Wesson thus gained an absolute monopoly in cartridge revolvers. The unfortunate White gained less than might be expected, since most of his gains from the royalties were expended in litigation against would-be copyists. Happily, he went on to invent a sewing machine and the famous White Steam Car, which somewhat

Horace Smith.

Daniel B. Wesson (1825–1906).

compensated him for his experiences in the firearms world.

The Rollin White patent, though vital in the U.S.A., could not be protected in Europe since an earlier patent of 1854, lodged by an unknown inventor through a patent agent in London, covered a pin-fire revolver with bored-through cylinders. This type of pistol had originated with Casimir Lefaucheaux of Paris who, in 1837, had developed the pin-fire cartridge. This used a capsule of detonating composition inside a cardboard case, which was fired by a pin passing through the side of the case and struck by a hammer. It was first developed for sporting guns but, by the early 1850s, the cartridge had become metallic and a number of bored-through revolvers had appeared. The 1854 patent covered one of these. The pin-fire revolver was adopted by the French Navy in 1856 and later by other governments on the Continent. Several thousand were to be used in the American Civil War, but the vulnerability of the pin feature to accidental damage and ignition always militated against widespread adoption of the pin-fire arm in military circles, and this form of ammunition eventually came to be associated with cheap pocket revolvers.

During the 'close season' in which Smith and Wesson enjoyed their monopoly, a third system of ignition evolved, the central or centre fire cartridge, in which a cap was fitted centrally in the cartridge base. This had considerable advantages. In the first place, it allowed heavier loadings to be used, since with rimfires there was always the danger of a heavy charge rupturing the cartridge rim. It also gave more

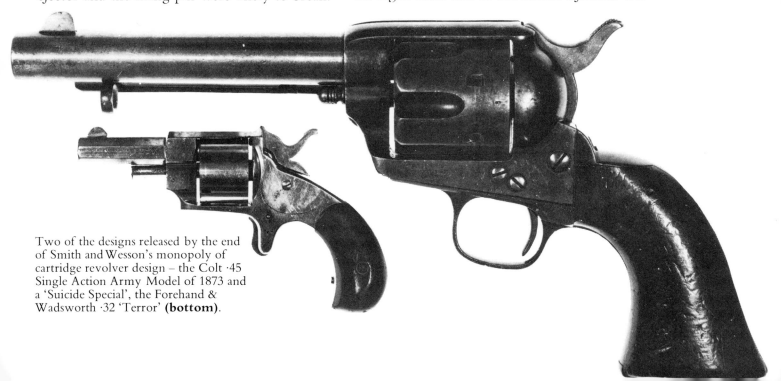

The first Smith & Wesson ·22 revolver was a hinged frame tip-up model. This solid-frame version is a licensed copy made by the Lowell Arms Company.

certain and regular ignition and it tended to improve revolver design. For the time being all such ideas had to remain dormant, and it was not until the expiry of the White patent that U.S. revolver manufacture and design moved forward. Once the patent did expire, it became a growth industry. The market was flooded with revolvers, some frank imitations of the Smith & Wesson design, others the cheap solid frame type which have since been categorised as 'Suicide Specials' from their lack of accuracy, reliability and finish.

Not surprisingly, Colt were among those whose talents were released, but the first designs from the company were not particularly clever and it seems to have taken them some years to find a good design. Once they had done so, the result became a legend. In 1873, the 'New Model Army Metallic Cartridge Revolving Pistol' appeared. It was better known as the 'Peacemaker', 'Frontier' or 'Single Action Army'. In the cold light of fact, it was not a particularly good design. The firing lock showed no improvement on Colt's early muzzle-loaders, parts which might have been expected to be forged integrally with the frame were screwed on as an afterthought, and both the ejector and the firing pin were likely to break.

For all that, the Single Action Army of 1873 became the epitome of the Old West and, except for a short break, has been in production ever since, as well as being the inspiration for innumerable copies.

With the arrival of metallic cartridges, either rim or centre fire, the designer was faced with the allied problems of loading the cartridges into the cylinder chambers and later extracting the fired cases. In the Smith & Wesson ·22 revolvers, the barrel and cylinder unit could be hinged upwards, pivoting in front of the hammer, so allowing the cylinder to be removed for emptying and loading. Where heavier and more powerful cartridges were to be used, this system was not liked, and the solid frame type of revolver had its cartridges loaded individually through a 'gate' on the right hand side of the frame. Ejection was

Two of the designs released by the end of Smith and Wesson's monopoly of cartridge revolver design – the Colt ·45 Single Action Army Model of 1873 and a 'Suicide Special', the Forehand & Wadsworth ·32 'Terror' (bottom).

Three basic revolver configurations. **Top to bottom:** the barrel hinged downwards, on an auto-ejecting British Webley, showing the operation of the star-shaped ejector plate; the solid frame, on a Ruger 'Super Single Six', one of many modern revolvers which owe their inspiration to the Colt New Model of 1873; the barrel hinged upwards, on one of the many Belgian freaks, with two barrels and a double row of chambers, giving a capacity of 16 shots.

Gate loading a Colt Frontier model.

done via the same gate, the cases being punched out one by one by a rod carried beneath the barrel or inside the axis pin of the cylinder itself. Various refinements to this simple system were introduced in order to avoid accidents. One of the most common mishaps was the falling of the hammer during loading, which resulted in any cartridge in the upper chamber being accidentally discharged.

Colt revolvers adopted the 'half cock' notch on the hammer. If the hammer was drawn partly back it could be locked by means of this notch, and no pressure on the trigger could lower it. A more elegant solution was that of a Belgian gunsmith named Abadie, who geared the gate to the firing lock so that as the gate was opened to load, the hammer was automatically drawn back, the trigger disconnected, and the cylinder released so that it could be indexed around for loading.

Gate loading was a cumbersome and slow business, and attempts were soon made to improve upon it. In 1865, W. C. Dodge, of Washington DC, patented a revolver design in which the barrel was hinged to drop down, exposing the cylinder for loading. He also obtained another patent for a star-shaped plate to be let into the rear face of the cylinder, from which it could be forced by suitable apparatus and, catching beneath the rims of the cartridge cases, would simultaneously eject the entire contents of the cylinder. Once again, Smith and Wesson were astute enough to obtain these important patents, and this time the protection was extended to Europe as well. Unfortunately, Dodge neglected to send the cheque for renewal in good time, the boat was delayed, and in 1868 the European patents were declared void. Dodge's failure allowed European manufacturers to use the star ejector plate from then on. It also gave several American writers the chance to upbraid Perfidious Albion and accuse the

British Patent Office of shady dealing. This accusation appears in several cases of disputed patents, and there seems to be little justification for such an attitude.

Armed with the Dodge patents, Smith and Wesson produced their 'Army Model 1869', or 'Number Three' revolver, in ·44 calibre, which is considered to be one of the finest revolvers in history. It was a heavy arm, with drop-down hinged barrel and automatic ejection by Dodge's star plate. The barrel unit was locked to the frame by a robust catch which interlocked with the hammer to prevent accidental opening. The design won numerous medals and awards, and in 1870 it was selected to be the standard sidearm of the Russian cavalry. For the next five years, Smith and Wesson were entirely concerned with filling this massive order – about 250,000 pistols were eventually delivered – and in that time Colt, who were actually producing an inferior product, had the American market to themselves. This allowed them to expand and gave the 'Colt' its place in the legends of the West.

used, the system adopted was to allow the cylinder to be drawn forward in the frame, axially, for a short distance; an extractor ring then stopped while the cylinder continued to move, so that the cylinder was, in effect, drawn from the empty cases. What happened then was that, inevitably, the bottom case failed to fall clear and jammed the whole mechanism. While the Enfield was a sound enough revolver in other aspects, its extraction system is a classic example of the problems which arise in trying to circumvent well-drawn patents.

In Germany, the Mauser company also essayed a military revolver with a difference. Instead of the cylinder being moved by the usual pawl and ratchet on the rear face, the outer surface was incised with grooves. Inside the frame, a rod and pin, connected with the trigger, reciprocated back and forth, riding in the grooves in the cylinder and thus rotating it every time the trigger was pulled. In order to load and extract, the barrel and cylinder were hinged at the top and broke open upwards. At the end of this opening stroke, a lever was pulled,

By this time, of course, the revolver was gaining a firm place in the military armouries in Europe. The British Army, after trying the Colt revolver, had gone over to the Adams, then, seeking a cartridge revolver, abandoned the trade and set about designing one within a Government establishment. The effort to avoid conflict with established patents resulted in a most peculiar design, the 'Enfield' ·476 revolver. It was a hinged frame weapon, but, since the extractor patented by Dodge could not be

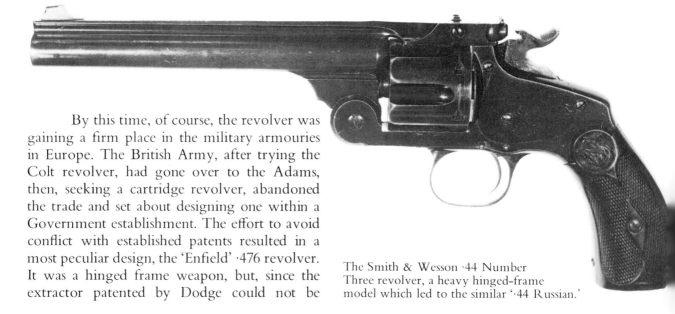

The Smith & Wesson ·44 Number Three revolver, a heavy hinged-frame model which led to the similar '·44 Russian.'

The Mauser 'Zig Zag' revolver of 1878, opened for reloading. Pulling the ring lever towards the muzzle operates the ejector plate in the centre of the cylinder.

Below: the Enfield ·476 revolver, opened to show how the cylinder slides forward, leaving the ejector plate in place.

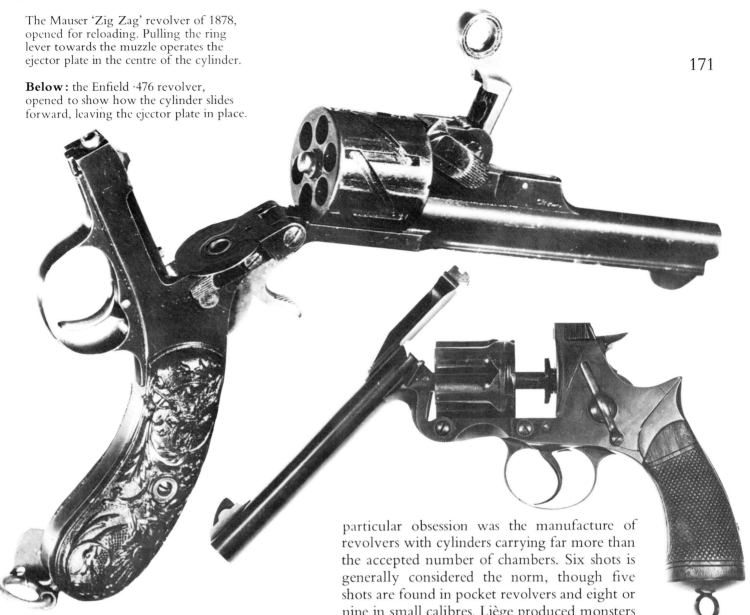

which drove out the extractor plate to eject the empty cases. It was an elegant engineering solution, but too complicated for service issue, and the German army preferred to accept a much more utilitarian solid-frame revolver in which the cylinder had to be completely removed for loading and unloading.

This form of upward-breaking automatic extraction is generally known, in Europe, as the 'Spirlet System', from the Belgian gunmaker who pioneered it in 1869. Belgium, and particularly the city of Liège owing to the proximity of coal and steel, had become one of the premier gunmaking areas of Europe, and small companies were producing cheap revolvers in great profusion by the 1880s. While most of them were unremarkable designs, largely based on other people's ideas, one must comment on some of the freaks which came from Liège, some of which still appear from time to time today. A

particular obsession was the manufacture of revolvers with cylinders carrying far more than the accepted number of chambers. Six shots is generally considered the norm, though five shots are found in pocket revolvers and eight or nine in small calibres. Liège produced monsters capable of firing 20 or more shots at one loading, either by making the cylinder of great diameter or making it with two circles of chambers and placing two superposed barrels in front. An adjustment to the hammer allowed the firing pin to strike either the upper or lower circle of chambers, discharging a bullet through the appropriate barrel. Owing to the physical dimensions of the cartridges, these weapons were invariably in small calibres, and they could hardly be called practical.

Other oddities worthy of note are revolvers capable of firing more than one sort of ammunition. The best-known among these is the Le Mat revolver, the invention of a French-born American physician, F. A. Le Mat. This revolver, which he first patented in 1856, used a normal form of cylinder but revolved it around a barrel which could be loaded with a charge of buckshot. By an adjustment to

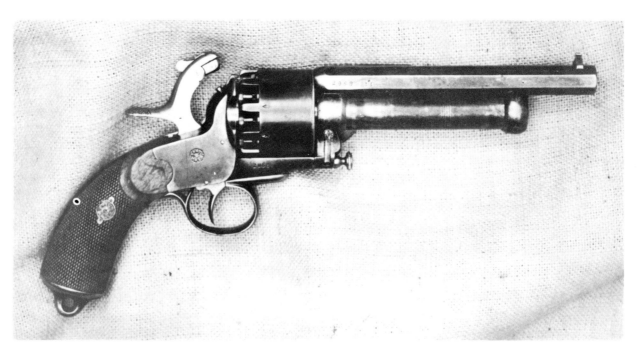

The combination revolver designed by
Jean Alexandre François Le Mat
(1824–c.1885) was produced in a variety
of different guises, from a baby revolver
to a carbine. Shown here is a late model
revolver.

the hammer, it was possible to fire the cartridges in the cylinder in the normal way and, in an emergency, switch the firing pin so as to fire the shot charge from the central barrel. Numbers of these pistols were made in France and supplied to the Confederate forces during the American Civil War. They continued to be made in Paris for some years, certainly until about 1880.

A similar weapon, less common today, is the Osgood Duplex revolver, made by the Osgood Gun Works of Norwich, Connecticut, in the 1880s. This was a ·22 calibre 8-shot hinged frame revolver, in which the cylinder turned around a tube containing a ·32 calibre barrel. A single ·32 rim-fire cartridge could be loaded into this central barrel and fired, as the Le Mat, by adjusting the firing pin on the hammer.

In Britain, the name of Webley now appeared in the revolver making world. After making a succession of sound pocket pistols, Webley managed to obtain an Army contract, the Enfield revolver having been finally dis-

The Webley RIC heavy revolver in ·476 calibre.

British Army's standard arm until the 1930s. Webley also became renowned for a smaller heavy revolver adopted by the Royal Irish Constabulary and hence known as the 'RIC' Model. With a short barrel, and chambered for such calibres as ·455, ·476 and even ·500, these robust weapons were widely bought and even more widely imitated by other manufacturers in the 1880s and 1890s.

credited and discarded. The Webley revolver was of hinge frame type, the barrel unit being locked to the frame by a particularly strong form of stirrup catch invented by a small gunmaker called Edwinson Green, who owned a small workshop in Cheltenham. This form of catch allowed the Webley revolver to be chambered for the most powerful loadings, and in ·455 calibre the Webley was to remain the

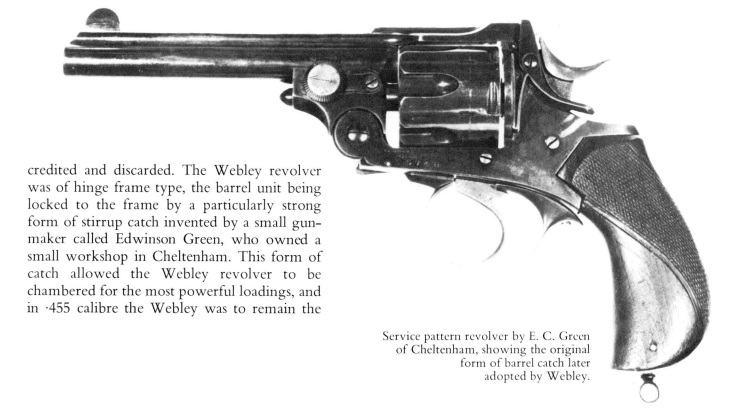

Service pattern revolver by E. C. Green of Cheltenham, showing the original form of barrel catch later adopted by Webley.

Two cheap revolvers of the 1890s, the Hopkins & Allen '·38 Safety Police Model' (**top**); and the Iver Johnson ·32 'Hammerless', which in fact had a hammer concealed in the rise of the frame behind the cylinder.

The Colt ·38 'New Army Model' of 1893, one of the first solid-frame side-opening revolvers. The cylinder is released by pulling back the catch below the hammer.

The Colt company, during this time, had continued to produce their solid frame, gate-loaded weapons, and were losing ground to the hinged-frame self-extracting pistols of Smith and Wesson and other manufacturers, such as Iver Johnson, Harrington & Richardson, and Hopkins & Allen, all of whom produced similar weapons. It was time for Colt to produce something more up-to-date, and in 1889 they introduced their 'New Navy' revolver which inaugurated a totally new approach to the extraction problem. Colt were reluctant to desert the solid frame. Indeed, they have never made a hinged frame revolver in their history. Their solution to the loading and extraction impasses was based on a patent granted to one W. Mason, an employee, in 1881. In this system, the cylinder was mounted on a 'crane' or hinged arm, pivoted at the lower front of the frame. By pulling back a spring catch on the left side of the pistol, the cylinder, on its crane, could be swung out sideways to lie alongside the frame. Once in this position, an ejector rod

quite content with the sales of their hinged-frame pistols and, in any case, could do little about the side-swinging cylinder pattern until the Colt patents expired in 1895. Once this occurred, they were ready with their own design, which differed slightly from the Colt in that the cylinder was released by pulling on the front end of the extractor rod, which lay beneath the barrel of the pistol. This was not entirely satisfactory – and neither was the Colt system, which retained the cylinder at its rear end and which was rendered less effective by the insistence of the U.S. Navy that the cylinder should revolve counter-clockwise. This meant that the pawl acting on the ratchet tended to push the cylinder out of alignment with the barrel. Colt appreciated this and eventually persuaded the Navy experts to change their specification. Smith and Wesson, however, developed a new system of locking which engaged the front end of the extractor rod with a lug forged beneath the barrel, and they have retained this system ever since.

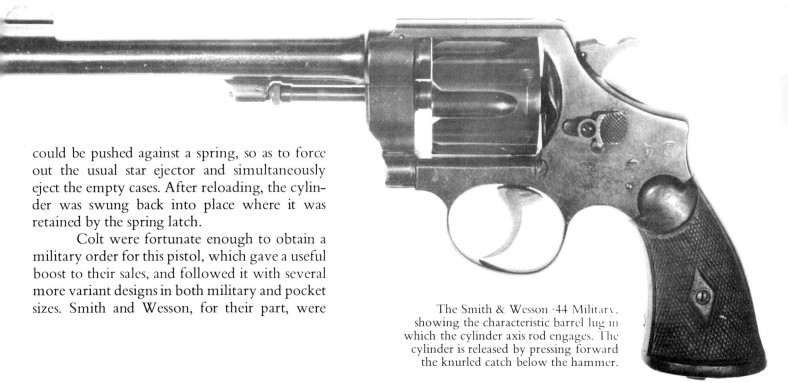

could be pushed against a spring, so as to force out the usual star ejector and simultaneously eject the empty cases. After reloading, the cylinder was swung back into place where it was retained by the spring latch.

Colt were fortunate enough to obtain a military order for this pistol, which gave a useful boost to their sales, and followed it with several more variant designs in both military and pocket sizes. Smith and Wesson, for their part, were

The Smith & Wesson ·44 Military, showing the characteristic barrel lug in which the cylinder axis rod engages. The cylinder is released by pressing forward the knurled catch below the hammer.

The Nagant gas-seal revolver of 1895.
The revolver is cocked and the cylinder
is thrust forward to engage the rear end
of the barrel.

In the 1890s, it seemed as if the revolver had gone just about as far as it could, and many inventors were turning to the automatic pistol in their never-ending search for improvement. There were, however, still some avenues to be explored and no shortage of people ready to explore them. One theoretical defect of the revolver is that there is a finite gap between the front of the chamber in the cylinder and the rear face of the barrel in the frame, and as the shot is fired the bullet leaps this gap, pursued by the propelling gases. Inevitably, some of the gas leaks from this joint; so, too, does noise, which is why no revolver can be successfully silenced. This theoretical defect attracted the attention of a Belgian gunsmith named Pieper as early as 1886. Pieper's design called for a special cartridge case, longer than normal, and for the front of the cylinder chambers to be recessed so that the case protruded. A lever beneath the frame was connected to the barrel, and operating this lever pushed the barrel forward and backwards. As it came back, the chamber end passed over the mouth of the cartridge case and entered the recessed face of the chamber. Thus, when the round was fired, the metal of the case bridged the gap and there was no gas leak.

Pieper manufactured some rifles to this specification, but for reasons lost in time he failed to renew the patent when it expired in 1890. He did, at a later date, make some revolvers based on these principles, but he was not so successful as Leon Nagant, another Liège gunsmith, who seized on the expiry of Pieper's patents to adopt the idea, modify it, and then re-patent it as his own. Having done this, he was astute enough to sell the idea to the Russian Army, who adopted the Nagant 'gas-seal' revolver in 1895. The principal change made by Nagant was to hold the barrel still and move the cylinder (though this had, in fact, been covered by Pieper in his original patent and was the system employed by him in his later revolver).

The cartridge was again special to the pistol and vital to its functioning. Of 7·62mm calibre, the case extended past the bullet and protruded from the front of the recessed chambers in the cylinder. There was a considerable gap between the face of the cylinder and the barrel in the 'rest' position, but when the hammer was cocked, either by the thumb or by pulling the trigger, a linkage came into action and thrust the cylinder forward bodily so that the end of the aligned chamber enveloped the end of the barrel and the mouth of the cartridge case was firmly lodged inside the end of the barrel. The hammer then fell and fired the round. As the hammer was cocked for the next shot, the cylinder was withdrawn, revolved, and thrust forward into engagement with the barrel once more.

Was it worth it? Was the gain in performance, due to the lack of escaping gas, sufficient to warrant the mechanical complications. The answer is not easy, since there is no way of directly comparing a gas-seal revolver with a 'non-gas-seal' of exactly the same characteristics of calibre, barrel length and so on. About 50 foot-seconds of initial velocity was gained and, since the nominal velocity of the cartridge was about 890 feet a second, it seems a small advantage and one which would hardly make an appreciable difference in actual combat. Nevertheless, the Russians were quite happy with it. They eventually obtained an exclusive license to the weapon and manufactured it for many years in their arsenal at Tula, and it remained in service use until after the Second World War.

The interest in the automatic pistol during the 1890s led many inventors to wonder what might be done to turn the revolver into an automatic weapon. As early as 1885 an engineer named Paulson, of Nottingham, England, patented a design in which gas was tapped from the revolver barrel to drive a piston

pistols. In 1895, he took out a patent for a modified Colt Single Action Army revolver in which he had separated the barrel and cylinder unit from the rest of the frame. The barrel section could slide back on the frame, in opposition to a powerful spring, and as it moved a pawl mounted on the hammer cross-shaft was forced back, cocking the hammer and thus rotating the cylinder.

The idea was practical, but only just, and it attracted the attention of the Webley and Scott company, the successors to P. Webley who had been supplying British Army revolvers since the demise of the Enfield. Fosbery and the Webley designers went to work to improve the basic idea and, in 1901, began to market a completely new design. This was based on the current Webley service revolver and, like the original idea, divided the weapon into two units, the barrel and cylinder section and the grip and frame section. The cylinder was incised on its

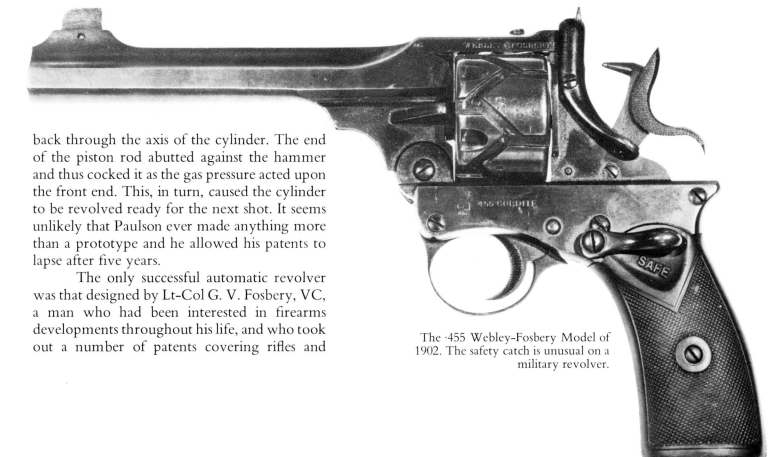

back through the axis of the cylinder. The end of the piston rod abutted against the hammer and thus cocked it as the gas pressure acted upon the front end. This, in turn, caused the cylinder to be revolved ready for the next shot. It seems unlikely that Paulson ever made anything more than a prototype and he allowed his patents to lapse after five years.

The only successful automatic revolver was that designed by Lt-Col G. V. Fosbery, VC, a man who had been interested in firearms developments throughout his life, and who took out a number of patents covering rifles and

The ·455 Webley-Fosbery Model of 1902. The safety catch is unusual on a military revolver.

Facing page: a sectioned drawing of the Ruger Single Six, showing the adoption of coil springs in place of the old time leaf springs and the use of a 'transfer bar' which lies between the hammer and the fixed firing pin. If the hammer is struck, for example through the pistol being dropped, it cannot touch the firing pin, since it will be jammed against the frame. Only when the trigger is correctly pulled will the transfer bar rise; then when the hammer falls the bar will transfer the blow to the firing pin.

outer surface with grooves, rather like those used on the earlier Mauser revolver, and these grooves engaged with a fixed pin in the pistol frame. Firing the pistol caused the barrel unit to recoil across the frame, and as it moved so the pin, acting in the groove, caused the cylinder to turn through one-twelfth of a revolution. At the same time, the pistol hammer was driven back to full-cock. The return spring then forced the barrel unit back across the frame top, and the pin, engaged in the cylinder groove, made the cylinder rotate another one-twelfth to complete the movement needed to bring a new chamber into alignment with the barrel.

Firing the Webley-Fosbery pistol was an unusual sensation. The arm had to be held firmly so that the recoil was used in actuating the mechanism. If the firer held the weapon at all loosely, then the recoil simply drove his wrist and arm back so that they 'soaked up' the recoil and the self-cocking action failed to take place. The revolver sold quite well, particularly for

the simplicity of a revolver with the magazine loading system of an automatic pistol. A magazine was loaded into the butt; in place of the normal cylinder there was a flat-sided block with two chambers, one in line with the barrel and one below. On pulling back an operating catch, a bolt was withdrawn, and on releasing the catch a cartridge was fed from the butt magazine into the lower chamber of the 'firing block'. When the trigger was pulled, the firing block revolved so that the loaded chamber came up into alignment with the barrel and the empty chamber went down underneath. As the chamber came to rest, a striker was released and the pistol fired. The bolt unit was then blown back by the explosion, extracting the empty case and reloading a fresh round into the lower chamber. The object behind all this was safety. Only when the trigger was pulled in order to fire a round did a round actually arrive in front of the firing pin and in line with the barrel. At any other time, the pistol was absolutely safe

target shooters – in fact, it was eventually forbidden in target shooting contests since it was considered to confer an advantage – and numbers were bought by British Army officers. In the test of battle, the Webley-Fosbery frequently failed through dirt getting into the mechanism, and manufacture ceased during the First World War. It was produced in the service ·455 calibre, but a small number of eight-shot versions chambered for the ·38 automatic pistol cartridge were also made for target work. These are extremely rare today.

Another approach was the Landstadt revolver of 1899, which attempted to combine

A modern Smith & Wesson 'K-22 Masterpiece' with target sights and grips.

Smith and Wesson differ little, in their appearance, from the pistols they were producing in 1907. Where the actual difference lies is under the skin: in 1907, the only way to make a revolver was to take a piece of steel and machine it into shape. Today, it may be cast, or components may be pressed from sintered metal. Coil springs replace the old-time gunsmith's leaf springs, and modern legislation demands safety features which were no part of the mechanisms designed years ago. Even with these manufacturing aids, good revolvers are expensive. The Colt Python ·357 costs $329, while the Colt M1911A1 automatic pistol in ·45 calibre costs $213. There is a 'feel' to a revolver which no automatic pistol will ever have, and so long as there are men who can detect this difference, revolvers will continue to be made.

against accidental discharge. Needless to say, few people were prepared to accept such a complicated procedure and the Landstadt pistol never got past the prototype stage.

Since the end of the First World War, there has been little advance in revolver design. This is largely a matter of economics. Revolvers are expensive things to make, they have reached a point where there is little value in trying to improve them – since practically every possible improvement has already been tried – and no manufacturer is willing to risk his reputation and money on a tentative idea. From time to time, it is true, new ideas have been put forward, but they have all fallen by the wayside, and the revolvers now produced by Webley, Colt and

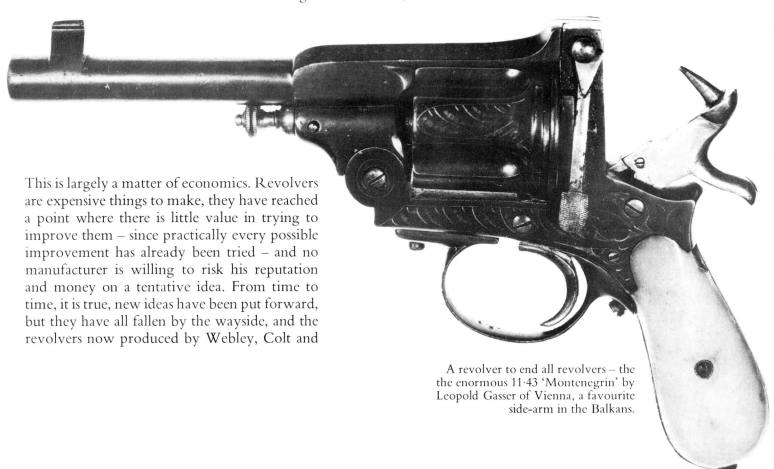

A revolver to end all revolvers – the the enormous 11·43 'Montenegrin' by Leopold Gasser of Vienna, a favourite side-arm in the Balkans.

Chapter Ten

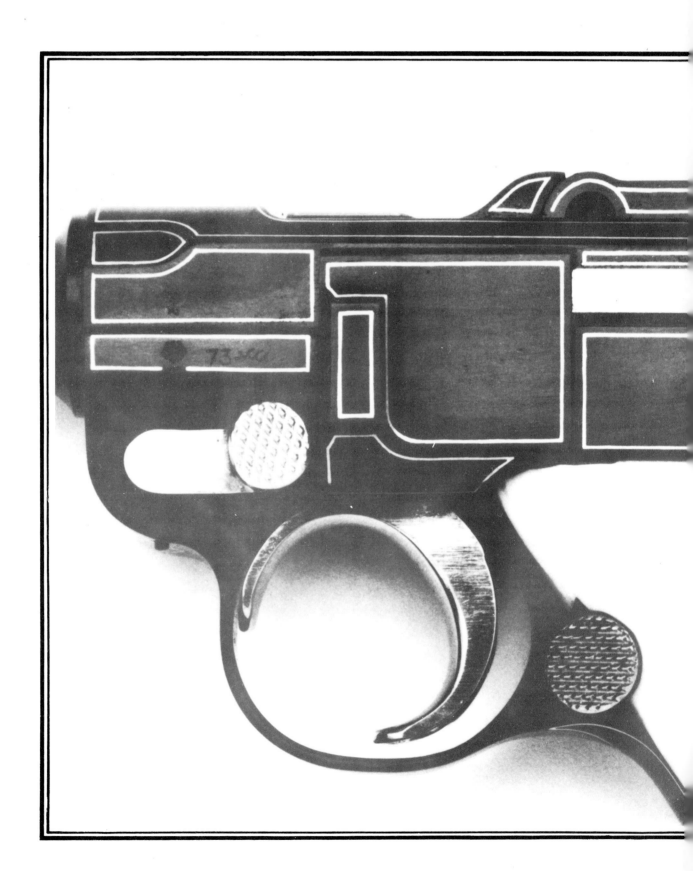

Automatic and Repeating Pistols

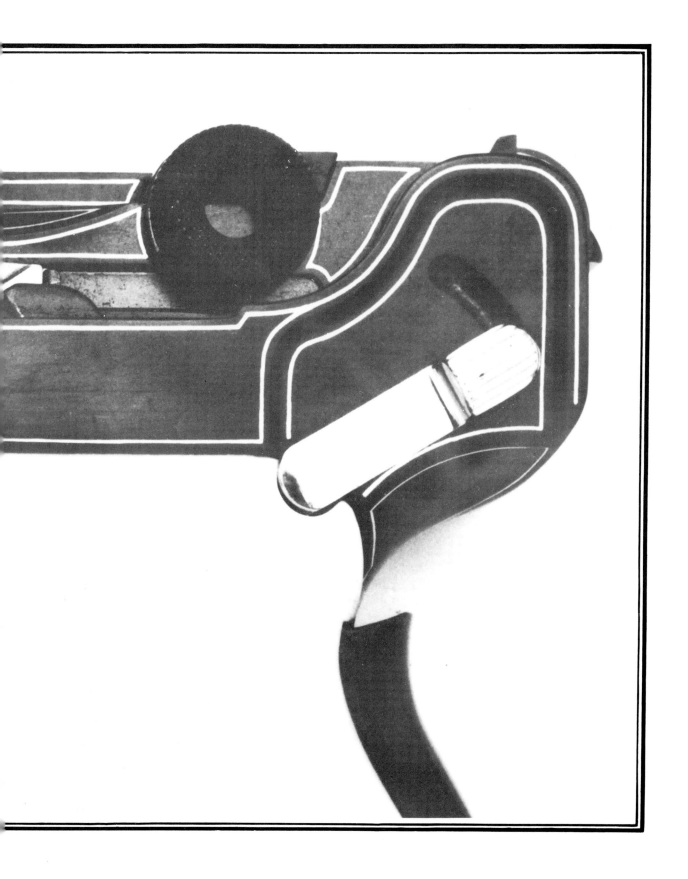

BY THE 1880s, the revolver was evidently reaching the end of its development. Remaining possibilities seemed to be thoroughly tied up by patents taken out by the bigger names in the business. Inventors began to look round and consider what other forms a hand gun could take. At the same time, the bolt-action magazine rifle was entering military service, so it

Krnka, a Bohemian resident in Vienna, Gustav Bittner, of Wiepert in Bohemia, and Schulhof, another Viennese. In Germany, Osterreich, of Berlin, and Mauser produced designs, while in the U.S.A. the Remington-Rider and the Volcanic can be placed in this class, although they used rather different mechanical principles. The customary method of operation, certainly

is not surprising to find this type of mechanism being explored in pistol form.

By some peculiar chance, most of the development of the 'mechanical repeating pistol' seems to have taken place in the Austro-Hungarian Empire, and it is difficult to determine precisely who invented what, since many of the ideas overlapped. Tabulating the patentees who never produced anything but a drawing would be a waste of time, but there were a handful of inventors who actually managed to produce working pistols. Some of these even got as far as being produced in relatively small numbers for commercial sale. Among the more successful inventors were Passler and Seidl of Vienna, Erwin Reiger, also of Vienna, Karl

for the European pistols, was much the same, and the Passler & Seidl design, patented in 1887, is as good an example as any. The breech is closed by an axially-moving bolt, similar to that of a rifle and locked into the breech by a rotary motion. Movement of the bolt, to close and open and to rotate it, is imparted by a lever protruding through the bottom of the pistol frame and ending in a finger-ring. By grasping the pistol butt, placing the forefinger in this ring and pushing it forward, the bolt is rotated and withdrawn to the rear. The spring-loaded magazine follower arm thrusts the cartridges upwards so that the topmost round lies in the path of the bolt, and by pulling the finger-ring backwards the bolt is closed, chambering the cartridge and leaving the striker inside the bolt cocked. The rear edge of the finger ring is slotted and, as it reaches the end of the closing stroke, it comes to rest with the firing trigger inside the slot, where an additional pressure of the forefinger can release this second trigger. This, in turn, releases the striker and fires the pistol, whereupon the whole cycle is repeated.

Theoretically, the design is impeccable. The breech is securely locked, which permits the use of quite powerful cartridges, while the mechanical components of the system are

Previous page: Detail of a modern Parabellum pistol produced by the Mauser factory (see page 189).

An early example of a 'mechanical repeating pistol' was the Schulhof 8mm Model 1884 **(above)**.

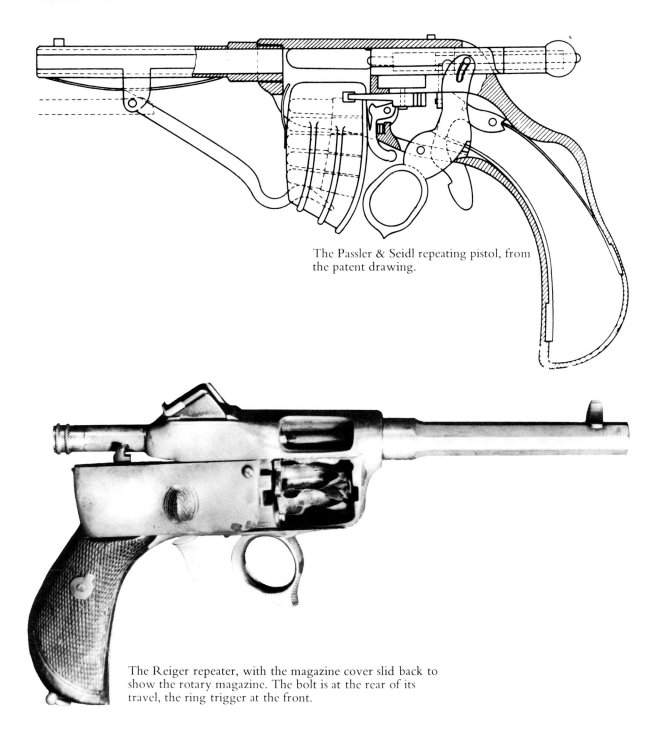

The Passler & Seidl repeating pistol, from
the patent drawing.

The Reiger repeater, with the magazine cover slid back to
show the rotary magazine. The bolt is at the rear of its
travel, the ring trigger at the front.

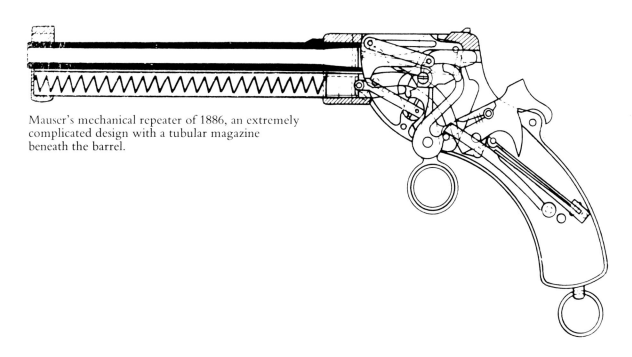

Mauser's mechanical repeater of 1886, an extremely
complicated design with a tubular magazine
beneath the barrel.

relatively simple and easily manufactured and assembled, leading to a cheap and reliable weapon. The principal drawback lies in the field of ergonomics. The human forefinger is ill-adapted to delivering much power in a pushing stroke, and it is likely that a fair amount of force would be needed to open the bolt in the event of a tightly-expanded cartridge case. Even allowing for the development of muscular power with practice, the mechanical repeater was scarcely a practical weapon. It had a short life; the first designs appeared in about 1885 and they had vanished by about 1895, with the result that they are now extremely scarce.

A smaller, more successful line of mechanical repeaters were those generally lumped together under the term 'palm-squeezer pistols' of which the French 'Mitrailleur' is a good example. These used low-powered rim- or pin-fire cartridges as a rule, although towards the end of their period they were being made for centre-fire rounds and, as the name implies, were to be concealed in the palm of the hand with the muzzle protruding between the fingers. By squeezing the palm an operating lever was compressed, chambering and firing a round. Releasing the grip retracted the lever to eject the empty case or, more usually, move it away from the breech before the next cartridge was presented. Many of these were carried by ladies and gentlemen, who would otherwise never have had dealings with firearms, simply as protection against footpads. As a result, they could frequently be found ornately decorated, cased in leather, inset with ivory or precious metals. They were in production for a surprisingly long time, from the middle 1880s until the beginning of the First World War, although they were gradually ousted by cheap pocket automatic pistols in the latter years.

The appearance of the latter type of weapon also explains the short life of the larger mechanical repeaters, and is the reason for their scarcity today. Their story starts with the development, in the late 1880s, of the Maxim gun, and Maxim's demonstration that the power inherent in the propelling charge could be put to use to operate the loading and extracting mechanism of a weapon as well as to propel the bullet. This led to research into the adaptation of automatic principles to hand guns, and in the early 1890s the automatic pistol was born. The first automatic pistol to be placed on the market was, in fact, a derivation based on a mechanical repeater.

This pioneer pistol was the Schonberger, although the reason for its name is far from clear. The design is due to a man named Laumann, who originated the weapon as a repeater, similar to the Passler & Seidl. He converted it into an automatic and had it manufactured at the Österreichische Waffenfabrik, Steyr. Schonberger was the factory superintendent at that time, and he may well have agreed to produce the weapon in exchange for having his name on the manufactured article.

The mechanical problem confronting Laumann was that of unlocking the bolt and withdrawing it, and he solved it in an unusual fashion. He lit upon a system which has scarcely been used since, and never in anything except prototype weapons. He relied on 'primer set-back' and this is so uncommon that some explanation is necessary.

When the charge in the cartridge is fired, the pressure generated acts in all directions and some finds its way through the fire-channel in the base of the case into the primer or cap, tending to thrust it backwards. In the majority of weapons, this rearward thrust is resisted by the face of the bolt or breech-block, but in Laumann's design, the cap was allowed to 'set back' a fraction of an inch. This forced back the firing pin so that a shoulder on the pin pressed against a cam surface to unlock the bolt, after which the remaining pressure in the case blew it back out of the chamber, carrying the bolt with it. In other words, once the bolt was unlocked the action became that of a 'blowback' pistol. Schonberger pistols are extremely scarce – no more than two or three are known to exist – and no ammunition has been seen for them for more than 60 years, so it is not possible to confirm the theoretical action by actual firing. However, they were undoubtedly made and sold, and take their place as the first practical automatic pistol.

As with most inventions, once the system had been proved practical, improvements flowed thick and fast. The Schonberger appeared in 1892, and a year later came first a still-born design from Andrea Schwarzlose and then the

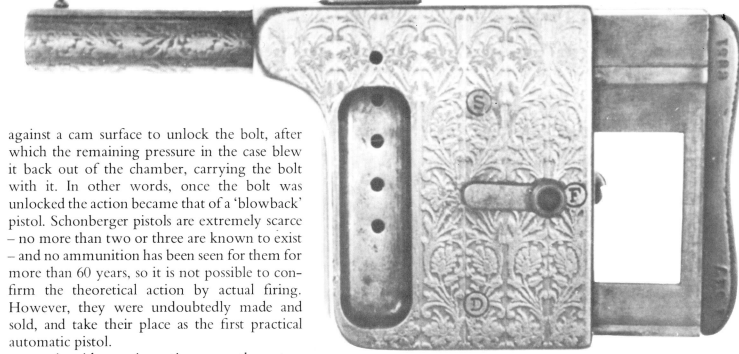

The French 'Mitrailleur' repeater, actuated by squeezing in the palm of the hand, and thus pushing the rear section inwards.

Two of the first automatic pistols to use the power of the charge to operate the loading and extracting mechanism: the Schonberger and the Borchardt (below).

The Borchardt mechanism, from a
contemporary text. Note the
cumbersome 'clock spring'
controlling the toggle.

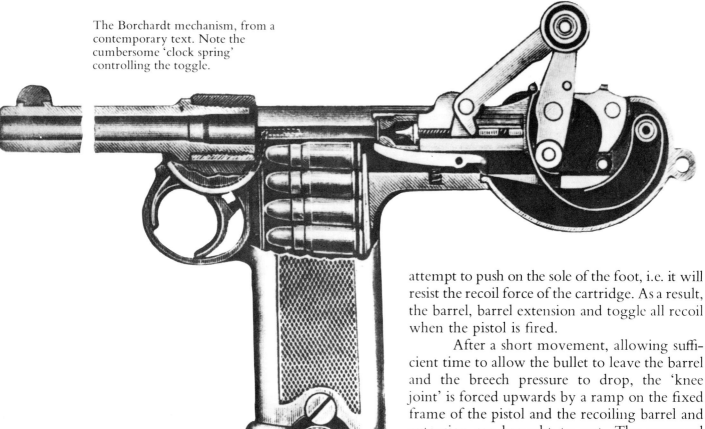

Borchardt pistol; 1894 saw the first of many
Bergmann designs, in 1896 the Charola-Anitua
and Simplex appeared, and in 1898 the Mauser.
Of these, the Borchardt and the Mauser are the
most important, since they were the two
weapons which had the greatest success. Hugo
Borchardt was a designer of some repute who
had worked in the U.S.A. and Europe for several
years, before going to Ludwig Lowe of Berlin.
During these years, he developed an idea for
an automatic pistol and his ideas were put into
production by Lowe. The heart of Borchardt's
design was the method of locking the breech,
using a folding toggle. This is generally likened
to the human leg – the 'hip' is connected to
extension arms running back from the pistol
barrel, while the 'foot' is the face of the breech.
As long as the 'leg' lies flat, it will resist any

attempt to push on the sole of the foot, i.e. it will
resist the recoil force of the cartridge. As a result,
the barrel, barrel extension and toggle all recoil
when the pistol is fired.

After a short movement, allowing sufficient time to allow the bullet to leave the barrel
and the breech pressure to drop, the 'knee
joint' is forced upwards by a ramp on the fixed
frame of the pistol and the recoiling barrel and
extension are brought to rest. The rearward
force of the cartridge then pushes the 'foot' – the
breech face – back, folding the 'knee' or toggle
joint upwards against the pressure of a spring.
Thus the breech is opened and the empty case
ejected. The spring then forces the joint down
again and as the breech face moves forward it
collects a cartridge from the magazine and
chambers it. The 'leg' is now lying flat once
more, securely holding the cartridge in the
breech ready to be fired.

The design of the toggle is the critical
factor, and it has to be matched to the design
of the cartridge, extremely carefully made and
fitted and of the finest materials. This was no
bar to manufacture in the 1890s and the Borchardt achieved some commercial success. As
a pistol it was relatively clumsy, but it was
always sold with a detachable buttstock and with
this fitted it was very accurate. More important
than the pistol was Borchardt's development of

A short-barrelled version of the 7·63mm Mauser pistol.

the 7·63mm cartridge which went with it, a bottle-necked cartridge firing a jacketed bullet at high velocity. The toggle joint relied on constant ballistics for its success and Borchardt's cartridge delivered a consistency which was quite unusual in those days. With revolvers, minor inconsistencies from round to round mattered little and were hardly noticeable, but the automatic pistol was more demanding.

As a result, when the famous Mauser company decided to look at automatic pistols, Mauser took Borchardt's cartridge as his starting point, making some minute dimensional changes to suit his own purposes, a fact which rather upset Borchardt. The Mauser pistol, one of the most recognisable pistols in the world, used an entirely different method of operation. A square-section bolt moved axially in the barrel extension and carried a striker, very much like the mechanical repeaters had done. The bolt was locked to the barrel extension, when closed, by a wedge block under the bolt, and as the barrel, extension and bolt recoiled, the wedge was allowed to disengage so that the bolt could continue to move independently and thus complete the loading cycle, collecting a fresh round from the magazine which was in front of the trigger. This was a much simpler mechanism than that of the Borchardt and it was less critical of consistency in its ammunition. Provided there was recoil, the Mauser would work, whereas if the amount of recoil were too little or too much, the Borchardt usually jammed. When these pistols began to become popular, commercial

ammunition makers began to produce their own brands of cartridge, and there was bound to be a certain amount of inconsistency from brand to brand.

The object of developing any powerful automatic pistol in those days was to interest a military force and obtain a contract to supply an army with weapons. Once this was secured, prosperity was assured, since military adoption was not only profitable in itself, but also gave a cachet of approval which was a valuable commercial asset. Neither Borchardt nor Mauser managed to achieve this desirable end. The Borchardt was far too cumbersome and delicate, while the Mauser was reliable but clumsy. Nevertheless, many officers equipped themselves with these pistols, particularly the Mauser, at their own expense.

At the Lowe factory, another designer, Georg Luger, came to the conclusion that if the Borchardt were redesigned it would stand a better chance of being adopted by the military. Borchardt turned down his suggestions, being

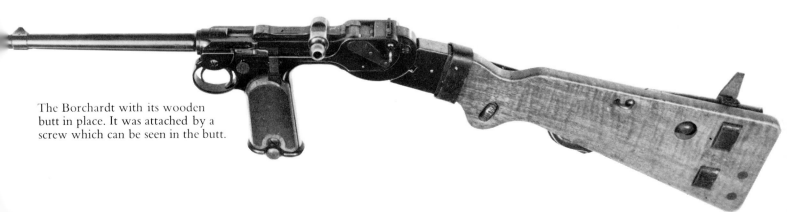

The Borchardt with its wooden butt in place. It was attached by a screw which can be seen in the butt.

German officers seeking a less cumbersome alternative to the Luger adopted this Mauser, firing a 7·65mm commercial round. Originally produced as a police weapon, it was used by the Luftwaffe and the Navy. This 1934 model has a German Navy badge.

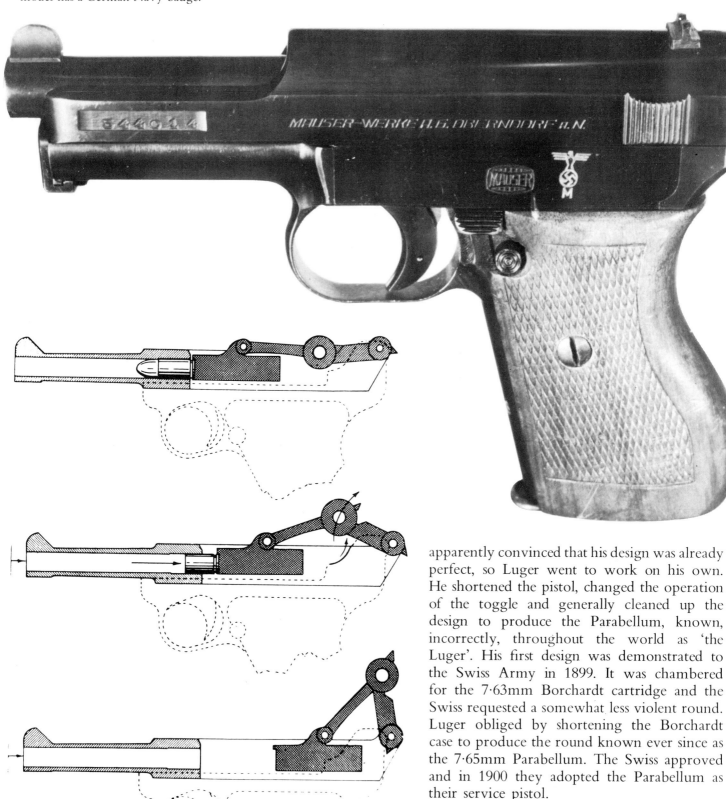

The sequence of operations of the Luger toggle lock. The top drawing shows that the centre joint lies below the end joints, so that a rearward force cannot open it. As the barrel and toggle recoil (second drawing), the joint is forced up by a ramp on the pistol frame. This allows the recoil force to complete the opening stroke.

apparently convinced that his design was already perfect, so Luger went to work on his own. He shortened the pistol, changed the operation of the toggle and generally cleaned up the design to produce the Parabellum, known, incorrectly, throughout the world as 'the Luger'. His first design was demonstrated to the Swiss Army in 1899. It was chambered for the 7·63mm Borchardt cartridge and the Swiss requested a somewhat less violent round. Luger obliged by shortening the Borchardt case to produce the round known ever since as the 7·65mm Parabellum. The Swiss approved and in 1900 they adopted the Parabellum as their service pistol.

Luger now took to the road as a salesman, attempting to interest other countries in the new pistol. Many European countries were interested, and even the United States bought a quantity for trial. It was not until 1904 that Luger achieved his big breakthrough, with the German Navy's adoption of the Parabellum. One feature which had delayed this success was the opinion that the 7·65mm bullet was too light for combat purposes, and to improve matters Luger opened out the neck of the 7·65mm cartridge case to take a 9mm bullet. With this, the German Navy accepted the pistol and in 1908 Luger's efforts were well rewarded when the German Army adopted it as the 'Pistole 1908' or 'P 08'. After this, its future was assured, and it was to remain in German military service until 1945. Several countries still use them, and they are still manufactured commercially by the Mauser company.

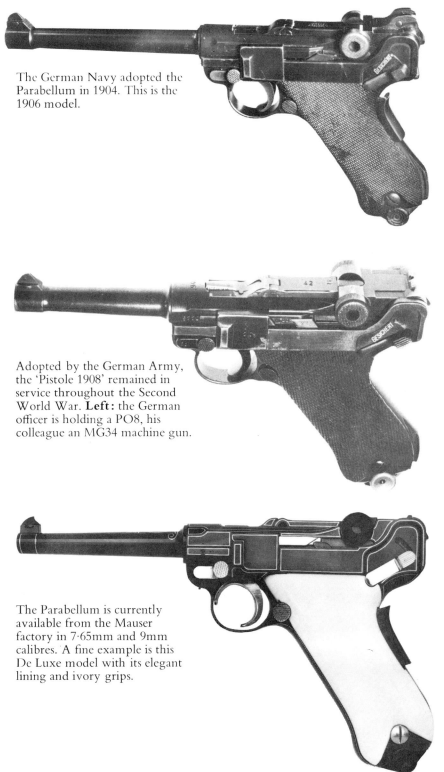

The German Navy adopted the Parabellum in 1904. This is the 1906 model.

Adopted by the German Army, the 'Pistole 1908' remained in service throughout the Second World War. **Left:** the German officer is holding a PO8, his colleague an MG34 machine gun.

The Parabellum is currently available from the Mauser factory in 7·65mm and 9mm calibres. A fine example is this De Luxe model with its elegant lining and ivory grips.

The Walther, a typical blowback pistol. The reaction of the cartridge case forces the slide, carrying the firing pin, to the rear. A fresh round is loaded on the return stroke. A coil spring around the barrel cushions recoil and returns the slide.

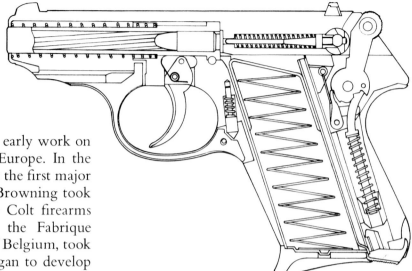

It will be seen that all the early work on automatic pistols was done in Europe. In the U.S.A. it was not until 1897 that the first major step was taken, when John M. Browning took out his first pistol patents. The Colt firearms company in the U.S.A. and the Fabrique Nationale d'Armes de Guerre, of Belgium, took licenses on these patents and began to develop pistols. The Colt company were primarily interested in a large-calibre pistol suitable for military adoption, and they began working on locked-breech designs. The Belgian company, on the other hand, saw as few others had done that there could be an enormous commercial market for light pocket automatic pistols, and they therefore channelled their development work in this direction.

Designing a commercial pistol to use a light cartridge was less of a problem than developing a locked breech, and FN had their first pocket pistol ready for sale in 1899. It was of the 'blow-back' type, which simply means that only the inertia of the breech held it closed while the cartridge fired, and that as soon as this inertia was overcome by the rearward thrust of the cartridge case, the breech opened and per-

formed the extracting and reloading cycle. In order to make this system work, the mass of the breech block needs to be substantially greater than the mass of the bullet, and this was done by making the breech block a part of the much greater component known as the 'slide', a metal casing which completely enclosed the barrel and the upper part of the pistol. The barrel was rigidly fixed to the pistol frame, and above it was anchored a strong spring. As the pistol was fired, the weight of the slide together with the pressure of the spring held the breech closed for enough time to allow the bullet to leave the barrel. Then the case pushed rearwards and the slide was forced back, compressing the spring as it went, until the amount of spring compression overcame the energy of

Two early blow-back automatics made by the Belgian Fabrique Nationale, the Browning Model of 1900, and (below) the Browning 1903 in 9mm calibre, widely adopted as a military and police pistol in Europe.

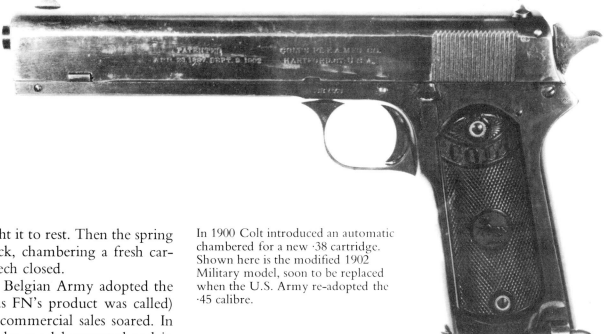

the slide and brought it to rest. Then the spring forced the slide back, chambering a fresh cartridge, and the breech closed.

In 1900, the Belgian Army adopted the Browning pistol (as FN's product was called) and from then on commercial sales soared. In 1903, an even simpler model appeared and in later years some improvements were made to the design. The simple construction of the 1903 model was so appealing to others that it was copied widely by Spanish gunmakers as well as other European companies, and it has been reliably estimated that some 75 per cent of the world's commercial pistols have been either Brownings or copies of Brownings.

The Colt company took their time about developing a heavy pistol. They were already supplying the U.S. Army and Navy with service revolvers, so they were in no hurry. Moreover, they had an enviable reputation and any automatic pistol they produced was likely to be good. It was not until 1900 that they placed a design on the market, chambered for a new cartridge, the ·38 Automatic Colt Pistol round. The design used the same enveloping slide as the Belgian models, but internally there was a great deal of difference. The barrel was attached to the pistol frame by two hinged links, one beneath the muzzle and one beneath the breech. On the top surface of the barrel were three raised lugs and inside the upper surface of the slide were corresponding recesses. Beneath the barrel was a powerful recoil spring, and a cross-pin through the slide passed ahead of this spring so that any rearward slide movement would compress it.

With the pistol 'at rest', the spring forced the slide forward. The breech-block was formed in the interior of the slide and this, pressing on the base of the chambered cartridge, forced the barrel forward on its hinged links so that it rose up and the lugs on the top surface engaged with the recesses in the slide. The barrel and slide were thus locked together. When the pistol was fired, the recoil caused barrel and slide to move back, still locked together, but as they moved the hinged links caused the barrel to describe a slight arc and move downwards as well as backwards until the lugs and recesses parted company. Once that happened, the slide was free to recoil, pushed back by the impulse already imparted to it and by the residual pressure in the breech forcing the cartridge case backwards. As the slide went back so it extracted the empty case and ejected it through a port, at the same time compressing the recoil spring. Then the spring forced the slide back, collecting a fresh cartridge from the magazine as it went. As the cartridge was chambered, so the pressure of the slide's forward thrust forced the barrel forward and upward until, once again, the lugs and recesses were engaged and the breech was then locked.

Some 3,000 of these were made, and today they are collectors pieces. Towards the end of their production run, in 1901, a few

The simplicity of design and construction of the Browning 1903 led to it being widely copied. This is a Spanish 'Action No. 2' model.

modifications appeared as different ideas were
tried out by the makers, and a year later a
slightly different model appeared which
remained in production until the late 1920s.
However, ·38 calibre, even though the cartridge was of relatively high velocity, was not
acceptable to the military. The U.S. Army had,
in fact, gone from ·45 calibre to ·38 calibre in
their service revolver in 1892, but the Philippine
Insurrection demonstrated that the ·38 revolver
lacked stopping power and there was a move
back to ·45. It followed from this that a ·38 automatic stood little chance, and in 1905 Colt
developed a suitable ·45 cartridge. Guns designed
around this cartridge were offered to and tested
by the U.S. Army. The soldiers were enthusiastic, but pointed out one or two details which
they felt could be improved. Colt went back
to the drawing board and the cartridge was
improved by increasing the bullet weight. A

grip safety was incorporated, so that the gun
could not be discharged unless it was being held
properly, and the double link system of holding the barrel was changed to one which used
a single link beneath the breech and supported
the muzzle in a special bush let into the front
of the slide. The recoil spring was also changed,
as was the slide contour. This was because one
objection to the earlier design had been that if
cross-pin connecting slide and spring broke,
the slide would be blown off the top of the
frame into the firer's face.

In 1907, the U.S. Army held a competitive trial of pistols. The Colt and Parabellum
were entered, together with designs by Savage,
Knoble, Bergmann, White-Merril, and some
revolvers. The Testing Board convened in
January and made its report by April, a remarkable example of alacrity. As a result of further
trials, some small modifications were made to
the Colt and it was adopted into U.S. service
as the Model 1911. Experience with it during
the First World War led to some cosmetic
modifications – the shape of the grip was
changed, the hammer spur altered and so forth –

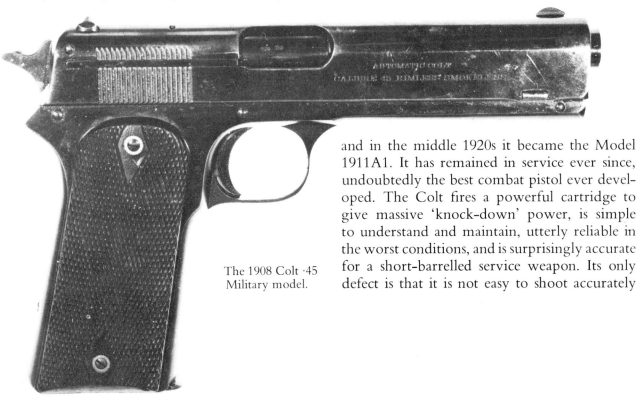

The 1908 Colt ·45
Military model.

and in the middle 1920s it became the Model
1911A1. It has remained in service ever since,
undoubtedly the best combat pistol ever developed. The Colt fires a powerful cartridge to
give massive 'knock-down' power, is simple
to understand and maintain, utterly reliable in
the worst conditions, and is surprisingly accurate
for a short-barrelled service weapon. Its only
defect is that it is not easy to shoot accurately

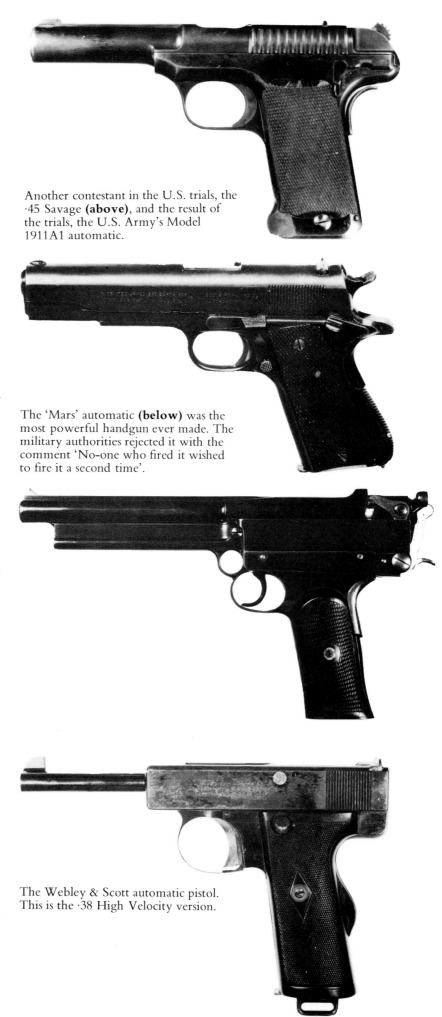

without adequate practice, but this drawback is easily overcome.

At this time, the British Army tried a number of automatic pistols but decided to stick with the heavy Webley revolver. However, in 1913, the Royal Navy adopted a Webley & Scott automatic. This was of ·455 calibre, a sturdy and reliable weapon provided it was used in clean conditions. As a sea service weapon it was satisfactory, but it was less successful when used in Flanders during the First World War.

Webley began their development of an automatic pistol with a somewhat remarkable and unfortunate weapon called the 'Mars'. This had been designed by a man named Gabbet-Fairfax, who took out innumerable patents for many forms of automatic weapon in the 1890s and early 1900s. In an endeavour to produce a pistol powerful enough to satisfy a military critic, he aimed for high velocities in small calibres and produced a monstrous weapon. The Mars used an unusual principle of operation known as 'long recoil'. The breech block was locked into the barrel by rotating lugs, and when the pistol was fired both barrel and breech block recoiled, locked together, the full length of the pistol frame. When this movement stopped, the breech was unlocked and the block held back, while the barrel was allowed to return to the forward position. As it came to rest a linkage released the block, which then ran forward, chambered a fresh cartridge, and locked into the barrel once again. The result of all this movement was that the pistol was well-nigh uncontrollable, leaping high in the air when it was fired. The ammunition was specially designed for it, and the 9mm version delivered a velocity of about 1,650 feet per second, an astonishing figure for a hand gun.

Webley decided against marketing the Mars themselves, but agreed to manufacture

Another contestant in the U.S. trials, the ·45 Savage **(above)**, and the result of the trials, the U.S. Army's Model 1911A1 automatic.

The 'Mars' automatic **(below)** was the most powerful handgun ever made. The military authorities rejected it with the comment 'No-one who fired it wished to fire it a second time'.

The Webley & Scott automatic pistol. This is the ·38 High Velocity version.

The 7·65mm Frommer 'Stop', service pistol of the Hungarian Army from 1912 onward.

it for Gabbet-Fairfax's 'Mars Pistol Syndicate'. Endeavours to interest military authorities were unsuccessful, though trials were carried out by the Royal Navy, and in 1903 Gabbet-Fairfax went bankrupt. Another syndicate was formed, but this had no better luck and the 'Mars' venture came to an end in 1904. No more than

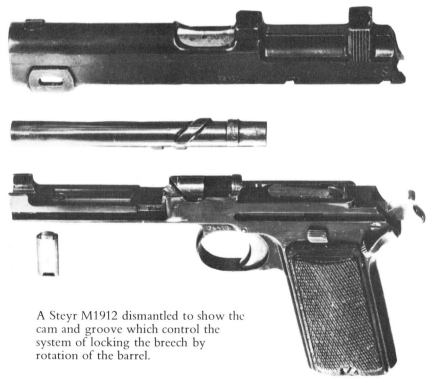

A Steyr M1912 dismantled to show the cam and groove which control the system of locking the breech by rotation of the barrel.

about 85 of these pistols were made, and they are probably the most scarce and valuable of all production automatic pistols.

The long recoil system of operation was later used by a Hungarian designer, Rudolf Frommer, to produce a service pistol for the Hungarian element of the Austro-Hungarian Army. This was the Frommer 'Stop', a long recoil locked breech weapon which used the 7·65mm Browning cartridge, although this was insufficiently powerful to justify a locked breech.

By the middle 1900s, the patents of Mauser, Luger, Browning and Bergmann had securely protected their methods of operating automatic pistols, but there was no shortage of inventors willing to try some new system. Almost every conceivable mechanical principle was explored, most of which never worked except on paper, but one or two managed to attain some success. One of the better methods to appear was that of using a rotating barrel, best exemplified by the Austrian Steyr Model 1912 pistol. Externally, this looked much like a Colt, with an enveloping slide and external hammer, but beneath the slide things were very different. The barrel was no longer attached to the frame, but merely rested on top, its movement constrained by two lugs, a square one beneath the breech and a helical one above it. The slide was provided with a helical groove inside the top section, engaging with the lug on the barrel. When the pistol fired, the barrel and slide recoiled, secured together by the engagement of the helical lug in its groove. The shape of these mating surfaces was such that the rearward movement of the slide attempted to rotate the barrel lug and thus the barrel, but rotation was prevented by the square lug beneath the barrel riding in a groove in the frame. After a short recoil stroke this bottom lug found itself at the end of the groove, which was then extended to one side. This allowed

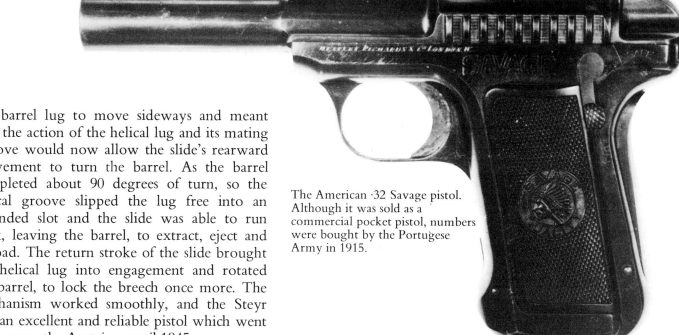

The American ·32 Savage pistol. Although it was sold as a commercial pocket pistol, numbers were bought by the Portugese Army in 1915.

the barrel lug to move sideways and meant that the action of the helical lug and its mating groove would now allow the slide's rearward movement to turn the barrel. As the barrel completed about 90 degrees of turn, so the helical groove slipped the lug free into an extended slot and the slide was able to run back, leaving the barrel, to extract, eject and re-load. The return stroke of the slide brought the helical lug into engagement and rotated the barrel, to lock the breech once more. The mechanism worked smoothly, and the Steyr was an excellent and reliable pistol which went on to serve the Austrians until 1945.

At about the same time, Arthur Savage, an American designer, aided by a Major Searle of the U.S. Army, produced a rotating barrel pistol which was rather more simple than the Steyr. No helical grooves were used, the slide and barrel being simply locked by a shaped cam surface. Resistance to opening was provided by the torque set up in the barrel by the passage of the bullet through the rifling. Once this resistance ended, when the bullet left the muzzle, the barrel was free to turn and the slide opened. This, at least, was the theory of it. In practice, it seemed not to be quite as secure as Searle and Savage thought. Certainly, one experiment, using spark-gap cameras, showed that the Savage actually opened its breech slightly faster than a common blowback pistol, so the claim that the Savage was locked seemed to be a thin one. The mode of operation is perhaps best described as a 'delayed blowback'.

After the First World War, there was a quiet period for firearms development. The armies of the world had vast stocks and were unlikely to require any new material for years, while they had disposed of sufficient surplus to satiate the commercial market for heavy calibre pistols. Only the makers of pocket pistols managed to continue, though they appear to

have done it on remarkably small profit margins. Many Spanish companies survived by entering the American mail order field, and with 7·65mm automatic pistols being sold in the U.S.A. for two or three dollars, it is obvious that the Spaniards were not likely to get fat very quickly.

As the world gradually returned to its usual state of irritability, the gunmakers found it worth their while to try a few new ideas. In the late 1920s, the Spanish Zulaica company, in Eibar, traditional home of the Spanish firearms

In addition to the large military pistols, Colt also produced pocket automatics such as this elegant model in ·25 calibre.

The Mauser Model 712, which Mauser
had to make in order to preserve their
markets in the face of the Spanish
machine pistols.

The Mauser Model 712, which Mauser
had to make in order to preserve their
markets in the face of the Spanish
machine pistols.

industry, were producing a replica of the
Mauser military pistol for export to China, and
it occurred to them to make a slight change to
the firing mechanism. In the usual automatic
pistol, one of the most important components
is the 'disconnector' which, as the name implies,
disconnects the trigger from the rest of the
firing mechanism immediately after a shot
has been fired. The connection can only be
re-made by the firer consciously releasing the
trigger before preparing to pull it for the next
shot. Without this disconnector, the gun would
continue to fire so long as the trigger were
held pressed. Zulaica placed a controlling
switch on the disconnector to bring it into or
out of action as the firer wished. With the
disconnector engaged, the pistol was the normal
one-shot-at-a-time automatic. With the disconnector thrown out of action, the weapon
became a fully automatic 'machine pistol'.
Since these Mauser copies were all fitted with
wooden butt-stocks and were sighted up to
1,000 yards, they were a sort of submachine
gun. This, at least, was the intention. The
reality fell somewhat short of this. The 'Royal',
the name of Zulaica's gun, fired the powerful

7·63mm Mauser cartridge, but was a lightweight weapon. Moreover, the light bolt and
short travel meant an extremely fast action, and
the result was that the rate of fire was astronomical and the gun barely controllable. The whole
magazine was emptied in less than a second, and
the violence of recoil forced the muzzle up and
away from the target after the first shot, so that
much of the ammunition was wasted.

Nevertheless, it was an impressive
weapon, noisy and spectacular, and it sold well
in some of the less technically competent areas
of the world. Other Spanish companies began
to copy the idea and eventually the Mauser
company themselves, seeing their markets
dwindling, were forced to produce a similar
model of their own, rather better designed and
engineered, in order to compete. Similar
machine-pistol conversions were made by
Echeverria, the Spanish Company who made
the 'Star' pistols. They were based on the Colt
design, and when turned into machine weapons
were even less attractive than the Royal, since
they were shorter than the Mauser copies and
less controllable. Except for a small quantity of
Mausers, bought by the German Army in the
middle 1930s when they were short of submachine guns, this type of pistol was not adopted
by a major army before the Second World War.

The most notable technical advance in
the years between the wars was the adoption of
a new type of firing mechanism for automatic
pistols. Arguments about the relative merits of
automatic pistols and revolvers had gone on
for years, and one of the advantages claimed
for the revolver was that it could be carried
safely, but fired immediately it was drawn
from its holster. This was due to the 'double-
action' firing mechanism which allowed a pull
on the trigger to raise and drop the hammer to
fire the first shot. The automatic pistol, on the
other hand, had either to be carried with a

The Astra 902, one of several Spanish copies of the Mauser which were modified to produce full-automatic fire.

round in the chamber and the hammer or striker cocked – a somewhat dangerous condition – or else it had to be cocked after drawing from the holster, by grasping the slide or bolt mechanism and pulling it back to charge the chamber and cock the hammer.

Several inventors had tried to get round this difficulty, and one popular line of approach was to provide some sort of a grip whereby the pistol could be cocked and charged by squeezing it as it was drawn. The only one of these to achieve any degree of success was the 'Einhand' pistol, invented by Witold Chylewski and manufactured by the Lignose company of Germany, successors to Bergmann. This had the forward end of the trigger-guard formed as a sliding component which, when gripped by the trigger finger and pulled back, caused the slide of the pistol to retract, cocking and loading in one movement. The finger was then transferred to the trigger and the pistol could be fired. This idea was only feasible in small-calibre blowback pistols, and attempts to apply the idea to heavy-calibre weapons with locked breeches always failed.

In 1908, a Bohemian inventor, Alois Tomiska, saw the obvious answer and applied the double-action system of the revolver to an automatic pistol, producing the 'Little Tom' pistol in 6·35mm and 7·65mm calibres.

Apart from the firing lock, it was a Browning copy, but it could be prepared for firing by pulling back the slide and releasing it, thus loading the chamber, and then carefully lowering the hammer against a stop. The weapon was then quite safe for carrying in the pocket, and, upon drawing it, a straight-through pull on the trigger would raise the hammer and then drop it in order to fire. Thereafter, the functioning would continue in the normal fashion for automatic pistols, the recoil of the slide leaving the hammer cocked after each shot.

Tomiska continued to make this pistol throughout the war years, and in 1920 sold the patents to a Viennese company who continued

The Lignose 'Einhand' pistol in ·35mm calibre, showing the ocking action.

The 'Little Tom', the first automatic pistol to make a success of a double-action lock.

with production until about 1925. It obviously sold well enough to give Tomiska a living, but it never seems to have become as popular as it deserved and specimens are relatively uncommon today.

With the demise of the Little Tom, the double action lock idea vanished until 1929, when it was revived by the Walther company, of Germany. Walther began making pocket blowback pistols in 1908, and produced a variety

The successful Walther 'PP' **(top)** was followed by the smaller 'PPK', and inspired a number of copies including this Turkish 'MKE'.

of excellent weapons, but by the late 1920s all their designs were looking elderly and they set out to design a more up-to-date weapon. This they did, and marketed it as the 'Model PP' or 'Polizei Pistole', in the well-founded hope of it being widely adopted by Continental police forces as a holster pistol. It was a blowback, in 7·65mm calibre – widely used as a police calibre – and incorporated a double action lock of considerable ingenuity. The safety catch of this pistol was on the slide, instead of on the frame as had previously been the case, and the sequence of operation was as follows. After inserting a full magazine into the pistol the slide was drawn back and released, loading a round into the chamber and leaving the hammer cocked. The safety catch was now turned to the 'safe' position, and as it turned an internal linkage first rotated a steel block to protect the end of the firing pin and then released the hammer so that it fell and rested on the safety block. When the weapon was required for action, all that was needed was to turn the safety catch to 'Fire' and pull the trigger, whereupon the block was removed and the hammer lifted and dropped.

The 'Model PP' was an immediate success, and was soon followed by the 'Model PPK' or 'Polizei Pistole Kriminal', a smaller version of the 'PP' intended to be carried by 'Kriminal Polizei' or plain-clothes policemen. There was only one slight drawback to this double action system and that was that accurate shooting when pulling-through the double action lock was difficult. The long pull of the forefinger usually upset the aim. Since the object was a fast snap shot at a fleeing criminal, there was little attention paid to this complaint. In 1938, one company thought enough to try to cure it. J. P. Sauer and Son, of Germany, produced a 7·65mm blowback pistol, which used a similar double-action system to that of the

Walther but controlled the hammer by a thumb-lever beneath the left grip, where it was easily reached by a right-handed shooter. With the pistol loaded and cocked, pressure on this lever would lower the hammer safely, after which it could be rapidly fired in the usual double action mode. As an alternative, a second pressure on the thumb-lever would raise the hammer to the full-cock position to allow a carefully aimed shot to be fired.

In 1936, German re-armament had begun in earnest, and the Army decided that the long-lived Parabellum was no longer the right pistol for service use. It was expensive to produce and the mechanism was prone to derangement

an external hammer, and it was accepted into German service in 1938 as the 'Pistole 38'. It was an immediate success and well over a million were to be made before production came to a halt in 1945. When the Walther company resumed business in post-war years, one of their prime tasks was to put the P-38 into production once again for the reconstituted German Army of the 1950s.

The most important step in pistol design in the 1930s was the overhauling of Browning's 'swinging link' locking system, which was attacked by a number of designers at more or less the same time. Before his death in 1926, Browning had made some changes, and these

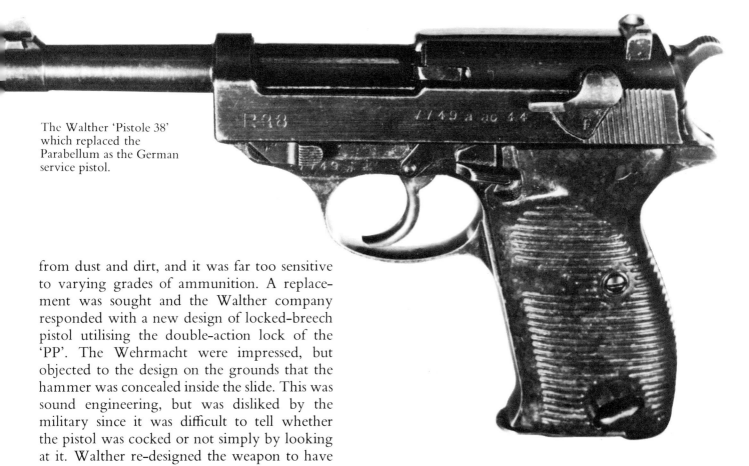

The Walther 'Pistole 38' which replaced the Parabellum as the German service pistol.

from dust and dirt, and it was far too sensitive to varying grades of ammunition. A replacement was sought and the Walther company responded with a new design of locked-breech pistol utilising the double-action lock of the 'PP'. The Wehrmacht were impressed, but objected to the design on the grounds that the hammer was concealed inside the slide. This was sound engineering, but was disliked by the military since it was difficult to tell whether the pistol was cocked or not simply by looking at it. Walther re-designed the weapon to have

The French MAS-35, designed by
Charles Petter.

The FN Browning GP-35, showing the
sight graduated to 500 metres and the
slot in the butt for attaching a holster-stock.

The Polish VIS-35. The catch on the
slide lowers the hammer safely on a
loaded chamber, while the catch at the
rear of the frame is to assist in
dismantling.

were taken by the Belgian engineers of the Fabrique Nationale as a basis for a new pistol. At the
same time, an enigmatic Frenchman named
Charles Petter, working for the Société Alsac-
ienne de Constructions Mechaniques, developed
a similar pistol. The basic change was the
removal of the hinged link beneath the breech
end of the barrel and its replacement by a solid
steel lug shaped into a cam form. This engaged
with a cross-pin in the pistol frame so that, as
the barrel recoiled, the cam profile would pull
down the breech end, thus disengaging the usual
locking lugs from the slide. Petter added another
refinement by making the hammer and firing
mechanism as a removable unit so that it could
easily be taken out for cleaning and repair. His
only mistake was to design the pistol around a
relatively useless cartridge, the 7·65mm Longue,
a peculiar French round which had too little
power to be of value as a combat cartridge.

The FN engineers used the same type of
cam, but did a better job by making the pistol
magazine capable of holding no less than 13
cartridges and chambering the pistol for the
universal 9mm Parabellum cartridge. The result
was introduced in 1935 as the 'Grande Puissance
Modèle 35' and was immediately adopted by
the Belgian Army. It was also adopted by
Lithuania, Latvia, Romania and Denmark.
Since most of the production was earmarked
for the Belgian contract, these other countries
received few before the war cut them off.

The third pistol of note in this period
came from Poland. The Poles were armed with
a varied collection of weapons left over from the
First World War and in the early 1930s they
decided to rationalise things by adopting a
common pattern. Invitations went out to
several makers, and a competitive trial was
held. The winner was a native design by two
Poles, Wilniewczyc and Skrzypinski, and once
again they had hit on the idea of replacing the

swinging link with a fixed cam. Otherwise there was little of note in the design, which was based on the Browning, but it was an extremely well-made pistol and entered service in 1936 as the 'VIS-35', though it is generally called the 'Radom' from the name of the Polish arsenal which made it.

One last pistol of the middle 1930s must be mentioned, a Finnish model designed by Aimo Lahti and named after him. At first glance, the Lahti resembles the Parabellum, with a similarly sloped butt and exposed barrel, but the mechanism is totally different, using a bolt sliding inside a square-section body. It fired the 9mm Parabellum cartridge, and the

Poland were occupied, both the Browning GP-35 and the VIS-35 pistols remained in production, and were adopted by the German Army to supplement their own P-38 supplies. Indeed, so great was the German demand for pistols that the Parabellum P-08, supposedly superseded by the Walther in 1938, remained in production until 1944.

The pistol was, of course, widely sought by various clandestine organisations: partisans, maquis and similar para-military forces, and vast numbers were procured and supplied to them, the markets in Spain and South America being scoured in order to produce the necessary number. One of the most remarkable weapons

The Finnish 9mm Lahti.

breech was locked by a yoke which engaged slots in each side of the bolt, locking them to the receiver. The Lahti was remarkable for using an 'accelerator' device to speed up the opening of the bolt, a device more common in machine guns than pistols, and one which it is virtually impossible to dismantle without recourse to a workshop. Nevertheless, it had a high reputation for reliability, particularly in extreme cold conditions, and was adopted by both the Finnish and Swedish armies.

The Second World War saw very little change in pistol design, largely because the principal combatants had enough to do in improving other types of weapon. The pistol is relatively little used in modern combat, and the designs in use at the start of the war were still there at the end. When Belgium and

The American 'Liberator' ·45 guerilla pistol.

was the 'Liberator' pistol, developed in the United States for distribution to resistance groups. It was a simple single-shot weapon with a hand operated breech, chambered for the standard ·45 U.S. cartridge. A trap-door in the butt carried a few extra rounds, but extraction had to be performed by opening the breech and poking a stick down the muzzle to push the empty case out. Originally called a 'Flare Projector' as a security cover, the 'Liberator' was stamped out of sheet metal by the Guide Lamp division of General Motors, who knew little about pistols, but quite a lot about stamping things out of metal very quickly. They produced a million of these devices in three months, a pistol every 7½ seconds, which is probably the only case in history where a weapon was manufactured more quickly than it could be loaded and fired.

After 1945, there was a lull in the pistol world, just as there had been after 1918, and for much the same reasons. The world situation did not remain quite so tranquil as it had done in the 1920s, and soon the armies of the world were looking to their equipment once again. The pistol had lost ground to the submachine gun, and those inventive talents which might have worked on pistols found a more profitable field in automatic weapons of the larger type. The only notable step in the 1950s was the adoption of an automatic pistol – the Browning GP-35 – by the British Army, who finally pensioned off the Webley revolver.

In the 1960s, things began to move once more, and the most remarkable event was the reappearance of the machine pistol. This idea, which most people thought to have been well and truly discredited by the Mauser and the Spanish weapons, now appeared from Russia of all places. The Soviet Army's standard pistol for several years had been the Tokarev, a 7·62mm weapon using the Colt swinging link system of breech locking. In the mid-1960s, however, the Tokarev began to fade away and two new pistols appeared, the Makarov and the Stetchkin. Both were chambered for a new cartridge, the 9mm Soviet or 9mm × 18 (18mm being the length of the cartridge case). This was slightly shorter and less powerful than the 9mm Para-

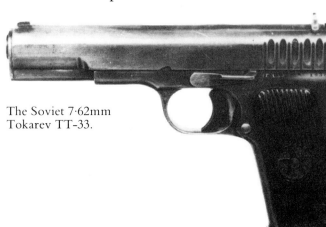

The Soviet 7·62mm Tokarev TT-33.

The Makarov, as made in East Germany. The resemblance between this and the Walther PP is considerable.

bellum, slightly longer and more powerful than the older '9mm Short' cartridge frequently used in police pistols in Europe and also by the Italian Army in their Beretta pistols. The object of this new cartridge was apparently to produce a round as powerful as could be handled without recourse to a locked breech, since both the new Soviet pistols were blowbacks. In fact, except for some small changes to suit manufacturing methods, both were more or less based on the design of the Walther 'PP', with double action locks. While the Makarov was quite conventional, the Stetchkin had a selector switch allowing full automatic fire and was provided with a shoulder stock, turning it into the usual quasi-submachine gun. It appears to have had little success, and recent information indicates that it has been withdrawn from first-line service.

A more promising line of approach has since been taken by the German company of Heckler and Koch. This company entered the pocket pistol field in post-war years, then went into the production of military rifles and machine guns. In the early 1970s they produced a double-action pistol, the P-9S, firing the

9mm Parabellum cartridge, and shortly afterwards a new model called the VP-70.

The latter introduced several important modern concepts into pistol design. Much of the frame construction utilises plastic material, with metal items bonded in as necessary, while the outer surfaces of the pistol are plastic-sheathed in order to simplify maintenance. While normally a hand-held pistol, it can be fitted with a plastic shoulder stock, and when this is clipped in place a protruding stud enters the body of the pistol and acts on the firing mechanism to produce what is called a 'burst-fire capability'. This means that one pressure on the trigger will produce a burst of three rounds. The trigger is then released and a fresh pressure will produce another three rounds. In this way the advantage of the full-automatic machine pistol is obtained, without the disadvantage of a runaway blast of fire upsetting the aim of the weapon.

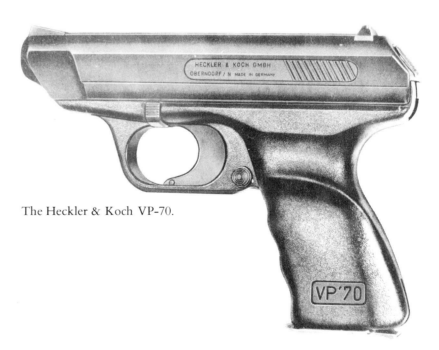

The Heckler & Koch VP-70.

Chapter Eleven

Machine Guns

ONE FACET of firearms design which intrigued inventors was how to get more firepower in a given time or how to produce sustained fire. Various 'volley guns' were put forward from time to time, usually enlarged revolvers of one form or another, but so long as the ammunition was formed of the separate components of powder, ball and cap there was little hope of producing the required answer. It was not until one-piece cartridges arrived that a multiple-fire weapon became possible.

One way round the problem was to prepare the ammunition components beforehand and this was done by an American inventor named Agar who developed a gun which was promptly nicknamed the 'Coffee Mill' due to the hopper and rotary handle which were the most prominent part of the mechanism. Steel tubes were prepared, each with a charge of powder, a lead ball and a percussion cap, and these were dropped into the hopper.

Turning the handle pushed one tube into the gun chamber, locked it, and then dropped a hammer to fire the cap. Continued rotation of the handle withdrew the empty tube, ejected it and then began feeding another. The gunner's assistant had to pick up the tubes, clean and re-load them, and then drop them back into the hopper so as to keep up the fire.

Agar patented his gun shortly before the American Civil War, but it was too revolutionary for the soldiers of the time and it is doubtful if as many as 50 were ever made. A similar fate awaited the 'Billinghurst-Requa Battery Gun', a rack of 24 rifle barrels carried on a wheeled frame. A like number of ·60 in prepared cartridges were held in a rack which was inserted behind the barrels so that the cartridges entered the gun breeches. A single percussion cap fired them all off at once in a ragged volley, after which the rack of empty cases was removed and a fresh one inserted.

This weapon was demonstrated in New York just before the Civil War and a number were purchased by both sides, notably for defending bridges with the sudden blast of fire.

One of these guns was taken to England in 1863 and subjected to trials by the Ordnance Select Committee, who reported that 'none of the rifle batteries could ever be effectually substituted for field guns ... and even as a device for multiplying and accelerating infantry fire from rifle barrels ... their utility would be very questionable ...'. This accurately reflects the dilemma in which the various authorities were placed when confronted with this type of weapon. Was it a field gun or was it an infantry weapon? How was it to be employed? It was the resolving of this problem which was the greatest brake on the adoption of the machine gun.

In Europe, at this time, a similar weapon was being perfected. A Belgian, Captain Fafchamps, had designed a multiple-barrelled weapon using a rack of prepared cartridges, similar in many respects to Agar's idea, and the design was taken up by a manufacturer named Montigny. He made some improvements and put the weapon into production as the 'Montigny Mitrailleuse' and eventually managed to interest the French Emperor Napoleon III. In conditions of great secrecy, the French Army were supplied with 156 of these guns, and in 1870 they were used against the Prussians.

The Mitrailleuse consisted of 25 barrels grouped inside a casing to give an external resemblance to a field gun. A lever on the side withdrew a heavy breech block and allowed a plate carrying 25 cartridges to be dropped behind the barrels, after which another stroke of the lever thrust the block home and chambered the rounds. Revolving a crank at the rear of the gun actuated 25 firing pins which fired the

Previous page: South Vietnam. An American machine-gunner in action near Bong Son, March 1967.

rounds in succession, faster or slower according to the speed at which the crank was turned. Unfortunately, the impact of the Mitrailleuse in action was a disaster. The French deployed the guns like artillery, using them in the open to fire on the Prussian infantry. As soon as they were seen, the Prussian artillery, which outranged them, opened fire and silenced them. This was very nearly the end of the machine-gun idea, but it was recognised as a tactical error and not connected with any technical shortcoming, so the idea survived.

A contemporary print of the Montigny Mitrailleuse on its field carriage and showing the plate, loaded with cartridges, being inserted into the breech.

he solved the problem by using six barrels which fired in turn. If the gun had a rate of fire of 600 rounds per minute, any one barrel would only have fired 100 and would have spent five-sixths of the time cooling down between shots. The six barrels were arranged on a rotating framework in front of the breech casing which contained the lock mechanism, the heart of Gatling's invention. Driven by a hand-rotated crank, the lock unit revolved with the barrels and a complex cam surface arranged for the various functions of feeding, locking, firing and extracting to take place in the barrels at different points in their rotation, firing always taking place when the barrel was at the topmost point in its circle of rotation. A strip of cartridges was inserted into the top of the breech casing, though in later years a more reliable rotary feed drum was adopted.

Although it was invented in 1861, the Gatling gun saw little employment during the Civil War. Military conservatism was still extremely strong and, morever, Gatling's sympathies appear to have been suspected by both the Union and the Confederate sides. Neither was willing to give him a respectable order in case he turned his coat and gave the guns to the others. In January, 1865, the U.S. War Department ordered 100 guns and, with that official recognition, Gatling began to sell guns throughout the world, licensing manufacture to companies in Europe. One of the more remarkable export sales was the supply of 400 guns to the Russian Government in 1871. A Russian officer, General Gorloff, was sent to the U.S.A. to oversee the production, and he astutely had nameplates made with his name on them, which were affixed to every gun before it was shipped. As a result the gun is always known in Russia as the 'Gorloff' and its invention is credited to Gorloff. Gatling is never given so much as a mention.

During the time of the Mitrailleuse's development, the U.S.A. brought forth the most famous of the 'mechanical' machine guns, the invention of Dr Richard J. Gatling. Gatling was concerned at the heating effect caused by firing several rounds in succession through one barrel, a point which several critics had raised when commenting on the Agar gun, and

Richard Jordan Gatling (1818–1903), inventor of the first successful 'mechanical' machine gun **(top)**; and a British Army ·45 Gatling gun on a field carriage in the Royal Artillery Rotunda Museum at Woolwich, England.

Some of the Gatling's rivals. A Gardener two-barrel gun in naval service, and **(top to bottom):** a three-barrel Nordenfelt on a field carriage; the Hotchkiss Revolver Cannon, which fired explosive shells of 37mm calibre; and the American Lowell machine gun, on which only one of the four barrels was used at a time, the others being revolved into position as the first became overheated.

In the next decade, a number of competing mechanical machine guns appeared. The Gardner, the Nordenfelt, the Hotchkiss Revolver Cannon, the Lowell and others were developed and adopted by various nations. All worked on similar principles, having multiple barrels fired in sequence by the operation of a handle or crank. Gatling went so far as to harness an electric motor to the rotary action of his gun and showed that a rate of fire of 3,000 rounds a minute could be achieved. Since this sort of power was not available on the battlefield, this was simply an interesting demonstration. Manpower was all that could be relied upon, and things might well have stayed that way but for the genius of one man, Hiram Maxim.

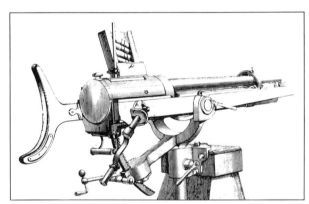

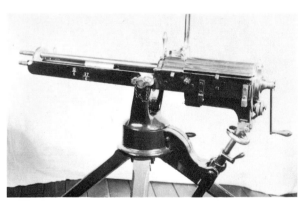

Hiram Maxim (1840–1916), inventor of the first recoil-operated machine gun.

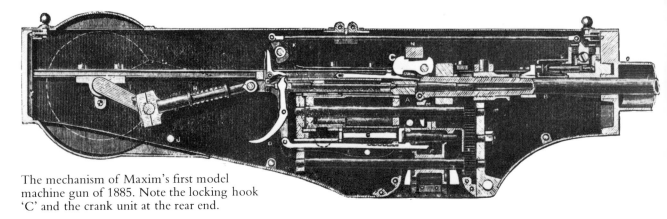

The mechanism of Maxim's first model machine gun of 1885. Note the locking hook 'C' and the crank unit at the rear end.

Maxim was a skilled engineer and inventor, and in 1881 his attention was drawn to the field of firearms. According to his own story, he was advised by a friend, 'If you want to make a pile of money, invent something that will enable these fool Europeans to cut each others throats with greater facility'. During the next few years he carefully examined the contemporary firearms and analysed every possible method of operating them. His contention was that much of the energy of the cartridge was wasted, and that somehow it must be capable of harnessing this energy to actuate the weapon.

In 1885, Maxim demonstrated his first model, in which the motive power was provided by the recoil force. It was chambered for the British ·45 Martini-Henry cartridge, and at the instant of firing the breech block and barrel were securely locked together by a large hook. Upon firing, the two units recoiled backwards, locked together for about half an inch, when the hook was disengaged and the barrel held. The breech block was then free to continue to the rear, extracting and ejecting the spent case as it did so. The block was linked to a crank by a connecting rod. As the movement of the block brought the crank to dead centre, the action was cocked and the momentum of the block's movement carried the crank past dead centre, reversing the movement of the block to send it back, loading a fresh round and closing the breech. The next shot fired would repeat this action, revolving the crank in the opposite direction until it stopped with the breech closed once more. Maxim adopted this system of partial rotation because of the danger of the crank accelerating and firing the gun faster and faster until something gave way if it were allowed to continue revolving in the same direction for every shot.

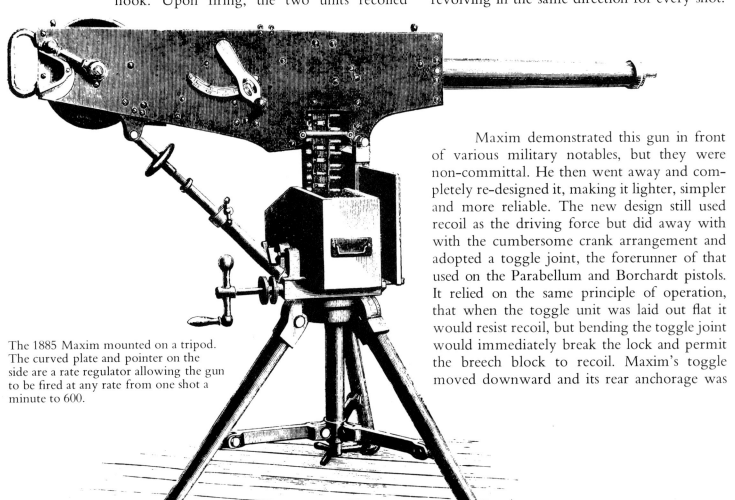

The 1885 Maxim mounted on a tripod. The curved plate and pointer on the side are a rate regulator allowing the gun to be fired at any rate from one shot a minute to 600.

Maxim demonstrated this gun in front of various military notables, but they were non-committal. He then went away and completely re-designed it, making it lighter, simpler and more reliable. The new design still used recoil as the driving force but did away with the cumbersome crank arrangement and adopted a toggle joint, the forerunner of that used on the Parabellum and Borchardt pistols. It relied on the same principle of operation, that when the toggle unit was laid out flat it would resist recoil, but bending the toggle joint would immediately break the lock and permit the breech block to recoil. Maxim's toggle moved downward and its rear anchorage was on a cross-shaft which terminated in a small crank. As the barrel and breech recoiled, this crank struck a projection on the gun body, which caused a rotation of the cross-shaft and a consequent folding of the toggle to open the breech. A spring, wound as the shaft revolved, then brought the toggle back into line, closing the breech as it did so. The gun was fed by a cloth belt carrying 333 cartridges, and a hook at the end of the belt allowed another to be hooked on so as to allow continuous fire.

Maxim toured Europe, demonstrating his gun to various astounded audiences, whose reactions were mixed. In Russia, the Tsar's officers listened to Maxim's explanation of how the gun worked, and laughed. Nobody, they said, could possibly work that little crank 600 times a minute. They stopped laughing when they saw what the gun could do by itself. In Denmark, the King watched Maxim empty a few belts into a target and then enquired how much each cartridge cost. On being told, he told Maxim that one of his guns would bankrupt Denmark in half a day. In spite of this, the gun was an instant success, and by 1890 it had been adopted by the British, German, Austrian, Swiss, Italian and Russian armies.

Early Maxim models: a British version **(above)** on its 'Overbank Carriage' designed to permit its being fired over parapets and walls; and the Russian Model 1910 on its 'Sokolov' mounting – the wheels could be replaced by sled runners in winter.

Apart from producing some notable pistol designs, John M. Browning (1855–1926) also invented a gas-operated machine gun.

Once Maxim had shown the way, other inventors crowded in to try and make similar weapons. Among the first was another notable American designer, John M. Browning. While he agreed with Maxim about using recoil, he thought there was more energy to be tapped by using the muzzle blast. His first idea was to put a plate in front of the muzzle, pierced to allow the bullet to pass through and connect this with the breech block via a system of levers. The violent rush of gas past the bullet would impinge on the plate and thus operate the breech. The idea worked and it was to be taken up with limited success by other inventors in later years. Browning soon abandoned it in favour of drilling a small hole in the underside of the barrel. The rush of gas through this hole, after the bullet had passed by, was used to blow down the tip of a lever, and this was suitably connected so as to operate the breech. By 1890, he had perfected the idea and offered the design to the Colt company. They produced working guns and, after tests, it was adopted by the U.S. Government as the M1895 machine gun. Because of the swinging arm beneath the front end, it was necessary to mount it well clear of the ground. Failure to do this produced some spectacular results, which led to the gun being nicknamed the 'Potato Digger'.

There are only three systems by which an automatic machine gun can be operated – recoil, gas, or blowback. The first two were now in use, and in 1893 the third was introduced in the Skoda machine gun from Austria. This had no positive lock on the breech at all, relying solely on having a heavy breech block supported by a powerful spring. In the same year another Austrian, Captain Odkolek, went to the French Hotchkiss company with a machine gun design. The American director of the company, Lawrence V. Benet, saw that the design had some merit and shrewdly bought the patents and rights to the gun outright, refusing to allow Odkolek any royalty deal. After some re-design this became the Hotchkiss gun and it was adopted by the French Army in 1897. The Hotchkiss was gas-operated, the gas being tapped off into a cylinder beneath the barrel where it drove a piston rod rearward to operate the breech block. The ammunition was fed into the gun from the right-hand side, by means of a metal strip in which the cartridge was held in clips. As the gun fired, so the cartridges were removed from the strip, which was pulled across the gun until it fell, empty, from the left-hand side. Although prone to over-heat, the Hotchkiss was moder-

The gas-operated Hotchkiss was one of
the earliest machine guns to see aerial
use, shown here in a Maurice Farman
biplane in the summer of 1914.

ately reliable and at least had the advantage
of weighing a good deal less than the Maxim.

One reason for the Maxim's weight was
the cooling problem. Firing 600 rounds a minute
delivered a vast amount of heat to the barrel,
and though Maxim's early guns were simply
cooled by the passage of air across the exposed
barrel, this was soon seen to be inadequate,
and the water-jacket, a prominent feature of
most machine guns since then, was adopted. A
gallon or so of water was poured into the jacket
and, as it gradually heated up, so it absorbed
heat from the barrel; when it boiled a tell-tale
plume of steam escaped, which was later
found to be a considerable embarrassment in

war, and so various condensers and water
supply pumps became standard accessories in
an attempt to keep the water temperature
down. The Hotchkiss, however, relied on air
cooling and had the barrel covered in fins in
an attempt to provide a greater radiating area.
The drawback to this system was that cleaning
the weapon invariably left a coat of oil between
the fins. This was heated by firing and burned
off, producing a blue haze above the barrel
which interfered with aiming the weapon.

The Maxim gun first saw combat in 1888
in The Gambia, being used by a British force
sent out to deal with some raiding tribesmen.
After that it appeared more and more frequently

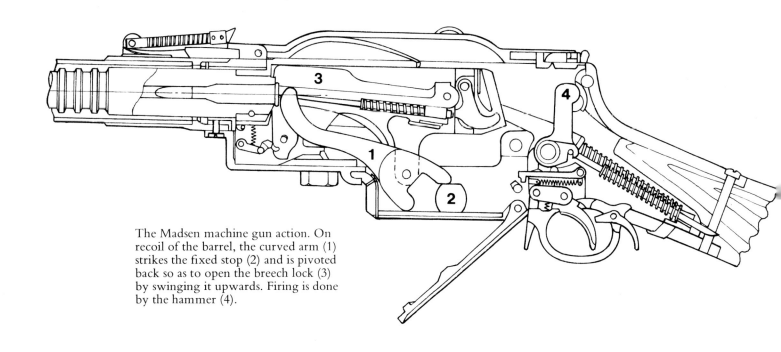

The Madsen machine gun action. On
recoil of the barrel, the curved arm (1)
strikes the fixed stop (2) and is pivoted
back so as to open the breech lock (3)
by swinging it upwards. Firing is done
by the hammer (4).

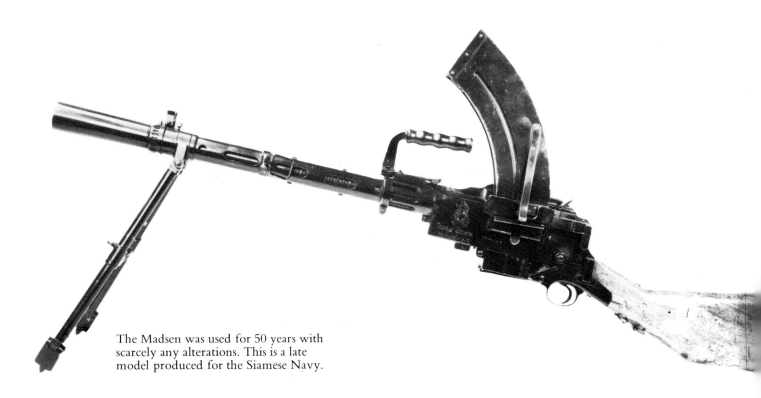

The Madsen was used for 50 years with
scarcely any alterations. This is a late
model produced for the Siamese Navy.

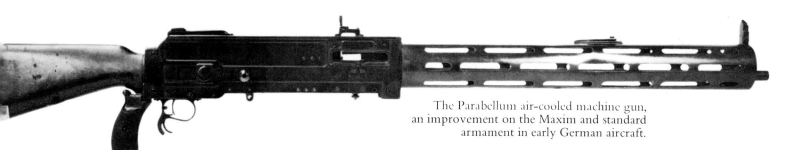

The Parabellum air-cooled machine gun, an improvement on the Maxim and standard armament in early German aircraft.

and with every action its fame spread. The most important step in the acceptance of the machine gun came with the Russo-Japanese War, the first of the modern technological-ideological wars. The Japanese used Hotchkiss guns, while the Russians were equipped with Maxim and Madsen guns. It was the first time that two major powers, each provided with machine guns, had met face-to-face, and the military of the rest of the world looked on with interest. The Russian Maxims, in prepared positions, at first outfought their opponents, but gradually the more aggressive tactics of the Japanese, using their lighter Hotchkiss guns in a more mobile role, paved the way for their eventual victory.

The Madsen gun, used by the Russian cavalry divisions, was one of the most remarkable machine guns in history and deserves special mention. It was invented by a Dane named Schouboe, and named after Madsen, the Danish Minister of War who was responsible for having it adopted by the Danish Army in 1902. It then remained in production for the next 50 years without major modification, was adopted by no less than 34 different countries, was used in almost every conceivable role, and was one of the most complicated and intricate mechanisms ever invented. The action is recoil-actuated and can best be described as an adaptation of the Martini rising-block breech mechanism. The block, however, does nothing except close the breech. The various actions of feeding and extracting which are performed by the block in other designs are done by separate mechanisms in the Madsen. As the gun recoils, the breech block swings up, allowing a separate extractor to extract the empty case and eject it, the firing hammer is cocked and a spring is compressed. At the end

of recoil this spring expands and forces the block and barrel forward. During this forward stroke, the block is lowered beneath the breech and an independent rammer pushes a cartridge from the overhead magazine into the chamber. The rammer is then withdrawn and the block swings up to close the breech ready for the round to be fired by the hammer. In spite of all this complication, the Madsen had an enviable reputation for reliability, and saw action in most of the major wars of this century.

The Russo-Japanese War and the South African War had allowed some lessons to be learned about machine guns and their tactical handling. One of the points which had emerged was that the Maxim, sound as it was, was a heavy piece of equipment to carry around the battlefield. Towards the end of the first decade of this century, it began to occur to designers that perhaps the Maxim could bear modification, and one of the first moves in this direction was due to another weapon of war making its first appearance: the aeroplane. In Germany, in 1909, the Army asked for a machine gun light enough to be carried on aircraft. The Government arsenal at Spandau had no time or staff to spare on such a request and a contract was given to a civilian firm, the Deutsche Waffen und Munitionsfabrik of Berlin, famous as the makers of the Luger pistol. After two years they produced their 'Parabellum' machine gun. The mechanism was basically that of the Maxim but the toggle was arranged to break in an upward direction and the water-jacket was abandoned, being replaced by a perforated screen around the barrel through which air could flow. A shoulder stock and pistol grip were fitted so that the gun could be used by the observer in an aircraft. It proved to be an excellent weapon and saw considerable service in the air in later years.

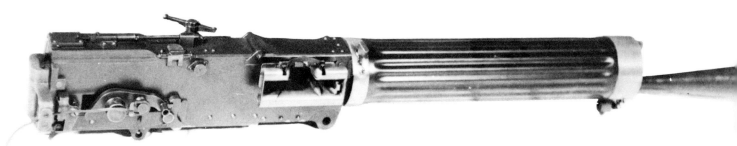

The impact of the machine gun during the First World War is well known. The Maxims and Vickers guns dominated No Man's Land and only the arrival of the tank broke the deadlock and made warfare mobile once again. In addition to the lessons learned in the tactical area, there were a number of technical lessons. One of the first was, quite simply, that what sufficed for peacetime equipment was not enough for the demands of an all-out war, and the numbers of machine guns demanded by the armies increased. Britain felt the pinch more than any other country, since its peacetime army was small, its requirement of guns less, and the manufacturing capacity corre-

spondingly small. While attempting to increase production, it became necessary to purchase guns in order to make up the required quantity.

Machine guns, though, were not a commodity to be bought at any hardware store, and most of the guns being produced were being made to government orders. There was, however, one weapon looking for a customer – the Lewis Gun. This had been designed by an American, Samuel MacLean, who had no success in interesting a manufacturer and eventually sold the patents in 1910 to the Automatic Arms Company of Buffalo. This company felt that MacLean's design could stand some improvement and they asked Colonel

The Maxim and its derivatives dominated the deadly trench battles of 1914–18: a German machine gun post on the retreat to the Siegfried Line, February 1917.

The Vickers **(left)** was an improved and lightened Maxim which became the standard British Army Machine gun in 1912. This version is a ·50 calibre model for mounting in tanks and armoured cars.

The French Army used the Hotchkiss machine gun. Here we see a French Hotchkiss gun team in August 1915.

The Lewis Gun (below) was adopted as the British light machine gun in 1915. Its light weight made it ideal for aircraft: one Vickers and three Lewis guns arm the Bristol fighter of RAF No. 22 Squadron shown at Agincourt, France, July 1918. Bottom of facing page: U.S. Marines in Flanders, July 1918; in this posed shot the Lewis gun has no magazine.

Isaac N. Lewis, recently retired from the U.S. Army, to undertake the task. In 1911, Lewis produced some prototype models, which were successful, and tried to interest the U.S. Ordnance Department in the gun, but without success. Eventually, he followed the same trail as John Browning and took his design to Europe, where he found a Belgian company prepared to produce and sell the gun. It was adopted by the Belgian Army in 1913, and later in that year the Birmingham Small Arms Company, of England, took out a licence and also began making the Lewis Gun. In 1914, when the British Army began to look for a machine gun, BSA were ready and willing. The entire production capacity of the Birmingham factory was switched to Lewis Guns and contracts were also let out to the Savage Arms Company of America.

After the Madsen, the Lewis was the first machine gun which could remotely be called 'light'. Gas-operated, and feeding from a round drum containing 47 cartridges, it weighed only 27lbs, a considerable improvement on the the 90lbs of a Vickers gun and its tripod. A gas piston beneath the barrel controlled the operation of a rotating bolt, and the most recognizable feature of the weapon was the large shroud around the barrel and gas piston. This was Lewis's unique cooling system, which has been a source of argument ever since he invented it. The barrel and gas cylinder were surrounded by an aluminium casing formed into a series of longitudinal fins, and around these went the smooth steel casing or shroud. When the gun was fired, the muzzle blast drew air through the casing, pulling it in near the barrel breech and allowing it to pass over the fins before it was expelled at the front; in this way a constant stream of cool air was directed across the barrel area. When the Lewis Gun was used in aircraft, the fin and shroud unit were removed, leaving the barrel and gas cylinder exposed to the airstream, which cooled the gun quite satisfactorily. In the Second World War, numbers of old aircraft guns were taken from store and used as ground guns and, to many people's surprise, they did not overheat. As one firearms authority said later, it looked as if the infantrymen of the First World War had been carrying around four pounds of useless metal purely in order to support an overrated theory.

Although the Lewis Gun was an American invention, and had been offered to the U.S. Army in 1911, it was never accepted by them during the First World War. Numerous excuses for this were put forward from time to time, but it seems that the heart of the matter was personal animosity between Lewis and General Crozier, Chief of Ordnance at the time. This was carried to such a degree that when the U.S. Marines, who had adopted the Lewis Gun, arrived in France in 1918, their weapons were taken from them and returned to base, and they were issued with the French Chauchat machine gun, which was undoubtedly the worst machine gun in history.

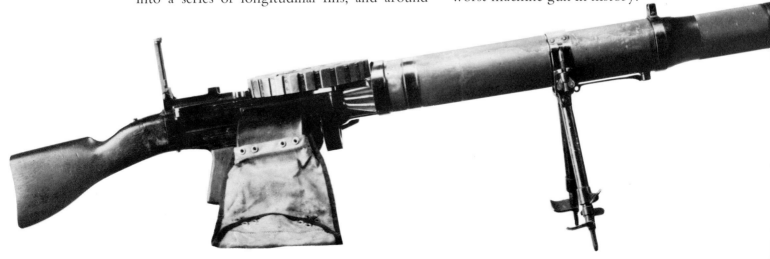

The typical Hotchkiss machine gun had heavy ribs on the barrel to dissipate the heat caused by prolonged firing. Bought by the U.S. Army before the First World War, it is seen in action with an anti-aircraft post at Raucort, France, October 1918.

When the U.S. Army found itself confronted with war in April 1917, it could hardly be said that it was 'equipped' with machine guns. In fact all it had was 282 Maxim guns, 158 Colt 'Potato Diggers' and 670 'Benet-Mercie Automatic Rifles', this being the American name for the French Hotchkiss gun. The Hotchkiss was a light, gas-operated, air-cooled gun which accepted its cartridges in metal strips. Of French manufacture, it was used in small numbers by the British Army, widely by the French and Belgian armies, and had been bought in pre-war days by the U.S. Army. Fortunately, John M. Browning was aware of the situation and he had been engaged in designing a machine gun for some time, so that when the war arrived, Browning was ready for it. By this time, Browning had abandoned his previous ideas on gas operation and had agreed with Maxim that recoil actuation made better sense in a heavy weapon.

The newly designed Browning machine gun was simple and robust, and in May 1917 the U.S. Army conducted a test in which one gun fired 20,000 rounds, non-stop, and then, after a short rest, fired another 20,000, all at a rate of 600 shots a minute. The testing board were reluctant to believe that this was anything other than a fluke, and so Browning produced another gun, loaded it, and continued to fire it non-stop until he ran out of ammunition. Browning stopped firing 48 minutes and 28,920 rounds later, had himself blindfolded by a spectator, and then proceeded to strip and re-assemble the gun. The board were convinced, and within a short period contracts were placed for the production of no less than 10,000 machine guns.

John M. Browning demonstrates his water-cooled machine gun, the U.S. Army Model 1917.

Browning had also anticipated the demand for a light weapon, and in this field he still felt that gas operation was the correct answer. At the same time as he showed his machine gun, he also showed this lighter weapon, which he called an 'Automatic Rifle'. Shaped like a rifle, it weighed 18½lbs and fired from a 20-shot box magazine placed below the action. A small bipod was fitted, though at the time of its introduction it was visualised as being fired from the hip, during the advance across No Man's Land. Although it was a good enough weapon in many respects, the 'BAR', as it will always be known, really fell between two stools: it was too heavy to be a rifle and insufficiently robust to be a good machine gun. Nevertheless, it was to remain as the U.S. Army's equivalent of a light machine gun for the next 50 years or so.

Designing machine guns was one thing; but getting them made and into the hands of the soldiers was another, and it was for this reason that the U.S. Expeditionary Force found themselves cursing the Chauchat. The French Army wanted a light machine gun; the Hotchkiss company were fully occupied in producing their heavy M1914 model for them and could not divert production to the lighter version, used by the U.S. Army as the Benet-Mercie. So a commission was instructed to develop a gun, and the result was the Chauchat. It operated on an unusual system called 'long recoil'. The barrel and bolt recoiled, locked together, for about four inches on the gun frame. At the end of this stroke, the bolt was opened and the barrel ran back, then the bolt was released, and ran back in its turn, collecting a fresh cartridge on the way from a magazine below the gun. Such a mechanism was extremely prone to derangement from dirt, of which there was no shortage on the Western Front, and to make matters worse it was poorly made of cheap material. Thousands were made, most of which appear to have been thrown away by their irate operators on the battlefield.

After the war, the French appear to have disposed of them and they turned up, for the last time, in the Spanish Civil War. A member of one of the International Brigades had this to say of them: 'It proved to be the most outstandingly useless weapon that I have ever seen and the whole lot were either lost or thrown away during the first day that we were in action. There seemed to be an almost unlimited number of ways in which it could jam itself, which it usually succeeded in doing before it had fired more than five consecutive rounds. Every time it jammed, it had to be completely taken apart and then put back together again. They were not one of the best buys.'

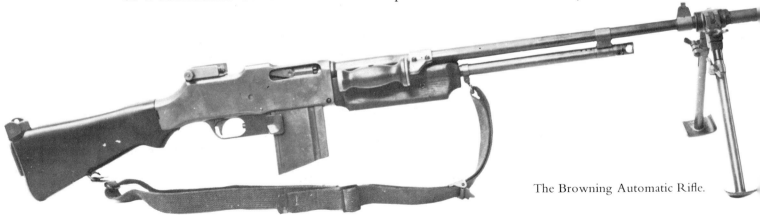

The Browning Automatic Rifle.

The Chauchat, generally regarded as one of the worst machine guns ever made. The peculiar semi-circular magazine was designed for the sharply tapered French 8mm cartridge.

The Chauchat in action: U.S. troops in the Battle of the Marne, July 1918, painted by Mal Thompson.

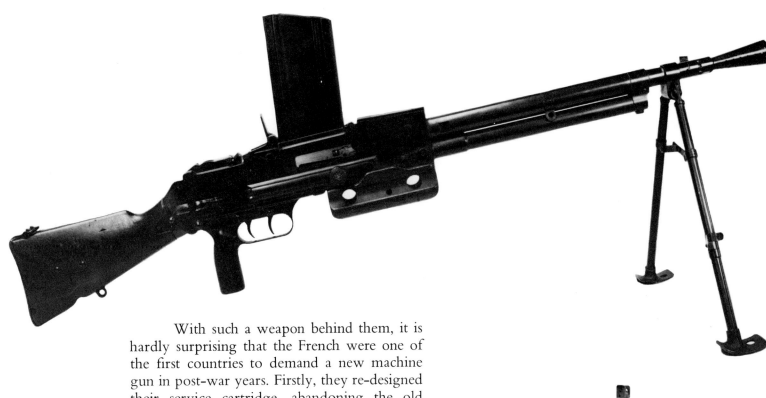

With such a weapon behind them, it is hardly surprising that the French were one of the first countries to demand a new machine gun in post-war years. Firstly, they re-designed their service cartridge, abandoning the old 8mm Lebel in favour of a modern rimless round based on the German 7·92mm Mauser cartridge. For reasons of their own they elected to go to a 7·5mm calibre, and with that settled produced a machine gun. Unfortunately, the design of the cartridge was far from perfect, and after a series of explosions and other accidents, the whole programme was stopped for the cartridge to be improved. Eventually, in 1929, the designers got it right and the new machine gun, known as the Chatellerault after the arsenal which produced it, entered service together with an improved cartridge. A modified version was also provided for use in the emplacements of the Maginot line and in tanks; this one had a peculiar side-mounted drum magazine instead of the simple top-mounted box of the infantry model.

Britain was also looking for a light machine gun, since it considered the Lewis to be too heavy and too prone to stoppage, though it was a paragon compared to the Chauchat. After considering the matter for some years, Britain organised a series of trials in 1930, in which all the current makes of machine gun were represented. Among them was a Czechoslovakian design made by the Zbrojovka

The Chatellerault M24/29 **(left)** was the French Army's replacement for the Hotchkiss and Chauchat models.
Big picture: The original version of the British Army's Bren gun, mounted on its rarely-used tripod. The mass-production model shortened the barrel and adopted a simpler sight.

Brno arms company as their ZB27 model. This had been seen by the British Military Attache in Prague and he had reported on it so favourably to London that a sample gun was purchased for the trial, at a price of £138 complete with 10,000 cartridges. The tests

zine on top of the gun. It could also be fitted to a tripod, though this was, in fact, rarely used. It was adopted throughout the British and Commonwealth armies and gained a formidable reputation for reliability and accuracy during the course of the Second World War. It is interesting to see that the German Army, after the annexation of Czechoslovakia, acquired a large quantity of ZB machine guns of similar pattern to the Bren and used them during the war, so that there must have been occasions when the same gun was in use on both sides of the front line.

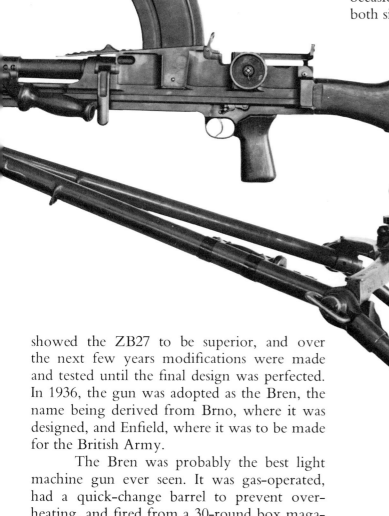

showed the ZB27 to be superior, and over the next few years modifications were made and tested until the final design was perfected. In 1936, the gun was adopted as the Bren, the name being derived from Brno, where it was designed, and Enfield, where it was to be made for the British Army.

The Bren was probably the best light machine gun ever seen. It was gas-operated, had a quick-change barrel to prevent overheating, and fired from a 30-round box maga-

The Bren gun in action in the Western
desert, 1940; and a Bren gunner of the
Durham Light Infantry firing from the
ruins of a house in Douet, France, in
June 1944.

The Germans put little faith in light machine guns, although they were not averse to using them in order to make up the numbers. They were the progenitors of the concept now known as the 'general purpose' machine gun, a weapon which was equally at home in the role of a light weapon accompanying the infantry section or a heavy weapon for delivering sustained fire. As a result of the First World War, the two roles had come to be filled by two distinct types of weapon: the heavy water-cooled gun, such as the Maxim, Vickers and Browning, and the light, magazine fed, air-cooled weapon such as the Bren, BAR and Chatellerault. The German Army, intent on re-writing the book of tactics to fit their brand of mobile war, were of the opinion that such hard and fast demarcation was dangerous. The light weapon of today might well be called upon tomorrow to act as a heavy weapon, and it was desirable that one gun should be able to fill both slots. Moreover, production of one gun for all purposes made economic sense, and also made training a good deal easier.

Bound by the requirements of the Versailles Treaty, German armament manufacturers resorted to a variety of stratagems to stay in business during the lean years of the 1920s. One company, Rheinmettal, bought up a moribund Swiss engineering firm to act as their sales outlet, so that weapons designed in Germany could be made and sold in Switzerland, and via this route a new machine gun was offered to the German Army in 1930. This, the MG30, was an advanced design in which the bolt was unlocked by rollers which followed a spiral cam track in the gun body as the barrel and bolt were driven back by recoil. A most ingenious feature was the facility for changing the barrel rapidly by twisting off the butt-stock and drawing the bolt and barrel back through the gun body. But the German Army, after buying a few, decided that it could do with some improvement, and they passed the weapon to the Mauser company to re-design. When Mauser had finished with it, it bore little resemblance to the original. The MG30 had used a box magazine clipped into the side of the gun; the new MG34 used a belt feed which, by changing the top cover of the gun body, could be replaced by a peculiar 'saddle' type of double drum. The rotating bolt of the MG30 had given way to one in which only the bolt head revolved and the barrel change facility was altered to one in which the gun body was hinged to the back of the barrel jacket, so that by swinging the body aside the barrel could be withdrawn without disturbing the bolt.

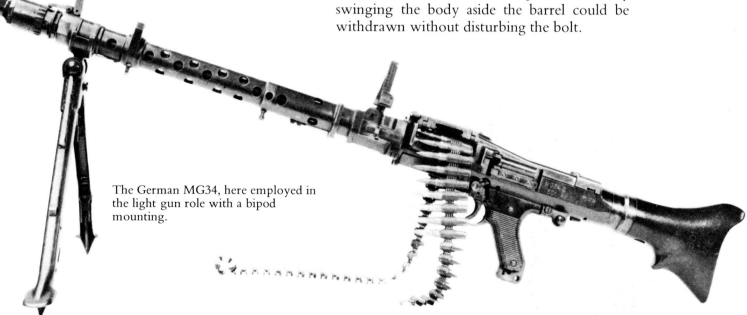

The German MG34, here employed in the light gun role with a bipod mounting.

The MG34 went into production as the standard machine gun. With a bipod and the saddle drum, it could function as the squad light machine gun, while on a tripod and belt-fed it was a valuable sustained-fire heavy weapon. The only defect was that it was too good. Manufacture was time-consuming and expensive. Once the Second World War got under way, it was found that even with five factories working as hard as they could, it was impossible to turn out MG34s fast enough, and Mauser were then asked to re-design the gun

Specially designed for mass production, the MG42 was mounted in tandem for anti-aircraft purposes.

with mass production foremost in their minds. They, in turn, called in an expert on metal pressing, who is said to have taken an Army machine gunner's course to find out what was wanted, and then set about developing a new weapon, the MG42. The method of locking was changed to a system in which two rollers at the side of the bolt moved out and jammed into recesses in the gun body. Unless these rollers were locked out, the firing pin could not pass through the bolt to fire the cartridge. The barrel change was slightly modified to make it even quicker. This was vital because the changes in design made the gun fire at the phenomenal rate of 1,200 rounds a minute – 20 shots a second – and prolonged firing at that rate would wear out a barrel in a very short time. The MG42 was one of the finest machine gun designs of all time, simple to make, extremely reliable in virtually any climatic conditions, simple to operate and maintain. More than 750,000 were made during the war, and it was widely copied in other countries afterwards, either as a whole or in some selected features. When the German Army was reconstituted in the 1950s, the MG42 was the gun they selected as their standard machine gun. In connection with this, it is amusing to note that the original drawings had been destroyed at the end of the war, and in order to produce working drawings, a captured MG42 was taken from an American museum, sent to Germany, and there dismantled and measured up in order to produce the necessary master drawings.

In the years since the Second World War the only major innovation in the machine gun world has been, in fact, a reversion. In a search for a fast-firing weapon with which to arm jet fighters, American engineers remembered that Dr. Gatling had strapped an electric motor to one of his guns. They borrowed a Gatling gun from a museum, harnessed an electric motor to it, and found that Gatling's ideas were perfectly sound. They then sat down to develop a multiple-barrelled machine gun powered by an an electric motor and capable of a rate of fire of 6,000 rounds a minute. The original versions were in 20mm calibre, firing high-explosive shells, but when the Vietnam war demanded fast-firing machine guns in helicopters, the weapon was reduced in size and chambered for the 7·62mm cartridge. This became known as the 'Mini-Gun' and it was later followed by an even smaller model, the 'Six-Pak', chambered for the 5·56mm cartridge.

While these weapons are quite practical, they do have some disadvantages, the most obvious being their appalling appetite for ammunition. They do have one advantage and that is that if a round of ammunition is faulty it is merely carried round and ejected without interrupting the fire. In any other type of machine gun, a misfire causes the gun to stop. The high rate of fire is, of course, vital where the target is a fast-moving aircraft, and so the 'Vulcan', as the general class of 'new' Gatlings are called, is found either as an aircraft weapon or an anti-aircraft weapon. Among the infantry soldiers, weapons of this type are unlikely to make much impression. They are heavy, they are cumbersome, and they demand a heavy source of power. When it comes to a machine gun that a man can pick up and carry on the battlefield, the designs of Maxim, Browning, Zbrojovka Brno and the others are still in use and are likely to be for a long time.

The MG42 in full array; the gun carries its bipod, although mounted on a recoil-absorbing tripod, and is fitted with a long-range indirect fire sight.

Chapter Twelve

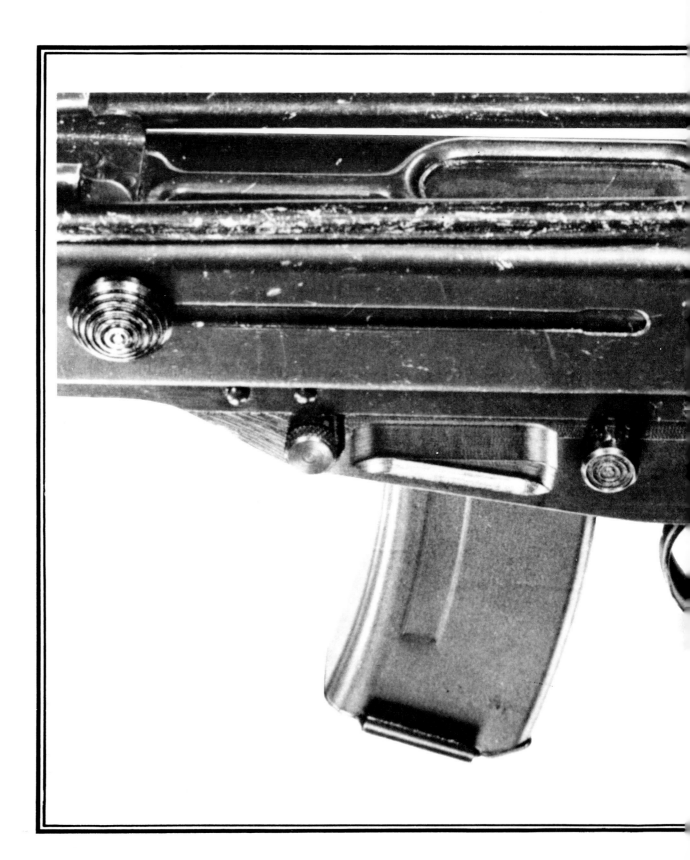

Submachine Guns

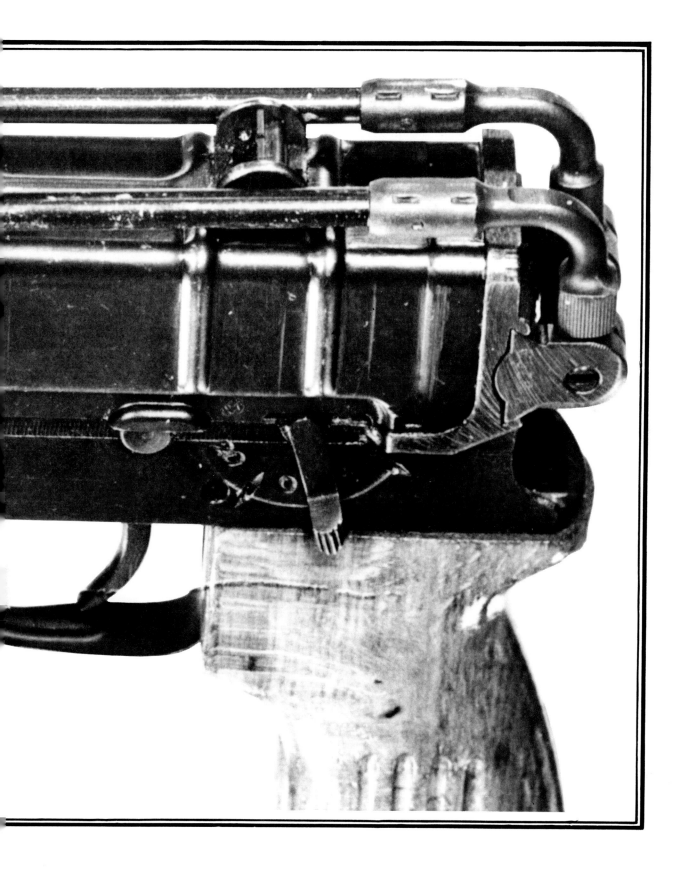

ALTHOUGH sometimes derisively referred to as a 'gangster weapon', the submachine gun is a military development. It was born during the First World War, came through a precarious adolescence in the inter-war years, and finally reached maturity in the Second World War. In the years since then, its influence has spread and it can now be found in every military armoury, but there are signs that its importance is on the wane, and some authorities believe that it is likely to vanish from military inventories by the mid-1980s.

In order to follow the history of the submachine gun and study some examples, it is necessary to define what a submachine gun is. Even the title has changed over the years. Many Continental nations refer to the weapon as a 'machine pistol', some as a 'machine carbine'. While both these expressions have some validity, they tend to confuse, since there are other meanings which can be ascribed to them. A 'machine pistol' can also be taken to mean an automatic pistol fitted with a butt and converted to fire full-automatic. These are not particularly efficient weapons and cannot be considered in the same class as a submachine gun. The term 'machine carbine' can also be held to cover weapons which are purely lightweight self-loading rifles, with or without an automatic fire capability, such as the U.S. Army's M1 Carbine.

The submachine gun, on the other hand, has certain definite and recognisable features: it normally fires a pistol cartridge; it is a magazine-fed automatic fire weapon which will continue to fire as long as the trigger is pressed and there are cartridges in the magazine;

and it is meant to be fired two-handed, either from the hip or from the shoulder. Any weapon which satisfies these three requirements can fairly be called a submachine gun.

With a few exceptions, submachine guns have usually been produced with the intention of arming many thousands of men in the shortest possible time and giving them overwhelming firepower. The requirement has therefore been for a weapon which is easily and cheaply made by mass production, but at the same time robust and resistant to the dirt and damage liable to be found on the battlefield. Consequently, the system of operation usually selected has been the 'blow back' or 'spent case projection' system.

In this system the gas pressure generated within the cartridge case on firing pushes the bullet through the barrel and, at the same time, exerts a rearward pressure on the breech-block or bolt which is supporting the cartridge in the breech. The difference in mass between the bullet and the breech-block means that the lighter bullet passes up the barrel and leaves the muzzle before the breech-block has managed to overcome its inertia; the gas pressure then exhausts through the barrel behind the bullet and the pressure within the breech drops to a level at which it is safe to extract the empty cartridge case. By this time, the block has begun to move and there is sufficient momen-

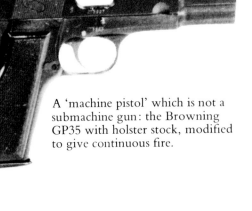

A 'machine pistol' which is not a submachine gun: the Browning GP35 with holster stock, modified to give continuous fire.

Previous page: Detail of a Czech Skorpion submachine gun (see page 247).

tum in it to operate the weapon. The impulse given to the block by the base of the case drives the block back against the pressure of a spring and an extractor in the block withdraws the spent cartridge case and ejects it. The recoiling block is stopped by the compression of the spring which then re-asserts itself and pushes

known variously as 'inertia locking' or 'differential locking'.

The cycle of operation is as outlined above, but the timing of it is so arranged that the charge in the cartridge is fired a fraction of a second before the breech-block reaches its extreme forward position; as the cartridge

A 'machine carbine'. Originally a self-loading rifle, the U.S. Army's Carbine ·30 M1 was later converted to fire full-automatic.

the block back towards the barrel, stripping a fresh cartridge from the magazine on the way and feeding it into the chamber. With the fresh cartridge chambered, the striker hits the cap and the cartridge is fired, starting the cycle all over again.

This is the simple blowback action, used in hundreds of small-calibre pocket pistols. The submachine gun is usually chambered for one of the more powerful pistol cartridges, of the type which demand a locked breech when used in a hand gun. The considerable difference in mass between the bullet and the submachine gun breech block favours the use of such a cartridge, but it is necessary to take some extra precautions to ensure that the breech supports the cartridge case for long enough to allow the chamber pressure to drop to a safe level. Another factor which has to be taken into consideration is the greater length of the submachine gun's barrel and the correspondingly greater time it takes for the bullet to leave it. The necessary additional safeguard is most usually obtained by making use of a principle

fires, the block is still moving forward, carrying the cartridge with it. Thus the pressure of the explosion must first arrest the forward movement before it can overcome the inertia of the block and start it moving backwards.

This advanced ignition is usually effected by making the chamber a tight fit around the case, so that as the case is pushed into it by the forward movement of the bolt it puts up some resistance when almost fully home and this allows the striker to hit the cap with sufficient force to fire it. Other systems have been used to achieve the same end, but even where they have been successful, they have not survived, and 'differential locking' is almost universal today.

Some designers have preferred to make use of systems which are more positive in checking the rearward breech movement, either fully locking or 'hesitation-locking' the breech, but with a few exceptions such complication has done nothing for the reliability or simplicity of the weapon and has shown no significant advantage over the simpler system. It is worth noting that one of the most successful 'hesitation-locking' weapons, the Thompson gun, was later changed to 'differential locking', and far from spoiling the weapon this actually improved it.

There are two schools of opinion as to which weapon can be claimed as the first submachine gun. The first weapon actually to fall within our quoted definition was the Vilar Perosa, developed in Italy in late 1915. However, it was far from being a submachine gun in appearance, whatever it may have been mechanically. It consisted of two machine-gun mechanisms, side by side, with overhead magazines, fired by spade grips in the manner of a heavy machine gun. It was a blowback gun with a form of differential locking, and it fired a pistol cartridge, the 9mm Glisenti round.

Its tactical application was not that of a submachine gun, but of a light machine gun for the support of infantry. This arose from the fact that during the First World War, the Italian Army had difficulties with machine guns, largely owing to the peculiar systems they espoused and the strange small-calibre cartridges used in their service rifles and machine guns. The standard weapon was the 6·5mm Revelli machine gun, a heavy and not particularly reliable weapon which was quite hopeless for use in mountain warfare of the kind in which the Italians were involved on most of their front with the Austrians. The Vilar Perosa was, therefore, intended to be carried as a mountain troop machine gun, mounted on a bipod or

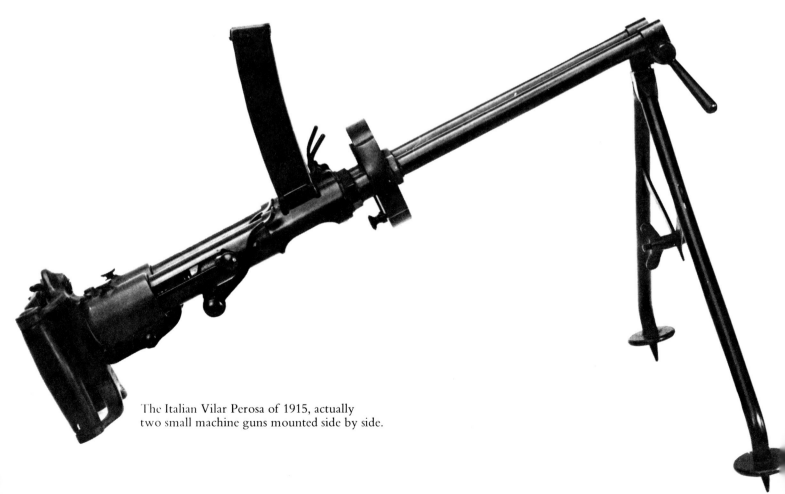

The Italian Vilar Perosa of 1915, actually
two small machine guns mounted side by side.

The first true submachine gun: the Bergmann Musquete, with its original 'snail' magazine.

tripod and even fitted with a heavy steel shield. Because of the relatively weak pistol cartridge used, it was not very successful in this role, and eventually found its best employment when slung from the shoulders of a walking soldier so that he could hold the spade grips and fire the gun as he advanced. The rate of fire was astronomical – 3,000 rounds a minute when both barrels were firing, though it was normal to fire only one barrel at a time in order to conserve ammunition. This was unfortunate, since the magazines held only 20 rounds for each barrel and did not take long to empty.

This, then, is the weapon generally credited as being the father of the submachine gun tribe. It will be clear from the above description that, while it may qualify on mechanical grounds, it certainly bears little resemblance to the weapons which came after it, either in appearance or in its manner of use. The first real submachine gun was probably the Bergmann 'Musquete' or 'Kugelspritz' which was placed in the hands of the German Army early in 1918.

Once again, the development of this weapon was due to shortcomings in the exist-

ing armament, but it was given an extra fillip by the emergence of a fresh tactical requirement. In an effort to conquer the stalemate on the Western Front, the German Army had begun to experiment with a tactic first suggested by General von Hutier and employed by him on the Eastern Front. This involved making up parties of 'storm troops', lightly equipped and well armed, who would advance in small bunches and infiltrate around obstacles under cover of smoke and gas bombardments, concentrating on carving a path for the reinforcing infantry to follow, instead of merely advancing in line like so many automata as had been the fashion until then. Such parties needed overwhelming firepower in order to deal quickly with anything in their path and they did not want to be burdened with the contemporary Maxim gun. A highly portable weapon was required, and this led to the development of the Bergmann Musquete.

The Bergmann, later to be given the more official title of Maschinen Pistole 18 or MP18, was designed by Hugo Schmeisser, a man who had been active in the small arms field for some years and who was to become

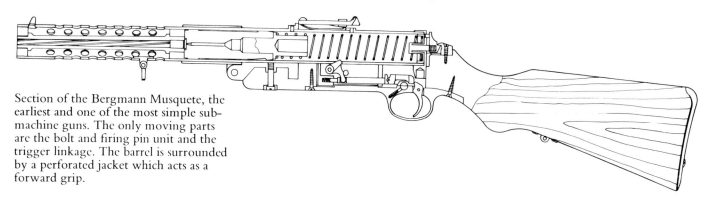

Section of the Bergmann Musquete, the earliest and one of the most simple submachine guns. The only moving parts are the bolt and firing pin unit and the trigger linkage. The barrel is surrounded by a perforated jacket which acts as a forward grip.

better-known in the future. It was a simple blowback weapon with differential locking, had a wooden stock and butt in conventional rifle fashion and, for convenience in supply, used the 'snail' helical magazine which had recently been introduced for use with the long-barrelled 'Artillery' Parabellum pistol. The Bergmann fired the 9mm Parabellum cartridge, the standard German pistol cartridge of the time, and it was a robust and reliable weapon of which some 35,000 were made before the war ended.

Once the war was over, the reaction to the submachine gun was varied. Most armies believed that what had obtained on the Western Front in 1916–18 was unique and such conditions were not likely to be repeated, and thus the weapon which had been born in those conditions would have no place in the future. The Allied Disarmament Commission removed submachine guns from the German Army and prohibited their future military use, though they did permit police forces to retain them, probably because of the street-fighting which was endemic in Germany in the early 1920s. In similar repressive vein, the few experiments the Allies had been making in this line were closed down, and that was the end of the submachine gun, so far as the major powers were concerned, for some years.

Some people, however, took the trouble to look at them more closely, and some private manufacturers began to make experiments. Soon the most famous of all was placed on the market for police use, the Thompson. It was this weapon which gave the phrase 'submachine gun' to the world. John T. Thompson was a Brigadier General of the U.S. Army who had begun work on what he called a 'trench broom', a fast-firing weapon to be used in trench warfare. The war ended before he had perfected the design, but during the 1920s the Thompson gun gradually found acceptance with various law enforcement agencies and then with criminal elements all over the world, turning up in the oddest places. It was soon on the scene in Ireland, and lingers there to this day. It appeared in the Baltic States during the various risings and putsches which ebbed and flowed in that area. It also found its way to South America for sundry revolutions. Above all, of course, it found its way into the hands of the Federal Bureau of Investigation – and the Capone mob and their contemporaries. Through the medium of Hollywood it became one of the most easily-recognised weapons in history. The association of the submachine gun with gangsters and crime was unfortunate, since it led to difficulties when it came to making armies believe in it as a military weapon.

The weapon which gave the submachine gun its gangster image, the Thompson M1928A1. It could use a 20-shot box or 50-shot drum magazine and was highly valued for its reliability.

In the Second World War, Britain
bought 'Tommy guns' from the U.S.
Below: troops armed with weapons
newly imported from America man
Britain's coastal defences, July 1940.

In 1926, Aimo Lahti, a noted Finnish arms designer, produced the 'Suomi', one of the best submachine guns ever made, and a little later the German company Rheinmettal, through their Swiss associate company Solothurn, placed a gun on the world market. The ball began to roll slowly as Swiss, Austrian, more German and finally Spanish companies began to make these new weapons, albeit in small numbers. The Gran Chaco War in South America, in 1932–35, saw the first major use of the submachine gun in combat, but this was soon overshadowed by its greater employment in the Spanish Civil War. Not only did both sides buy whatever they could lay their hands on, but local manufacturers turned out their own designs. Germany, Russia and Italy, intent upon having their latest products tested in the field, were not slow to provide stocks.

It takes a shrewd analyst to draw conclusions from the confused and bloody actions of the Spanish Civil War. All civil wars are bitter and convoluted, but this one was overlaid by so many political cross-currents that untangling the course of even a minor action demands a knowledge of dialectics and political economy as well as one of tactics. Most of the volunteer forces employed appear to have been more enthusiastic than knowledgeable, and in these peculiar circumstances the submachine gun showed itself to some advantage. It was easy to train men to use it, it rarely went wrong and, when it did, it was either easily mended or cheap enough to throw away – and it was fairly catholic in the ammunition it fired. These aspects were particularly noted by the Germans and the Soviets, both of whom were looking at the problem of having to arm a lot of men fast in the future, and both these countries set to work to develop military submachine guns. The Italians gave it rather less attention, as did the British and Americans.

Three machine guns of the 1930s. **Top to bottom:** The Finnish Suomi M1932 set new standards of quality and reliability; the Steyr-Solothurn was designed in Germany, but perfected in Switzerland and made in Austria in order to evade the restrictions of the Treaty of Versailles; the 'Labora' submachine gun was produced in a Catalan factory during the Spanish Civil War.

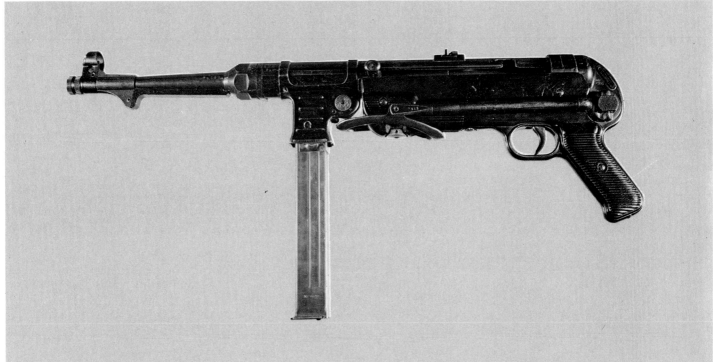

Submachine guns of the Second World
War. **Facing page, top to bottom:** the
PPSh (Machine Pistol of Shpagin),
produced by the million to become the
most common infantry weapon in the
Soviet Army; the German MP40, an
innovative design made entirely of steel
and plastic; the British Lanchester,
based on the original Bergmann design.

Germany and Russia had, in fact, been
experimenting with submachine guns for some
years, but now they set to work in earnest and
in 1938 both began mass production, settling
on a standard design and producing it in vast
numbers. Eventually, the Soviets became the
foremost employers of submachine guns, since
they saw in it the ideal weapon for arming large
numbers of conscript soldiers in a short time
and providing them with heavy firepower.
The Germans, although they employed large
numbers of submachine guns, never had the
the quantity in service that the Russians did,
largely because they never had quite the same
problem of equipping a massive army of
peasants virtually overnight.

Contrary to common belief, the British
Army had not closed its eyes to the submachine
gun and, during the 1930s, tested just about
every model then in existence. The stumbling
block was its tactical use, how to fit such an
individualistic weapon into the rigid framework of tactics and drill. Moreover, the testing
authorities had, over the years, become condi-
tioned to look for long-lasting attributes in
service firearms – quality in manufacture that
would ensure it could pass every possible test
and virtually never break down, factors of
safety in the design which guaranteed that no
accident could ever occur, and a quality of
finish and appearance worthy of the best products of the gunsmith's trade. This was not the

sort of weapon which was being produced in
the submachine gun field, and consequently
the British Army were always being told that
as soon as a good enough design appeared, they
could have some, but until then they would
have to wait.

When the war broke out in 1939, the
Army were, at last, in a position where they
could demand weapons immediately, and the
authorities considered that the best of the
submachine guns was the Finnish Suomi. By
the time they had deliberated over this and
made up their minds, Russia had invaded
Finland and the Finns had better things to do
with their Suomis than sell them, so Britain
had to buy the Thompson from America. It
remained in service for the rest of the war,
though in diminishing numbers as the Sten
replaced it. Once the Thompson was adopted,
a hunt began for something with which to
replace it, largely because the Thompson was
an expensive weapon and slow to manufacture,
and after many trials it was decided to copy the
German, Schmeisser-designed, MP28, which
was little more than a cleaned-up version of the
original MP18. With some slight changes to
suit British methods of dimensioning and
manufacture, it was approved for service as
the 'Lanchester'. However, just as production
was about to begin, the Royal Small Arms
Factory, at Enfield Lock, produced the Sten
Gun. This was immediately accepted for the

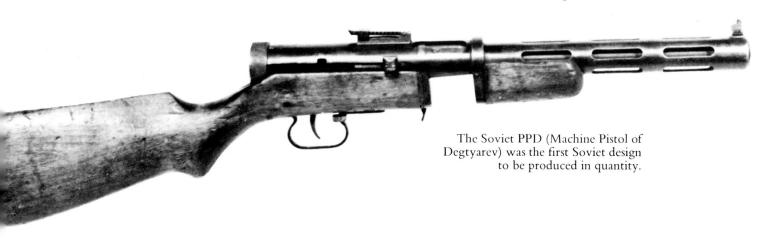

The Soviet PPD (Machine Pistol of
Degtyarev) was the first Soviet design
to be produced in quantity.

The Sten symbolized a new approach to gun manufacture and inspired many imitations. **Top:** the Sten Gun Mark II with a German-made copy below. The principal difference is in the position of the magazine housing.

The German 'Machine Pistol 3008', another Sten copy, made by Blohm & Voss of Hamburg in 1944.

The Austen, an amalgamation of the best features of the Sten gun and the German MP40, for use by the Australian Army.

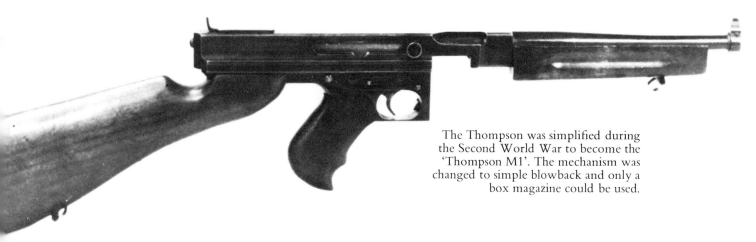

Another Australian gun, the Owen, which Australian soldiers preferred to the Austen despite its curious appearance.

Army, the Lanchester going to the Royal Navy.

The Sten Gun was all things to all men. Some hated it for its cheap appearance and dangerous habits, others thought it was the the greatest invention since the wheel. While its original versions were strictly utilitarian in appearance, later models were developed which improved safety and appearance until the last models were as good as anyone could ask. They were produced by the million, distributed all over the world, and were even copied by the Germans and by secret partisan workshops. Hundreds of thousands must still exist.

While the Sten was important as a weapon of war, it was equally important as a symbol. It broke what might be called the 'gunsmith barrier'. Here for the first time was a weapon adopted in vast numbers by a major power which was stamped out, welded up, and produced with scant regard for niceties of form or finish. Abandoning the traditional methods and standards of fire-arms manufacture, the Sten represented a totally new philosophy. It was designed to be used, hard, until it broke down or wore out, and then to be thrown away. Replacement was cheaper and quicker than repair.

This system soon became accepted as logical, and since that time the submachine gun has been a weapon designed more with production and replacement in mind than long service life. In point of fact, few have been quite as inferior as the Sten or some of the war-time Soviet designs. The U.S. Army, faced with the same problem of providing a sub-machine gun in large numbers, tested a wide variety of offerings, most of which had obviously been influenced by the Thompson and most of which were dubious manufacturing propositions because of their traditional design methods. Some, on the other hand, leaned too far in the direction of simplicity. An official report on one example said: 'This gun performed so erratically that it was impossible to determine the causes of the malfunctioning, the possibilities being so numerous'.

The Thompson was simplified during the Second World War to become the 'Thompson M1'. The mechanism was changed to simple blowback and only a box magazine could be used.

246

Facing page: Two widely used modern submachine guns, the compact Czech Skorpion (top left), and the Swedish Carl Gustav.
The Armalite rifle was widely used by American forces in Vietnam: the black infantryman is on a 'search and destroy' mission in Quang Ngai Province, June 1967; at the bottom, repelling a Viet Cong attack on Tan Son Nhut Air Base, January 1968.

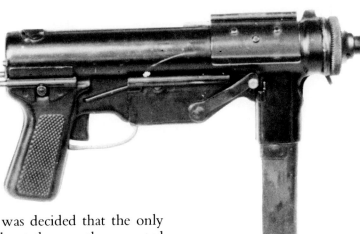

The U.S. Army's design for a cheap and robust submachine gun – the M3, known popularly as the 'Grease Gun'.

Eventually it was decided that the only way the Army could get the gun they wanted was to sit down and design it themselves. This they did and the resulting weapon went into service. Officially known as the 'M3', unofficially as the 'Grease Gun' from its shape, it was another from the same stable as the Sten, simple, easily made, robust enough for its purpose and without unnecessary frills.

After the war ended, armies were more or less content to keep the submachine guns which they were left with. Economy and retrenchment were the watch-words of the day. The gunmakers, however, appreciated that sooner or later the wartime stocks would run out and the soldiers would be back in the market-place, so they began to take suitable steps, designing new weapons, testing them and ironing out some of the more glaring defects of the wartime rush-jobs. They produced designs which, while observing the basic requirements of cheapness and easy manufacture, were better engineering jobs, more reliable and better looking.

One of the desirable attributes of a new design was that it should be compact. Some of the submachine guns used during the war were scarcely smaller than normal rifles or carbines and there seemed little justification for such dimensions. The problem lay in the mechanics of the blow-back system. In order to absorb the recoil force, it was necessary to use a heavy bolt and allow it to recoil some distance against a spring. Given this movement, the dimensions of the gun body more or less automatically resolved themselves into sufficient space in which to fit the bolt. Reducing the size of the gun meant radically re-thinking the whole design.

As usual, the same idea seems to have occurred to different designers at more or less

The French MAT49, typical of the first post-war generation of submachine guns.

Another postwar design, the Italian Beretta Model 5 incorporated a deflector at the muzzle which helped to keep the aim steady during continuous fire, and a grip safety unit behind the magazine to prevent the weapon being fired unless it was properly held.

the same time; in fact two or three seem to have begun looking at bolt configuration during the war. Probably the first was an Italian named Oliani. In 1942, he produced a protype sub-machine gun called the Armaguerra. No specimen is known to exist today, but a later model, the Armaguerra 44, has survived and certainly has a bolt of unusual design. It can best be described as a letter 'L' turned on its side, clockwise through 90°. It is, in effect, a short bolt with a long overhanging arm, reaching well forward of the breech and lying along the top of the barrel when the bolt is closed. The greater part of the weight and bulk of the bolt is in front of the actual bolt face, and the amount of metal behind the breech is enough only to hold the firing pin and with-stand the force of the explosion of the cartridge. As a result, little space is needed behind the bolt for the recoil stroke and the gun is quite compact. Oliani seems to have been more concerned with reducing the shift of gravity as the gun fired and the bolt moved back and forth, than with reducing the size of the gun. His design solved this particular problem very well, and it was a very stable weapon to fire.

However, the overhanging portion of the bolt had to be accommodated in a special casing above the barrel, which gave the Armaguerra a peculiar appearance.

A Czech designer named Holek is said to have worked on a similar design of 'over-hung' bolt during the German occupation and certainly the first post-war Czech guns used bolts of this type. Also worthy of note is the Polish designer, Podzenkowski, who worked at the British Royal Small Arms factory during the war and in 1945 designed the experimental EM2 submachine gun. This used a bolt which was hollowed out so that it enveloped the barrel at the moment of firing, and had slots cut in it to allow feed and extraction.

Whatever the source of these designs, they were rapidly developed, and a number of extremely compact guns using the 'over-hung', 'telescoping' or 'wrap-around' bolt were soon available. At much the same time,

The Armaguerra OG44. The elongated casing above the barrel is for the 'overhung' bolt.

The modern generation of submachine guns.

The Czech CZ23 model designed by Holek. The overhung bolt has allowed the design to contract and the magazine is fitted inside the pistol grip, making for easier loading.

The Israeli Uzi, one of the most compact weapons in current use.

The Chinese People's Army Type 64 silenced submachine gun.

Two submachine guns based on 5·56mm assault rifles: the Heckler & Koch HK53; and the Colt Commando **(bottom),** stemming from the Armalite design.

the political situation began to deteriorate and new submachine guns began to appear in in the hands of military forces around the world. The Madsen, the Carl Gustav, the Uzi and several others were well distributed and they were followed by many more.

The war, which saw the flowering of the submachine gun, also marked the birth of another type of weapon, the assault rifle. In its earliest form, it was actually called a machine pistol, although this was no more than camouflage for political reasons. The assault rifle used a smaller cartridge than the normal infantry rifle, but one which was still a good deal more powerful than a pistol cartridge and which demanded some form of breech locking. It was light and handy and had the ability to deliver either single shots or automatic fire. Indeed, except for the cartridge, the characteristics of the assault rifle are practically those of the submachine gun, so it comes as no surprise to find military thinkers asking why it was necessary to have the two types of weapon.

Shortly after the war, the Soviets produced an assault rifle, the Kalashnikov AK47, and set about producing it in hundreds of thousands in order to replace the submachine guns which had been so conspicuous a feature of the wartime Red Army. As a result, the submachine gun has all but vanished from sight in Soviet Army circles.

This lead has since been followed elsewhere. The U.S. Army adopted the Armalite design of ·223 rifle, and since then the submachine gun has been relegated to the Reserve. The German company, Heckler and Koch, produce a submachine gun called the HK53 which is actually chambered for the same ·223 cartridge as the rifle. The division between submachine gun and assault rifle has almost vanished, and the submachine gun as a separate species may very well vanish with it.

Index Figures in *italics* refer to illustrations

Bibliography

Part One

Atkinson, J. A.: *Duelling Pistols and some of the affairs they settled*, London, 1964.

Blackmore, H. L.: *British Military Firearms 1650–1850*, London 1961.
Guns and Rifles of the World, London, 1965.

Blair, C.: *European and American Arms c. 1100–1850*, London, 1962.
Pistols of the World, London 1968.
'Scottish Firearms', *Bulletin of the American Society of Arms Collectors*, No. 31, Dallas, Texas, 1975.

Cossé-Brissac, Charles de; Rolland, J. F.; Druène, B.; Devantour, Charles, etc.: *The Ancient Art of Warfare*, Paris and Turin, 1966.

Dillin, J. G.: *The Kentucky Rifle*, New York, 1959.

Firth, Sir Charles Harding: *Cromwell's Army*, London, 1902.

Gaier, C.: *Four Centuries of Liège Gunmaking*, Liège, 1976.

Hawkins, Peter: *The Price Guide to Antique Guns and Pistols*, Woodbridge, Suffolk, 1973.

Hayward, J. F.: *The Art of the Gunmaker*, 2 vols., London, 1962–3.
European Firearms (Victoria and Albert Museum), London, 1955.

Lavin, James: *A History of Spanish Firearms*, London, 1965.

Mann, Sir J.: *European Arms and Armour* (Wallace Collection catalogue), 2 vols., London, 1962.

Neal, W. K., and Back, D. H. L.: *The Mantons: Gunmakers*, London, 1967.
Forsyth and Co. Patent Gunmakers, London, 1970.

Partington, J. R.: *A History of Greek Fire and Gunpowder*, Cambridge, 1960.

Peterson, H. L. (ed.): *The Encyclopedia of Firearms*, London and New York, 1964.

Pollard, H. B. C.: *A History of Firearms*, London, 1930.

Stone, G. C.: *A Glossary of the Construction, Decoration and Use of Arms and Armour in all countries and in all times*, Portland, Maine, 1934.

Tarassuk, L.: *Antique European and American Firearms at the Hermitage Museum, Leningrad*, Leningrad, 1972.

Tout, T. F.: 'Firearms in England and in the 14th Century', *English Historical Review*, Vol. XXVI, London, 1911.

Winant, L.: *Early Percussion Firearms*, New York, 1959.

Journals: *Journal of the Arms and Armour Society*, Leatherhead, Surrey; *Journal of the Royal Armoury Stockholm*, Livrustkammaren, Stockholm; *Vaabenhistoriske Aarbøge*, Copenhagen; *Zeitschrift für Historische Waffenkunde*, 1897–1944 (from 1923 *Waffen- und Kostümkunde*), Berlin.

Part Two

Hobart, F. W. A.: *A Pictorial History of the Machine Gun*, London, 1971.
A Pictorial History of the Submachine Gun, London, 1973.

Hogg, Ian V., and Weeks, J. S.: *Military Small Arms of the 20th Century*, London, 1977.

Lugs, J.: *Firearms Past and Present*, Bingley, Yorkshire, 1973.

Smith, W. H. B., and Smith, J. E.: *The Book of Rifles*, Harrisburg, Pennsylvania, 1972.

Taylerson, A. W. F.; Andrews, R. A. V.; Frith, J.: *The Revolver, 1818–1865*, London, 1968.

Taylerson, A. W. F.: *The Revolver, 1865–1888*, London, 1966.
The Revolver, 1889–1914, London, 1970.

Walter, J.: *Luger*, London, 1977.

Wilson, R. K.: *Textbook of Automatic Pistols*, London, 1975.

Acknowledgements and thanks are due to
Mr Claude Blair of the Victoria and Albert
Museum for reading the manuscript of Part One
and making helpful comments and suggestions;
also to Peter Macdonald and Stanley Eost for
special photography of weapons in Part One; to
those private owners who have given permission
for items from their collections to be photographed;
and to the Pattern Room, Royal Small Arms
Factory, Enfield Lock, Middlesex, for providing
facilities to photograph modern small arms.

PHOTO CREDITS: Ambrosiana, Milan, 26;
American History Picture Library, 146, 148, 157b,
225b; Antikvarisk-Topografiska Arkivet,
Stockholm, 12–13, 14b; Austrian National
Library, Vienna, 16b, 18b; Bayerisches
Nationalmuseum, Munich, 29b, 30t; Birmingham
City Museum and Art Gallery, 87; Bradford City
Museum, 62t; Christie, Manson & Woods Ltd.,
53b, 66c, 68b, 69b, 79b, 102, 104, 114t, 115t, 120b,
128t; Department of the Environment, copyright
H. L. Blackmore, 74–75, 83; Department of the
Environment, Crown copyright reserved, 19t, 44,
45t, 47, 53t, 65, 67c, 79t, 80–81, 99, 101b,
116, 117, 118l, 120t, 121, 123, 126, 131; 164;
Edinburgh Castle, 15b; Germanisches Museum,
Nuremberg, 30c; Gunshots, 139, 141, 143b, 172b;
Historical Picture Service, 72b, 137r, 144;
Historisches Museum, Bern, 15t; Historisches
Museum, Dresden, 37; Ian V. Hogg, 149b, 150t,
151t, 152, 154t, 156, 157t, 158, 159, 162, 165, 167,
168, 169, 170, 171, 173, 174, 175, 176, 177, 178,
179, 183, 185, 186, 187, 188, 189t & c, 190, 191,
192, 193, 194, 195, 196, 197, 198, 199, 200, 201,
202, 203, 209t, 210, 212, 213, 215, 216b, 217, 218t,
220, 222t, 223, 224, 225t, 226, 227, 229, 230, 231,
232–233, 234, 235, 236, 237t, 238, 240–241, 242,
243, 244, 245, 246, 247tl & c, 248, 249; Robert
Hunt Picture Library, 136–137c; 151b, 153,
189bl, 218b, 221, 222b, 228, 247tr & b; Levens
Hall, Cumberland, 42b; Livrustkammaren,

Stockholm, 36b, 40t, 125b; Mansell Collection,
71b, 72t, 73; Mauser Jagdwaffen GmbH, 135, 142,
180–181, 189br; Musée de l'Armée, Paris, 36t;
National Army Museum, 56(border), 57, 60, 113,
114b, 211; W. Keith Neal, 64, 76; Palazzo
Ducale, Venice, 29t, 127; Pitt-Rivers Museum,
Oxford, 42t; Popperfoto, 204–205; Private
Collections, 27, 43; Quarto Archives, 4, 7, 8–9, 10,
11, 16t, 18t, 19b, 20, 21, 22–23, 28, 34, 38–39,
40b, 51, 55b, 56c, 82, 115, 130j, 172t, 208, 209b;
Radio Times Hulton Picture Library, 151c, 207,
219, 239; Real Armería, Madrid, 32;
Rijksantikvarieämbetet och Statenshistoriska
Museer, Stockholm, 93c; Schloss Konopiste,
Czechoslovakia, 133; Sotheby & Co., 49b, 66t & b,
67t & b, 71t, 78b, 88c, 89c; Tøjhusmuseet,
Copenhagen, 14t, 93t, 97c & b, 112, 128b; Tower
Armouries, 50, 100t, 138, 155, 166, 214; Victoria
and Albert Museum, Crown copyright reserved,
endpapers, frontispiece, 24–25, 30b, 31, 33, 35, 41,
45b, 46b, 48, 49t, 52, 54, 55t, 58–59, 61, 62b, 63,
68t, 69t, 70, 84–85, 86, 88l & b, 89r & b, 88–89c,
90, 91, 92, 93b, 94, 95, 96, 97t, 98, 100b, 101t, 102,
103, 105, 106, 107, 108, 109, 110–111, 118r, 119,
122, 124b, 125, 132, 133t; Western Americana
Picture Library, 136l, 143t, 145, 147, 149t,
160–161, 163b.

Special drawings by Helen Downton.